HOMEOWNER'S GUIDE TO BUYING, EVALUATING AND MAINTAINING YOUR HOME

HOMEOWNER'S GUIDE TO BUYING, EVALUATING AND MAINTAINING YOUR HOME

BY

Joseph G. McNeill, P.E.

VNR **VAN NOSTRAND REINHOLD COMPANY**
NEW YORK   CINCINNATI   ATLANTA   DALLAS   SAN FRANCISCO
LONDON   TORONTO   MELBOURNE

Van Nostrand Reinhold Company Regional Offices:
New York Cincinnati Atlanta Dallas San Francisco

Van Nostrand Reinhold Company International Offices:
London Toronto Melbourne

Copyright © 1979 by Litton Educational Publishing, Inc.

Library of Congress Catalog Card Number: 78-26241
ISBN: 0-442-23607-7

Manufactured in the United States of America

Published by Van Nostrand Reinhold Company
135 West 50th Street, New York, N.Y. 10020

Published simultaneously in Canada by Van Nostrand Reinhold Ltd.

15 14 13 12 11 10 9 8 7 6 5 4 3 2 1

Library of Congress Cataloging in Publication Data

McNeill, Joseph G

   Homeowner's guide to buying, evaluating and maintaining your home.

   Includes bibliographical references and index.
   1. House buying—Handbooks, manuals, etc.
   2. Dwellings—Maintenance and repair—Handbooks,
manuals, etc. I. Title.
TH4817.5.M25   643   78-26241
ISBN 0-442-23607-7

This book is dedicated to

My family,

My colleagues,

My many client-homeowners,

And my students.

Their experiences have made this book possible.

PREFACE

Welcome aboard! If you're reading this book, then you are taking the first step toward reducing the costs of homeownership. Knowledge, preparation, and good professional advice will insure that your home is a dream house and not a headache. I can tell you right now that it is better to lose a house because of your knowledge than to gain one through ignorance.

So you've decided to buy a home. Now you are confronted with the exasperating and frightening dilemma of deciding which new home will best suit your needs and pocketbook. You need a guide that will address itself to assisting you in the task of intelligently buying and maintaining a house. This manual is such a guide, and it may save you hundreds of dollars and secure for you the peace of mind that comes from a sound investment.

For the past eight years, my firm, AMC Home Inspection Service, has inspected and warranted thousands of homes and paid numerous claims. From this experience, I have come to know the home buyer and homeowner and the problems they face in selecting, evaluating, and maintaining their homes. In this age of rising prices, the huge investment one makes when buying a house can never be taken lightly. It is quite possibly the largest single investment you will make in your lifetime. Repairs alone in a poorly selected home can be completely beyond the average home buyer's means. Although more consumers today are aware of the need to be informed before purchasing a home, all too often I am still confronted with unhappy homeowners who say, "I had no one to turn to, no one to talk to, no one to answer my questions." This book will answer many of those questions.

I want to share with you, in layman's terminology, the same information I give weekly to professional home inspector trainees. Of course, if the advice of a home inspector or engineer is available, it would be wise to seek his or her services. An expert's knowledge and years of experience in the field will be well worth the fee. However, if no one is available to advise you, then this manual will provide you with the necessary information.

This book will show you how to look beyond the cosmetic aspects of your prospective home. Unweeded gardens and torn wallpaper are merely temporary eyesores easily renewed, but poor foundations or a structurally unsound house can give you years of heartaches. Herein you will learn how to evaluate the major components of your residential home and property. These major components include the site, roof, heating, air conditioning, structure, foundation, basement, kitchen, electric service, and plumbing, as well as the exterior appurtenances.

If you are selling a home you may wish to turn right to Chapter 34 for complete details on preparing to sell. For those who are considering buying a house, read the first five chapters of Part I that give an overview on buying a house plus a complete checklist to use in locating and inspecting the house. Part II contains details on how to evaluate your home's systems, and Part III discusses how to maintain your home. Each chapter gives a general introduction to the system, then discusses the technical details, outlines the problems you may encounter, tells how to inspect the system, and then summarizes the maintenance suggestions.

The potential homeowner or buyer, the real estate salesperson, as well as the home inspector and the student in construction class, will find this manual a valuable reference source. Much of this information has been the basis of classes I have taught at University Extension as well as company training programs. It is the result of fifteen years of personal experience in many aspects of the residential inspection field, through which I have been able to view thousands of case situations.

I sincerely hope this book will be of great value to you, and if you, the reader, have any suggestions concerning this book or the home inspection field, or questions concerning your own home, I encourage you to write to me and share your ideas. By sharing problems and ideas in this way, you can be assured that other homeowners will benefit.

In closing, I would like to extend my sincerest gratitude to the many people whose homes, problems, and successes form the basis of this book. To my colleagues, far too numerous to mention, my warmest thanks; special thanks to Helen, my typist, to Lori for editing, and to Eileen, my researcher and associate.

Joseph G. McNeill, P.E.
Bound Brook, New Jersey

Contents

HOMEOWNER'S GUIDE TO BUYING, EVALUATING AND MAINTAINING YOUR HOME

PART I.
BUYING YOUR
HOME

1.
Introduction: The Book's Philosophy and Use

This guide is written for that group of people involved in buying, selling, evaluating, maintaining, or inspecting single family dwellings. The great American dream is to own a home on a plot of land. Some people will want a new home but the great majority will buy resale homes. Frequently, this means revitalizing an older house. For most of us, our home is the largest single expenditure we will make. If it is not done with good planning and thought, the price of ownership may easily exceed our means.

Most home buyers, whether buying their first or fourth home, are inexperienced in the process of searching for and closing on a home. Choosing and financing are challenges that cost a great deal of money. These costs may be in the form of rent or mortgage payments plus property taxes, insurance, and municipal assessments. A homeowner also has to pay for utilities, repairs, and decorating. Many decisions in unfamiliar areas have to be made, and the home buyer must deal with people who use unfamiliar terms and procedures. This may make buying a home one of the most traumatic experiences of your life.

Because preparation and information are the keys to the success of a new venture, this book should make the decisions easier.

GOAL

My aim is to help you with buying, evaluating, and maintaining a home by providing you with experience you may be lacking. Upon completion of this manual, you should be able to:

3

Define your housing needs;

Develop a plan for selecting a neighborhood, locating a house, negotiating the price, and keeping the closing costs low;

Understand the common problems in residential dwelling-house components and systems;

Inspect the house or have others determine the condition under your direction;

Develop a maintenance plan for your home; and

Plan to sell the home as a step to retirement or a newer, larger home.

WHY WRITE THIS BOOK?

Over the past ten years, I've inspected thousands of homes and commercial buildings to determine the condition of the structural, mechanical, and electrical components. I've been called out on numerous complaints against builders and remodeling contractors. Homeowners have written to me about their problems, in response to my newspaper column and radio programs on home maintenance. From these experiences, I prepared a series of home system maintenance guides for inspection clients, attorneys, and realtors. The response was excellent, and it became apparent that there was a need for a homeowner's guide that would combine these experiences: a one-stop "how-to-do-it" reference book on how to buy, inspect, and maintain a single family dwelling.

Over a period of time, I've collected an extensive library of books and articles on residential construction and inspection in the United States and Europe. This includes many excellent books and pamphlets written by the Department of Agriculture, HUD, and other government agencies. (Some of these are listed in Appendix B.) This material was used extensively in training home inspectors.

As you read along, if you have any questions or comments, please write. Many of my students have done this in courses I've taught for University Extension in home inspection and structural problems.

WHO IS THE READER?

If you are a potential home buyer or homeowner, then this guide will help make the process easier and will save you money; if you are a student in civil technology or engineering, then this book will give you insight into the dynamics and problems of dwelling-house ownership; if you are a home economics teacher, this should serve as a handy textbook for your students; and for the municipal building and home inspector, this provides a guide to the spectrum of problems involved in homes in your community. This manual can also be a handy reference for architects and engineers, lawyers, and realtors who deal with the home buyer.

WHO IS THE HOME BUYER?

Psychologists say that people involved in real estate transactions generally are very anxious and seem to be under almost as much stress as they would be after learning about the death of a spouse. Because real estate buyers or sellers are under such stress, they usually develop negative opinions of everyone involved in the sale of property, and their anxiety causes them to become suspicious even of those who are there to help. Therefore, the buyer or seller should plan the move carefully and take full advantage of all the services available: doing it all alone only makes matters worse.

The Census Bureau has published a wealth of data on the home buyer. According to this data, buyers of new homes are a bit older and have slightly larger incomes than buyers of resale units. Previous renters account for almost one-half (48%) of all single family home buyers. Previous owners, often selling one home to buy another, account for 42%; newly formed households made up the remaining 10%. In 1977, 91% of all homes were bought by households headed by a man, but since 1973, single women are buying more homes and this percentage will rise accordingly. This supports my findings that the buyer is usually new at the homeowning process and needs all the help he or she can get.

Almost four out of ten home buyers are between 25 and 34 years of age, with roughly a quarter between 35 and 44. The median home buyer is 36 years old, compared to 47 years old for all households. The average home buyer generally has a higher than average income, which is understandable today as the price of homes and homeownership skyrocket.

People move for a variety of reasons: employment or job change, family, desire to become a homeowner, wanting to live in a better neighborhood, a desire to upgrade one's housing standards, or a need for a larger or better house. In 1977, new home buyers purchased properties valued at twice their annual incomes. Previous owners purchased properties at 2.2 times their annual incomes because of the equity from a previous sale.

PLAN OF THE BOOK

This book is written for the person who wants to carefully plan the buying and ownership of a home. Its purpose is to save buyers money and help them avoid the problems that so many people fall into because of inexperience. It shows how to ask questions and get money-saving answers. The appendix has an extensive glossary of terms and some further suggested readings.

Part I is devoted to buying your home. The chapter on basic house construction discusses the structural parts of a dwelling-house and how it is built. As a home buyer, you could engage a realtor, attorney, home inspector, appraiser, and insurer prior to completing a closing or settlement, and one chapter discusses these services. There is also a chapter with a step-by-step map to buying and negotiating for the home. Chapter 5 discusses common house ailments as a broad introduction to those components that need special attention. Finally, a detailed buying and inspecting checklist is presented for your use in finding the neighborhood, buying the house, and assessing all the structural, mechanical and electrical components.

Part II concerns the exterior and interior system components. Each chapter has an introduction, a technical section, a listing of possible problems, maintenance suggestions, inspection sequence, and a summary. This will make it easy for you to find information on these systems.

Part III tells you how to buy services, and explains the economics of remodeling and repairs. One chapter is an exhaustive list of energy-saving methods that, if followed, can easily cut your energy bill by 20%. Household emergencies and how to cope with them are discussed. Another chapter suggests methods for home security and how to prevent fire, burglary, and noise pollution. Also given is an extensive preventive maintenance checklist. This periodic attention to details will increase the value of your home.

Part IV discusses selling your house. Here you will discover there are as many decisions involved in selling as there are in buying. Proper care will increase the amount of capital you will have available for the next house or your retirement nest egg.

HOUSE COMPARING KIT

Whether you are house comparing or planning home maintenance, you will need tools. Start to accumulate a basic set of hammers, screw drivers, wrenches, and saws, and store them in a sturdy tool box. When you are ready to search for a house, have the following additional items with you.

A camera. After you look at a few homes, you will need a picture to refresh your memory. Get a copy of the multiple listing data sheet (MLS) from the realtor. This has the house facts you will need.

Graph paper and a clipboard. You can use this to sketch the rooms' sizes and their relation to one another.

A tape measure: 50 feet. This is handy for measuring, but you can become a human yardstick yourself. Learn to pace at an average three feet. Measure your shoe length—usually about ten inches for a woman and 12 inches for a man. Your outstretched hands reach almost your height. These statistics can let you quickly measure a house.

A notebook. Carry a pencil and note paper and clip them to your clipboard. Use this with the picture, MLS data sheet, and graph paper to record features about the house that please you. After you've viewed 15 or more homes, even the major features will be a blur in your mind.

An inspection checklist. Prepare an inspection checklist from the Part I Summary.

A maintenance checklist. Chapter 33 lists the suggested periodic maintenance checks. Bring a copy along to discuss with the owner of the home you select. Get a list of the tradespeople he or she uses.

This kit is based on some of the items our home inspectors carry when they inspect a home. Since they see thousands of homes, an accurate report is the only way they can recall a dwelling.

REFERENCE MATERIALS

This guide should answer most of your house buying questions. If you would like to do some further reading, consult Appendix B. Also consider getting on the mailing list for the free Consumer Information Bulletin that is an index of selected federal publications of consumer interest. Write to Consumer Information Center, Pueblo, Colorado 81009. Tell them your interest is residential housing.

SUMMARY

This is a "how to" book. I believe if you've persisted in reading this far you have overcome one of the roadblocks to good planning—namely, procrastination. You are willing to give the book a try. You have a willingness to gather data, to establish a plan, and to carry it out. Good luck!

2.
Basic House Construction

INTRODUCTION

The purpose of this chapter is to provide you with an overall introduction to the component parts of a wood frame dwelling. Also discussed are the elements of good construction and the steps usually taken in building a house. The principle function of a house is to furnish protection from the elements. In its current stage, our society requires that the home provide not only shelter but also privacy, safety, and reasonable protection of our physical and mental health.

Figure 2.1 shows the parts of a residential dwelling-house. This represents the parts you will find in most resale homes. Carefully examining each part and noting its relationship to others will provide you with insight into construction procedures. It is important to have a knowledge of these construction elements when you plan the maintenance and operation of your home.

TECHNICAL INFORMATION

Preplanning Details. A construction project requires a great deal of planning. A plan may range from a simple list of dimensions to a detailed drawing, depending upon the nature of the project and the degree of accuracy required. The basic design can be done by an architect or you can purchase standard plans from a plan group. The municipal zoning and housing boards must approve the plans and the site.

Choose the house site carefully. By doing so, you can avoid future

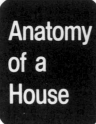

Anatomy of a House

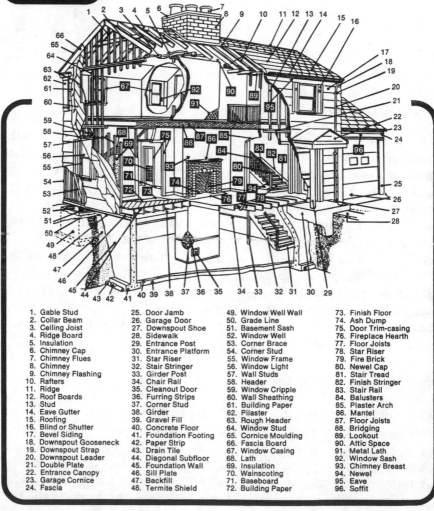

Figure 2.1. Anatomy of a house. Source: AMC Home Inspection and Warranty Service.

1. Gable Stud
2. Collar Beam
3. Ceiling Joist
4. Ridge Board
5. Insulation
6. Chimney Cap
7. Chimney Flues
8. Chimney
9. Chimney Flashing
10. Rafters
11. Ridge
12. Roof Boards
13. Stud
14. Eave Gutter
15. Roofing
16. Blind or Shutter
17. Bevel Siding
18. Downspout Gooseneck
19. Downspout Strap
20. Downspout Leader
21. Double Plate
22. Entrance Canopy
23. Garage Cornice
24. Fascia

25. Door Jamb
26. Garage Door
27. Downspout Shoe
28. Sidewalk
29. Entrance Post
30. Entrance Platform
31. Star Riser
32. Stair Stringer
33. Girder Post
34. Chair Rail
35. Cleanout Door
36. Furring Strips
37. Corner Stud
38. Girder
39. Gravel Fill
40. Concrete Floor
41. Foundation Footing
42. Paper Strip
43. Drain Tile
44. Diagonal Subfloor
45. Foundation Wall
46. Sill Plate
47. Backfill
48. Termite Shield

49. Window Well Wall
50. Grade Line
51. Basement Sash
52. Window Well
53. Corner Brace
54. Corner Stud
55. Window Frame
56. Window Light
57. Wall Studs
58. Header
59. Window Cripple
60. Wall Sheathing
61. Building Paper
62. Pilaster
63. Rough Header
64. Window Stud
65. Cornice Moulding
66. Fascia Board
67. Window Casing
68. Lath
69. Insulation
70. Wainscoting
71. Baseboard
72. Building Paper

73. Finish Floor
74. Ash Dump
75. Door Trim-casing
76. Fireplace Hearth
77. Floor Joists
78. Star Riser
79. Fire Brick
80. Newel Cap
81. Stair Tread
82. Finish Stringer
83. Balusters
84. Balusters
85. Plaster Arch
86. Mantel
87. Floor Joists
88. Bridging
89. Lookout
90. Attic Space
91. Metal Lath
92. Window Sash
93. Chimney Breast
94. Newel
95. Eave
96. Soffit

problems that could be expensive to correct. For example, poor soil drainage could lead to a wet or damp basement. Choose a firm, well-drained site. Avoid poorly drained or unstable land. In some cases, it may be necessary to provide good drainage with tile and ditches. Well-drained sloping sites are ideal for basements.

Avoid building in low valleys where the air may be trapped. A house needs good air circulation. Look for good accessibility to roads. Long private roads and driveways are expensive to build and maintain. There should be good availability of gas, water, electricity, and sewage disposal. If the site is not convenient to a public sewer system, check with local health authorities to make sure that the soil is suitable for a private sewage disposal system. Sewage disposal must be downgrade from the house and well away from the house water supply. If you must drill a well, be certain beforehand that water is available.

Design or plan the house to meet your family's requirements. Too small a house would be false economy, so be sure to consider your future as well as your present needs. In time, you may need more bedrooms or another bathroom or two. The space for additional bedrooms can be an unfinished attic or a clean, dry basement. The heating and electrical work can be roughed in. For future bathrooms, you can rough in the plumbing in the attic or basement or in a large walk-in closet. This work will increase the initial cost of the house, but it will be more economical in the long run because such work can usually be done less expensively at the time the house is built. As with the overall house design, plan the interior arrangements to insure your family's comfort and satisfaction. To economize, make rooms multi-purpose: for example, combine family room and kitchen or family room and dining room.

Steps in Building a House. Once the preliminary planning is complete, the house is ready to be built. The following steps are usually taken in building a dwelling-house.

Laying out the foundation. A licensed surveyor is hired to prepare a survey, lay out the lot and building lines, and stake the grade levels. In some cases (not always), batter boards are set up around the building layout stakes. Excavation and grading is then done to prepare for the footing. You should take advantage of the sun in placing the house on the lot. Laying out a foundation is the critical beginning in house construction. If you make sure the foundation is square and level, you will find that all later jobs—from rough carpentry through finish construction and installation of cabinetry—are made much easier.

Footings.   A trench is dug around the perimeter or foundation line of the house. The spread footing or base for the foundation usually consists of poured concrete. Normally, it is as thick as the foundation wall and twice as wide. Footings distribute the weight of the foundation and the weight of the building structure to the ground. Reinforcing rods should be embedded in the concrete footings but rarely are in small construction.

Foundations.   These are constructed of poured concrete, cinder block, or concrete block. They should be waterproofed on the exterior. Design of foundations must take the bearing load—weight of structure and contents—into consideration. In older structures, stone, wood, and brick foundations were used. The exterior surface is waterproofed.

Sills and girders.   After the concrete or block has been set, wooden sills are bolted to the top of the foundation. Then solid or built-up wood or steel girders are set in place, extending from one side of the foundation to the other. They are supported along the length by vertical steel or wooden posts called lally columns. The size and length of the girders is determined by the distance to be spanned and the weight of the superstructure to be supported.

Floor joists.   Floor joists are installed on top of the girder and extended from the girder to the wooden sill plate on the foundation wall. Cross-bridging is used to stiffen the floor joists. The open spaces between the joists at the foundation are covered by box sills or headers. Floor joists are set on 16-inch centers.

Subflooring.   Subflooring is installed on top of the joists as a base for finish flooring. In new construction, plywood is used. In older construction, diagonal tongue and groove boards were used. Sole plates (2 x 4 or 2 x 6 inches) are nailed on top of the subflooring along the line of contemplated interior walls. These form the base for the studding which will make the skeleton framework of the walls. The 2 x 4 studs are placed perpendicular, from 12 to 16 inches apart, and nailed at the bottom of the sole plate. Construction practice today calls for platform construction or braced framing. Older homes used balloon framing, where the studs extended in one piece from the sill plates to the rafters.

Rafter and ceiling joists.   Rafter plates are usually doubled and placed on top of the stud wall around the perimeter and along the line of contemplated interior walls. These plates are usually 2 x 4 or 2 x 6 inches and support the lower ends of the rafters or roof joists. Installed next and in the same direction as floor joists are the ceiling joists. Unless the structure is to be more than one story, ceiling joists are usually 2 x 6 or 2 x 8 inches.

Sheathing and wall types.   Walls that are load bearing are those that bear a load and support other framework and finish members. In contrast, nonbearing walls or partitions act as enclosures but bear no load. Bearing walls support the roof and ceilings or the floors above. Bearing walls are usually above the main girder and the foundation. Sheathing—either plywood, composition board, or tongue and groove boards—is applied on the exterior of the outer wall studding. This forms the base for whatever type of exterior siding or exterior finish called for by the plans.

Roof joists.   The next step is the installation of the roof structure. Roof rafters or joists are placed parallel to each other, from 12 to 24 inches apart, extending upward from the outer wall top or rafter plate at a predetermined angle to the ridge pole. Similar rafters are extended upward from the opposite exterior wall to the ridge pole. Rafters may be 2 x 4 to 2 x 8 inches, depending upon length and load. Sheathing is then applied to the rafters as a base for nailing the roofing. Here plywood or composition board is used.

Roofing.   The roof surface is covered with building paper to act as a moisture barrier. Finish roofing could be wood shingles, slates, asphalt or composition shingles, or rigid asbestos shingles. Roofing is applied by the square (100 square feet).

Siding.   After the roofing has been installed, the next step is the application of the exterior finish. Heating ducts, roughing in of plumbing and wiring, insulation, and the installation of doors and windows can be done at the same time. Materials vary from one area to another. For the most part, the product used depends upon personal choice.

Exterior paint work.   For exterior painting, one must wait for the proper weather, while interior painting can be done once the heat is on or the weather is warm. If wood siding is installed, it must be primed and sealed prior to painting. Hardboard siding has a factory applied finish, but should be painted following installation.

Backfill.   Once the exterior work is completed, dirt can be placed against the exterior walls of the foundation. This backfill should be packed to avoid too much absorption of rain water. Care must be taken to keep from damaging the walls.

Interior surfaces. Ceiling and interior wall surfaces can be plaster, wood, stucco, or gypsum board (wall board). Plaster walls are rarely used today. The need to cut costs dictates the use of dry wall or some other type of interior panel wall finish in lieu of plaster. This dry wall finish is nailed directly to the interior studding.

Trim and flooring. After the walls have been allowed to properly dry or cure, interior trim is installed around windows and doorways and baseboard is placed around the perimeter of walls. Finish flooring may consist of linoleum, tile, or wood. Though oak is commonly used for flooring, other woods which can be used include maple, fir, and pine. Wood flooring is sanded and finished. Care in fitting and application must be taken to avoid binding in damp weather and gapping in dry weather. Many new homes use carpeting over a plywood base.

SUMMARY

Construction details and practices do vary among builders and in different sections of the country. New and different materials and construction practices are introduced from time to time. However, five basic elements are necessary for construction to achieve soundness and durability: good design, efficient planning, good materials, efficient workmanship, and proper supervision. Whether a structure is simple or elaborate, these five elements must be present.

The visible interior and exterior parts of a dwelling-house have a bearing on the soundness, state of repair, and safety of the dwelling, both during intended use and in the event of a fire. Your understanding of these parts will aid you in the selection or construction of your home. Part II discusses the components of a home in detail, including how to inspect and evaluate them.

3.
Home Inspection, Appraisal, and Other Services to Aid the Home Buyer and Owner

INTRODUCTION

Professional help is available to assist you in planning and buying a house. If the house buying process has become a major headache for you, this chapter will provide you with some relief. It simply introduces you to the people involved in home buying and the services they provide. An understanding of their functions will make home buying much easier and a more enjoyable experience for you.

Proficient expert advice is the most effective way to get help in an area you are not familiar with. The fees are high but the advice and the savings in time and money more than offset the expense. You may decide to use only a part of the services but you should know what is available to help you.

RELOCATION SERVICES

In the past ten years, numerous independent relocation services were started to help corporate transferees with both selling and purchasing homes. As companies relocated executives, there was a need to help the employees select neighborhoods, and to provide financing and home inspection assistance, as well as other services. The names of some relocation firms are Homerica, Homebuyers Assistance Corp., Equitable, and Executrans. Your personnel office will have the name of the relocation firm they use and the extent of the services provided.

At the same time, cooperative real estate organizations were started to aid in real estate referrals across the United States. Century 21,

E.R.A., and Gallery of Homes are a few of these national groups. Relocation services will refer you to these groups or to local reputable realtors.

BROKERS

You should use a broker to buy or sell a home. Unless you have the knowledge and skill required to make a house sale, a broker's services are indispensible. A broker works for you to provide a buyer for your home at realistic prices and terms acceptable to you.

You will have to sign a listing contract. This is an employment contract with a broker. The contract should include the broker's commission, the house price, and terms of sale, whether or not you will be required to pay the broker's commission if you find the buyer yourself, whether you are responsible for the broker's expenses if the contract is cancelled, and the signature of the person who agreed to pay the commission. Your lawyer should review this prior to signing.

There are different types of listing contracts: the exclusive listing, the joint broker listing, the open listing, and the multiple listing. It is generally thought that the multiple listing provides the fastest and most efficient service. Multiple listings are successful since they promote greater advertising exposure and therefore increase the chances of finding a buyer. Multiple listing people pick up prospects from open houses and from advertising other houses. Prospects want a choice. In fact, buyers generally don't take the open or advertised property; they usually buy a less expensive one—which may well be yours. If you sign a six-month listing, insist upon a three-month cancellation clause to protect yourself should you become disenchanted with the action or service.

The broker is bound by state law to fairly represent the sales of the property. He will also conduct any bargaining sessions with clients. Make sure you are doing business with a reputable broker. More often than not, he or she will be a realtor, a member of the National Association of Realtors.

Finding the right broker to handle the sale or purchase of your home is almost as difficult as selecting the right doctor or lawyer. Find out what services the broker is prepared to offer. To find a good real estate broker, ask your friends or call the mortgage officers of local banks and savings-and-loan associations. Notice which brokers run the most newspaper advertisements for houses in the neighborhoods you prefer. Often, brokers will specialize in a particular neighborhood.

If you are buying a home, a broker will give you general information about a community and specific information about schools, churches, and stores. He will help you get financing and will know how to expedite settlement services. You should advise the broker of your price range, the amount of cash available, and your other requirements of a home. He will show you a number of houses. When you find the one you like, the broker will usually conduct the negotiations with the seller, unless you agree to pay the asking price.

Of course, it is possible to buy or sell a home without the services of a broker. However, this would require great time and knowledge on the part of the buyer. Unless you are quite skilled in the complexities of the house sales market, it is best to take advantage of the broker's offerings.

MUNICIPAL OFFICERS

In your house search, be sure to consult the various municipal authorities who can inform you on the state of the neighborhood, taxes, assessments, flooding, and other local problems. These people are available in the municipal building and have titles like building inspector, tax assessor, water and sewage clerk, sanitarian, health officer, zoning officer, and town clerk.

ATTORNEYS

Choose an attorney who specializes in the field of real estate. A lawyer who is experienced in these matters will save you money and problems in years to come. You are responsible for paying his fee, so be sure to ask the rates in advance and determine the method of payment. Many lawyers charge a percentage of the purchase price, but this can become quite expensive. A more desirable arrangement is to pay your lawyer an hourly rate based on the amount of time he works for you. This attorney will represent you at the closing. Have a clear agreement with him that he represents you and only you.

In many large cities, closings are held at offices of title insurance companies who provide insurance against anything being wrong with the title. Again, your attorney can be invaluable, especially if you are inexperienced in real estate or business dealings. He will make certain that the many fees and charges involved in the settlement are legitimate. The attorney also supplies the abstract of the title, drafts the deed to the property, checks the sales contract, and represents you at the closing.

Before signing the sales contract, have your attorney read it over to determine that it fully protects your interests. The contract should include the Parties to the transaction, the Price to be paid, the Closing date, the Description, any Personal items included in the sale, representations by the seller as to the status of title, and the rights and obligations of the parties in the event the transfer is not consummated.

The "title" to real estate is the right of the owner to its possession and use, free from the claims of others. There are a number of ways your use of the property may be limited. One is by local zoning laws or restrictions in the deeds. Such limitations may enhance the value of the home to you, or they may frustrate your purposes in buying it. If property taxes are not paid, this can result in loss of title. There are special assessments or levies for paving, sidewalks, sewers, drainage, or other improvements. These constitute a charge against the property similar to that for general property taxes. The purchase agreement will require the seller to transfer to the purchaser a marketable title to the property free from all indebtedness or limitations on its use, except for those you may have agreed to accept. It is up to you, the purchaser, to be certain the title you get is marketable. This will require a title search in which a title or abstract company or a lawyer will search through records of previous ownership and sale to establish the right of the seller to sell the property to you.

APPRAISERS

An appraisal is an impartial opinion of the value of real estate prepared by an expert who knows all the factors that make up the current real estate market. It is an opinion by a recognized professional appraiser. There are many good reasons for having an appraisal made of your property. You may want to obtain a professional opinion of the present value of a home or property you wish to buy or sell, or the value of the home you want to build. An expert's opinion of the value of a home or other property is useful as a prudent safeguard against excessive tax assessments, capital gains payments, and other taxes; an appraisal is needed to verify damage claims resulting from fire, rain, hail, wind-storms, and other disasters; and an expert's opinion of value for a home or other property can be the basis for "just compensation" in cases where property is to be taken for future public use.

The professional appraiser must acquire all the facts about the property. He or she will gather comparative selling prices for similar property in the area, and will calculate the square or cubic footage of the buildings and apply a replacement factor. In all cases, an appraiser will thoroughly inspect the interior and exterior of the property, and pay close attention to the condition of the structure and mechanical and electrical equipment. The appraiser considers the location of the property in reference to stores, schools, churches, and recreational areas. He evaluates the neighborhood, applicable zoning regulations, and the trends in property taxes. From this body of information, the appraiser will set a dollar value figure to be used as a basis for negotiation between buyer and seller.

You can select an appraiser by consulting the Society of Real Estate Appraisers for the name of a certified appraiser in your area. Your real estate agent may be of some assistance to you in the selection process. Once you have selected a qualified appraiser be sure your instructions include the reason for your appraisal, the type of report you want, and the date that you need the report. Allow sufficient time for the appraiser to complete his inspection, do his research, and then analyze the data to write the report. This could vary from two days to two weeks. The fee will vary, depending on the nature of the assignment, and will run from $75 up.

HOME INSPECTION AGENCIES

Once you have signed the closing papers on your new home, the house is yours for better or worse. The time to discuss problems is before you buy the house. Many people could have been saved countless hours of frustration as well as increased costs if only they'd had their homes inspected by professionals before buying. Residential housing inspection firms evaluate property for potential buyers and sellers. The inspectors, many of whom are engineers, evaluate the home and property to disclose the condition of the major elements, to note the items that require maintenance, and to estimate when certain components may need replacement. The components of a home include the site, roof, heating, air conditioning, structure, foundation, basement, kitchen, electric service, plumbing, and exterior appurtenances. Residential inspection is presently done in a community by inspection firms on a local or national basis and by individual professional consultants. Inspection fees start at $125 and an inspection lasts about two hours.

WARRANTY PROGRAMS

Many firms, in response to consumer demands, provide warranties that the equipment and structure in new and resale homes will operate satisfactorily for a period of one or more years. Your relocation firm or broker can provide you with information on these programs, or consult the yellow pages under "Building Inspection."

Home inspection firms will inspect your home to determine the condition of the structural, electrical, and mechanical components, and then for an extra fee of $75 to $150, provide a warranty that those items found satisfactory will continue to be so for a 12-month period. If not, the firm will cover the repair or replacement cost from $100 to $25,000. This provides good overall protection, and certain firms are approved by the National Association of Realtors.

Other firms offer a non-inspection warranty for a set fee of $200 to $300, covering electrical, mechanical, and plumbing components. The roof and structural elements are not covered, which is a drawback to these programs.

On new homes, some builders' associations and insurance carriers offer a warranty where the builder agrees to repair, replace, or pay to you the reasonable cost of repairs or replacement of all defects in your home during the initial warranty period. The initial warranty periods for various elements of your home will differ. On appliances, equipment, and fixtures (including their fittings, attachments, controls, and appurtenances) the warranty is equal to the manufacturer's warranty, but not for more than one year. Some of these items, therefore, may be covered for a full year, and others for 90 days. Structural problems are covered for up to ten years—and that is good protection.

INSURANCE AGENTS

Consult with your local agent on the type of coverage he recommends. This is usually a comprehensive homeowners policy. Discuss the expansive riders that cover equipment failure. If you are in a flood plain, be sure to get federal flood insurance, which is available at a low cost.

Depending on the practice in your state, title insurance should be obtained. This is a policy that protects the lender's interest in the property against any title defects not disclosed by the title search. Whether the buyer or seller pays for this varies with local custom. Only one premium payment is required and it is due when the insurance policy is issued. In most areas, the transfer of title from the seller to the buyer is accomplished by a "warranty deed." Through the warranty deed, the seller guarantees the title against claims of other persons.

MORTGAGE LENDERS

Mortgage loans are obtained from savings banks, commercial banks, savings-and-loan associations, mortgage bankers, insurance companies, and from the seller or relatives. Shop around, compare, and find where you can secure a mortgage loan on the best terms for your financial condition. Do this before you start your search for a house.

A mortgage is a loan contract. A lender agrees to provide the money you need to buy a specific home. You promise to repay the money based on terms set forth in the agreement. The contract should state the amount of the loan, the interest rate, the size of the payment, and the frequency of payments. It may also include other provisions, such as penalties and prepayment privileges. As the borrower, you pledge your home as security. It remains pledged until the loan is paid off. If you fail to meet the terms of the contract, the lender has the right to foreclose.

It is wise to find out as much as you can about terms and payment plans of as many different lending sources as possible. Your lawyer or broker may be able to advise you on lending institutions or you can go directly to the lending institution for information. As you obtain information, note differences in interest rates, differences in method of making payments, the length of time given to repay the loan, and the effect of a large cash downpayment.

Various types of mortgage loan plans are available, such as the conventional loan, the Veterans Administration loan, the Federal Housing Administration insured loan, and flexible loans. Conventional loans are made strictly between you and a private lender. You offer your home and your credit as security. Conventional loans vary widely in form and are the most common type used to buy and build homes.

V.A. guaranteed loans are made to eligible veterans by private lenders. If you are a veteran, check with the Veterans Administration for information on home financing benefits available to you. A local bank also can tell you what you are entitled to under the law.

F.H.A. loans are made by private lenders and insured by the Federal Housing Administration. These loans are available to buy a new or existing home or to refinance a home built by the owner. To pay expenses, and cover possible losses, F.H.A. charges an insurance premium on the unpaid balance of the loan. The charge is included in the borrower's monthly mortgage payment. The F.H.A. appraises each home to determine its value and to make sure it is structurally sound and does not present conditions that endanger the health, safety, and well-being of the occupants. F.H.A. loans usually have longer repayment periods and have interest rates fixed by the Department of Housing and Urban Development. Points must be paid by the seller of the home to the bank if an F.H.A. loan is used by the buyer; the amount depends on local interest rates.

At the lending institution, ask to talk with the mortgage loan officer. Tell him you want to buy a home and how much you want to borrow. If the lender wants your business, he will suggest that you file an application. In filling out the forms, you will have to answer questions about the property you wish to buy and about yourself as a prospective home buyer. After a few weeks, you will be notified whether or not your application has been approved. If your application is approved, the lender will arrange the closing of the loan with you. Don't be afraid to negotiate with your lender to try to get the best deal.

Today, a Flexible Loan Insurance Program (FLIP) is available, with graduated payments keyed to family income. Monthly payments are lower at first, and increase slowly as a family's income rises. Just how much monthly payments will be is determined by careful assessment of the buyer's assets and projected income. Though bank acceptance of FLIP mortgages was slow at first, many national banks have become involved; in addition, the service has spread to state banks. Check with your banker.

If ever you experience difficulty in keeping your mortgage payments up to date, you may want to make use of one or more sources of help in your community. Although money may not be available to you from community sources, your local bank can offer the kind of assistance that might help you out of your financial bind. You already know the first place to go for help—to the bank that holds the mortgage on your house. Be sure to tell your bank if you expect to fall behind in your payments. Or if you are already behind, call for an appointment to see the loan manager of your bank. Give him all the details about why you can't pay on time. He may be able to work out a plan to make up back payments at a rate you can afford or a plan to delay future payments until you can make other arrangements.

MOVER

On the national average, the moving experience can be uneventful, but it also can lead to frustrations and uncertainties. The key to a successful move is preparation. The preparation must include the best information available to suit your particular needs.

There are three types of moves.

While *local moves*, within a single metropolitan area or county, can be the easiest type of move, the degree of protection for the consumer often is minimal. Calls to local consumer assistance offices, better business bureaus, and neighbors who have used a local moving company are good first steps. The last step before any move, however, is to make certain the contract between mover and consumer is fully understood by both parties.

Transfer of household goods *within a single state* is similar to a local move, except longer distances and greater times will generally prevail. At the same time, state governments usually are better organized for the licensing or certification of household goods movers. The state's public utility commission or state corporation commission often can provide guidelines to consider before you engage a mover.

Because of the time and distance involved, movement *across state lines* represents the most complex type of move. At the same time, this kind of move is backed by the most precise set of requirements and rules for the protection of the consumer. If household goods are being transported across state lines by a carrier, the movement comes under the jurisdiction of the Interstate Commerce Commission. Information on their rules is available through their Washington office.

Try to be flexible in your moving plans. Try to avoid moving during the summer season and those days preceding the first of the month when many households are being shifted. Consult your moving company for their standard moving checklist. This will be of invaluable assistance in your planning. Decide what you intend to move; which material you will transport yourself; which articles you will pack; and which will be packed for you at a fee. Select a moving company with a good reputation in the community and ask for written estimates. Determine what degree of legal protection is needed for the safety of your household goods. Be sure that agreements between you and the carrier are in writing and on the order of service and the bill of lading which the carrier will provide.

When the driver arrives, and before loading begins, obtain his name, home office location and telephone number, vehicle license and equipment numbers, the location of the scale he will use to weigh your shipment, his route, the expected arrival time, and where he can be reached *en route*. Also let him know your plans and provide an address and telephone number where you can be reached.

An inventory will be made of your goods and their condition. Have someone accompany the mover's representative as he writes up the inventory. Note in writing any disagreement over the described condition of an article before signing off after completion of inventory. Examine the bill of lading carefully. It serves as a receipt and represents the contract of carriage. Be certain you understand the portion setting forth the liability of the mover for any loss or damage to your goods. Verify the tare weight of the vehicle before your goods were loaded. The difference between the loaded and tare weights will establish the weight of your shipment.

Plan to be at the delivery site on or before the agreed delivery time. Movers need only wait three hours for you to accept your shipment. Upon delivery, have a family member check each article against the inventory and examine for any damage. Before signing the delivery receipt or the inventory, make sure they include written notations of loss or damage, and be specific. Good planning with a reputable carrier will make the move easier.

SUMMARY

Use the services of experts in both buying and selling a house. Many pitfalls can be avoided this way. When you settle in the community of your choice, you gain a stake in its future, its plans, and its problems, so select carefully. Consult the detailed checklist that covers all the points discussed in Part I.

4.
Buying the Home

INTRODUCTION

Careful research avoids pitfalls in buying a house. Relying too strongly on emotion can lead to your dream house later turning into a nightmare. Choosing and financing a home can be a challenging undertaking for a family. Many unfamiliar decisions must be made, and money can be saved if you are well prepared.

This chapter outlines the steps to take in buying the home: listing your family needs, selecting a community, deciding on the house, and financing and closing on the house. There is a comprehensive checklist in the Part I summary that will guide you through the steps in buying and inspecting the house. Refer to this after reading the first five chapters.

NEEDS

Once you've decided to buy a house, you must draw up a list of the fundamental requirements of your family and the type of home and community in which you are interested. The personal needs will be dependent upon the size of your family, the ages of your children, your requirements for basic shelter, your place of work, your need of a home for social and entertainment purposes, the nearness of community services, and the price you are able to pay. There may be special needs, such as studio or office space, or special interest, such as gardening or other outdoor activities. You may require land and outdoor space for the family. You may have special educational needs. You or your wife or husband may want a view.

These requirements should be carefully listed by priority, before starting any searching. The way you want to live should determine the location and type of dwelling you chose. You will probably have to make compromises, and the priority list will help you decide what you're willing to do without.

INFORMATION CHECKLIST

In preparing for your house hunting, you will need basic financial data to establish your credit. Make a list of the value of your checking accounts, savings accounts, stocks and bonds, savings certificates, charge accounts, real estate holdings, insurance, automobiles, annual income, and any debts you may have. This profile will produce your net worth and will be requested by the mortgage lender. Next, prepare a budget of your present income and expenses for both renting and owning a home.

RENT OR BUY

At some time, you must make a choice between renting or owning a house or other shelter. Both renting and owning have advantages and disadvantages. In deciding which is best, you will want to consider such factors as the size and age of your family, your finances, your job, your family's likes and dislikes, the costs involved, and the housing available in your community. The major advantage of owning a home is the fact that the price of homes have outpaced the rise in inflation. A house is a wise investment, but you must be able to come up with the downpayment.

HOW MUCH CAN YOU AFFORD?

Your ability to pay for a new home is dependent upon your job, your savings, your ability as a handyman, and also your willingness to sacrifice extras like travel or expensive entertainment. To plan wisely, estimate how much money you will have available for monthly mortgage, utilities payments, and property maintenance by subtracting monthly living expenses from monthly income. Keep in mind that the price of the home should not exceed two to two and one half times your annual family income. A young couple should stay on the low side of this estimate. If income is substantial and job prospects good, the upper level can be applied.

A homeowner should not pay more than 25% of income for monthly housing expense, which includes the mortgage payment plus the average cost of heat, utilities, maintenance, and equipment replacement. The bank and seller can provide typical monthly mortgage payments for homes in your price range and can give you some tips on estimating house operating costs.

The downpayment will vary from 5% to 30%, depending on the type of loan and local lending conditions. The obvious source of money for a downpayment is either your savings or the proceeds from a sale of a home you already own. But there are other sources, like life insurance cash value, profit and pension funds, and a working spouse. You should start accumulating this downpayment as part of your marriage plans.

COST OF HOMEOWNERSHIP

One of the common errors made in buying a house is to think that the only cost will be a small downpayment plus monthly mortgage payments. Before you buy, be sure your income is large enough to cover all the costs for today and into the next few years. Make up a budget and include the initial cash outlay for closing costs, which can run over $2000. Then consider mortgage payments, taxes and insurance, heat and utilities, maintenance, equipment replacement, and other debts. Get a total cost figure and work out a budget for the next three years. Budgets and savings plans go hand in hand.

WHAT KIND OF A HOME?

The choices depend on the section of the United States you live in and whether you want an old or a new home. You can select a single family house, a multiple dwelling, a cooperative, or a condominium. House styles include the Cape Cod, ranch, split level, contemporary, colonial, Tudor, Spanish, and variations of these. Keep an open mind and explore as many possibilities as you can before you narrow your choice to fit your particular needs.

Statistics show that two out of every three buyers select a used house.

The one person out of three who buys a new house is likely to purchase one that is already built rather than have one built. This is a choice each home buyer must make for himself.

The age of a house should not necessarily limit your choice. Although some older homes may require more repair work, many have received excellent care from previous, long-time owners. Usually two of the biggest advantages an older house offers is more space for the money and an established community. Many older homes have ample bedroom space. The lot may have been planted with trees and shrubs and therefore present relatively few landscaping problems. Of course, some older houses are located in neighborhoods that have started to deteriorate. Before purchasing a house in an older neighborhood, be sure to check on any future plans for neighborhood improvement.

THE COMMUNITY

Before beginning your search, be sure to consult the experts discussed in Chapter 3. The relocation firm and local brokers can supplement the information you gather from local friends and municipal officials.

If you are new to the area, make a systematic search to find two or three communities that suit your family needs. Spend a few days touring areas to get a feel for the towns. Keep your price level in mind as you look around. Read real estate ads for those communities. Determine the quality of municipal services. Note the physical appearance of the homes and streets. Is the area convenient to your work?— try to stay within a 15-minute drive, or better still, be near public transportation.

When you purchase a home you are not only getting a place to live; you are making an investment. The best way to protect your investment is to pick a location that is desirable now and will continue to be desirable in the future. You should find out as much as possible about different areas and neighborhoods before you decide on one. Ask questions of responsible persons who know the answers, study the zoning map, shop in the stores, visit the schools, and try the commuting routes. Don't learn about the problem areas after you move in.

QUESTIONS TO ASK THE MUNICIPALITY

The municipal engineer, building inspector, and other officials can supply you with good information about the town. Question the proper officials about local problems. Ask about the adequacy of the public sewer system, the septic systems, the water supply, the rate and trend of taxes, what municipal facilities are provided, the size of the police and fire protection, the location of the hospitals, the trash removal and snow removal schedules, transportation and shopping convenience, recreational activities, and cultural opportunities. Find out if real estate taxes are rising. Ask what the current assessing practices are. Are there problems with water run-off and drainage? Is the character of the town changing? Is there a master plan? Are there many break-ins or acts of vandalism? Make a list of questions from the information in this book.

INSPECTING THE HOME

Keep in mind when house hunting that there is no such thing as the perfect house. There are certain factors that need to be considered from the point of view of your personal needs and the resale value of any house you are considering. In many cities, there are reputable inspection firms that will examine the home and its components. Their expertise and experience will be well worth the price. At AMC, we have uncovered numerous defects that the buyer could negotiate with the seller. Other times, all we found was an excellent house. In your inspection, the key points to remember are these: Is the foundation good? Is the house frame square and free of decay and insect damage? Is the house arranged for good livability and does it fit your needs? What is needed to bring the house up to your standards and what are the costs?

Real estate law makes it incumbent upon the seller and his agent to tell the buyer of any defects they know of which are not apparent. They are liable to restitution if they do not reveal these defects. You may also want to avail yourself of a home inspection warranty plan as an added protection. AMC has been successful with these plans in protecting the consumer from large unexpected expenditures when they move in. If, after the inspection, you are unsure of the selling price, then hire an appraiser. But first discuss this with the realtor, who is your agent in the negotiation process.

BUYING THE HOUSE

You've found a resale house. Now you make an offer, the first step in the negotiating process. New homes usually have a set price. To make an offer, you will sign a sales agreement indicating a price and submit a small returnable deposit to show that you are earnest in your desire to buy. Before you sign the contract, read it carefully and understand each detail. All verbal agreements go in the contract and these should include an engineering and termite inspection. Have the lawyer and realtor review this document.

In making an offer, be sure to gather data on the recent sales of comparable homes. Your realtor can help, or you can engage an appraiser. When all these facts are in, make the offer. Depending on whether it is a seller's or buyer's market, you will stay close to the appraisal or selling price. With the offer made, the realtor will act as a go-between for you and the seller. Over the next few days, be prepared to compromise on this offer price. When you agree on a price, you and the seller are ready to go to a more final contract.

Before signing any contract, have your attorney read it over to determine that it fully protects your interests. The contract should include: the parties to the transaction, the price to be paid, the method of payment, the amount of deposit, the financing requirements and contingencies, the closing date, the property description, any prior title recitals (optional), the personal items included in the sale, the representations by the seller as to the status of the title, and the rights and obligations of the parties in the event the transaction is not consummated.

The "title" to real estate is the right of the owner to its possession and use, free from the claims of others. The property may be limited by local governmental zoning laws or restrictions in the deeds, by general real property taxes which if not paid can result in loss of title, and by special assessments of levies for paving, sidewalks, sewers, drainage, or other improvements.

The contract will require the seller to transfer to you a "marketable" title to the property free from all indebtedness or limitations except for those you may have agreed to accept. A "marketable" title assures its ready acceptance by a future purchaser or lender. This will require a title search to establish the right of the seller to sell the property to you. Title insurance should also be obtained; it protects the lender's interest and your interest in the property against any title defects not disclosed by the title search. Only one premium payment is required, due when the insurance policy is issued at closing.

CLOSING

The closing is the transaction where you receive all of the documents required to convey the title of your home and your right to occupy it. The closing may take place in the office of the lender, the lawyer, or the title company. Both spouses should attend the settlement as their signatures will be needed. If you are traveling, your lawyer can represent you. The keys to your new home are turned over at the closing.

Under the Real Estate Settlement Procedures Act (RESPA), your lender must supply you with a booklet called "Settlement Costs," within three days after you apply for a mortgage loan. He must also give you a written estimate of all closing costs. These costs are all the charges and fees incurred in transferring ownership of your new home to you, in processing the loan papers required before your lender will forward to your seller the money being provided to help you buy your home, and finally, in taking the steps necessary to assure that your lender will have a valid lien against your property as security for the repayment by you of your home purchase loan. Other costs which must be paid at the closing are the adjustments to be made between you and your seller for certain yearly payments which may be charged on a *pro rata* basis.

On the day before closing, you have the right to inspect the original closing statement. Most costs are firm by then. Depending on where you live, some of the charges you may find in the closing statement are for: title insurance, the title search, the attorney's fees, a survey of the property, preparation of documents, the closing fee, a credit report, a termite and engineering inspection (sometimes paid when done), the lender's origination fee, the appraisal fee, the recording fee, state and local transfer taxes, mortgage insurance premiums, escrow fees, and *pro rata* charges like taxes and fuel. There will be a lot of paper signing and other things going on at the closing and your attorney and lender will make this as smooth as possible. When finished, take your spouse out to dinner. You both deserve it!

MISCELLANEOUS CONCERNS

There are a number of things you must do prior to moving to make the move as smooth as possible. Consult your moving company for their standard checklist. Other items to consider include the following. From the homeowners, get all instruction booklets and warrantees. Get the names of the service people they have used. Check to see if the Town Building and Health Inspector have to inspect the home prior to purchase for conformance to the minimum property maintenance code. If the home is to be left empty, are all systems protected from the elements? Has the well water been checked for potability and capacity? Do you have a well log containing well statistics? Has the septic tank pump record been checked? Do you have a map of the system? Call the utility and fuel companies for a utility usage check. Have all appliances been checked and serviced? Have you availed yourself of a fire prevention check and a security check by the local municipality? Check on peculiar weather conditions such as floods, high water table, poor soil drainage, heavy rains, heavy snows, severe icing at the gutters, and infestation. Call the Town Building Inspector and Health Officers to see if there are any reported violations or problems in your house or the area.

SUMMARY

Careful research and planning will help you avoid the pitfalls in buying a house. Use the checklist in the Part I Summary plus the maintenance checklist in Chapter 33 as a guide for your plans. Moving is a stress-provoking process and good preparation will tend to make it a smoother operation. Once you've successfully purchased your new home, you will have a new problem: maintaining it. In fact, you agree in your mortgage to keep the property in good condition. This is only common sense. Why sacrifice to buy an expensive house and then allow it to lose value through your neglect? Regularly put aside an amount for annual upkeep, allowing for the fact that maintenance costs will vary from year to year.

Enjoy your new home!!

5.
Common House Ailments

INTRODUCTION

The purpose of this chapter is to give an overview of the common house ailments that will be discussed in detail in Part II. Figure 5.1 illustrates these problems. Of course, not all houses are faced with all problems; however, an awareness of the difficulties you may encounter will be invaluable to you as a homeowner. For your convenience, a list of approximate repair or replacement costs is included in Chapter 28 (Home Improvement Economics).

If you buy a new or resale home, you should be absolutely sure the house is in sound condition. Get expert advice, if necessary, from an impartial person who has house construction experience—a home inspector or engineer. You don't want to buy a house with a leaky roof, termites, a wet basement, a poor foundation, aluminum wiring, poor lot drainage, a faulty sewage system, an inadequate water supply, or a sagging structure, without knowing what you are getting into. If you do find defects, then the seller may agree to correct these or adjust the sale price of the home. Nothing can be done after you move in except for you to correct it at your expense.

The following common house problems are the key points you should evaluate. Once you have a good basic structure, many ways are open to improve the house appearance and comfort. Painting and landscaping improve the appeal of any home.

THE NEIGHBORHOOD

Location, location, and location are the three most important points in selecting a home! Choose your location very carefully because it

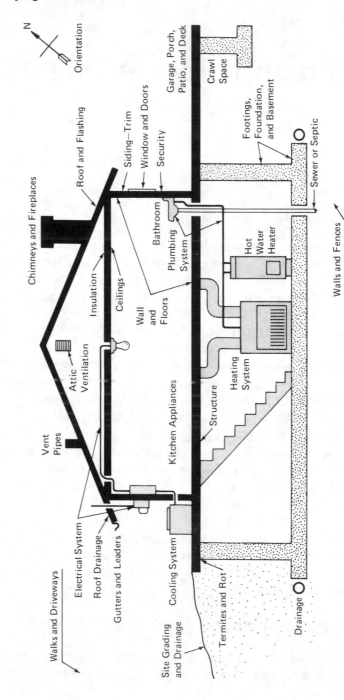

Figure 5.1. Common problems found in resale houses.

will determine your ability to sell the house at a price commensurate with or better than the rise in inflation. All areas will eventually decline in time and your objective is to determine the early warning signs. Your lawyer, realtor, and relocation service can be of invaluable help in defining suitable locations.

SUITABILITY OF THE HOME FOR THE FAMILY

Before you buy, determine your housing needs over the next 10 to 15 years. Buy a house that will meet those needs so you won't have to move because the house is too small or too large. Houses can be expanded and unused space can be converted to living space. Check to make sure you have ample storage space. In houses with no basement, be sure there is storage in the attic or utility room. It is costly to move— so select the home carefully.

GROUNDS AND LANDSCAPING

Make sure you are going to be satisfied with the size and shape of your lot, and with the existing or proposed lawn, shrubbery, walks, driveways, and garage. If you want to have a garden or play space for the children, make sure that sufficient space is available. Is the land properly graded to provide diversion of water away from the building and property and to prevent soil saturation detrimental to the structure? Is the house located in a flood plain? If it is a resale home, take careful notice of the slope of the ground around the house. It should slope away from the house so that water will be carried away from the foundation; otherwise the water may cause trouble. If any additional work on the lot is to be done, make sure the purchase agreement lists all the improvements the builder or owner will make as part of the purchase price. Rough grading and landscaping can be very expensive.

FOUNDATION PROBLEMS

Few homes experience foundation problems but those that do are costly to repair. The weight of your house rests upon the foundation, which consists of the footing and the foundation wall. Foundation walls are subject to a wide variety of stresses and strains. The base of the wall maintains a fairly constant temperature, whereas the top portion is subject to extreme temperature changes which cause concrete and other masonry to expand and contract. This can result in several problems; namely, cracks, condensation, and leaking. Foundation cracks may also be due to uneven distribution of house loads over footings, from footings of inadequate size, or from unstable soil conditions. If you see cracks larger than 5/16 inch, have an expert analyze the cause.

STRUCTURE AND SETTLEMENT PROBLEMS

All houses settle. Rare is the house that does not develop some wall and ceiling cracks. Masonry materials as well as lumber will shrink to some degree. Shrinkage occurs in masonry material during the settling or curing period after installation. It occurs in lumber as the moisture content is reduced. Changes in the weather will cause wood to shrink or expand, resulting in cracks in walls and at joints in woodwork and floorboards. Plaster walls and ceilings that crack because of wood or concrete shrinkage do not present a structural hazard. Cracks that develop in basement or foundation walls or in exterior walls usually indicate structural deficiencies of some kind. Have these evaluated.

If you have a choice, avoid buying a house with extreme structural cracks. Such cracks are usually large, extending across the surface and through the plaster or concrete. The best thing one can do about a house with a defective frame is not to buy it. If the house you choose has a defective frame, seek the advice of a competent expert as to what may be done to arrest the problem.

ROOFING SYSTEMS

The condition of the roof is usually apparent upon close examination. Most roof leaks are caused by leaking flashings or a poor roof drainage system. A roof leak is most likely to occur where the roof joins chimneys, dormers, or in the valleys where two roof slopes meet. These areas are protected by metal flashings that should prevent water from leaking into the house. But flashings become loosened, rusted, worn, or pitted with holes and need sealing. If the valleys of a roof become filled with snow and ice, a temporary roof leak may result from water backing up under the shingles. Clogged downspouts or gutters may also cause roof leaks, and they should be kept clean from leaves, trash, and other material.

Water may leak through the roof for other reasons. Asphalt shingle roofs may leak in a high wind. As these shingles get older, they curl, tear, and become pierced with holes. Wood shingles curl, loosen, and fall off the roof, and asbestos shingles crack, break, and become lost. Metal roofs become rusted; built-up roofs become torn and worn through. If a leak develops, look for water stains on the ceilings and be suspicious of any ceiling that has been recently repainted.

EXTERIOR SURFACES

Most wood or masonry siding materials remain structurally sound. Exterior finishes wear at various rates. Natural finishes need renewing every few years by applying a fresh, penetrating coat when wear begins to show. When repainting, use the type of paint originally applied. A different type of paint may be incompatible and fail to wear satisfactorily. There are many causes of poor paint wear. Most common are vapor or condensation problems, which occur in tightly built insulated houses lacking vapor barriers. Other causes are rain or other water behind siding, an improperly applied priming coat, too frequent repainting, or use of an incompatible type of paint when repainting. Whatever the cause, find and correct it before repainting.

Like other woodwork, doors and window frames tend to swell, shrink, and rot. However, a warped door or stuck window may straighten itself in warm weather.

EXTERIOR APPURTENANCES

These include detached garages, porches, stairs, decks, walks, patios, retaining walls, fences, areaways, and driveways. Weathering, excessive moisture, wood insects, poor installation, and no maintenance are the causes of appurtenance problems. Inspect these items carefully as replacement can be costly.

SWIMMING POOLS

Don't let a pool scare you off. There is some work in maintaining a pool, but if you plan for it you can have a pleasant family activity. In-ground pools should be checked by a pool company for structural soundness of the concrete, or for the condition of the plastic liner and the metal framing and supports. Rot, aging, settlement, corrosion, and weathering are the problem areas.

WET BASEMENTS

These are caused mainly by poor roof drainage and poor foundation grading. A leaky basement wall is annoying but it is usually easy to repair. Variations in climate, soil, and drainage conditions in your locality govern the degree of moisture and dampness that threatens your home. Be especially wary of houses located in flood plains or near streams; most of them have periodic water problems. It is important that your lot be graded away in all directions from the house. If water is allowed to form pools near the foundations, it will eventually find its way into the building.

If there is moisture in the basement, don't conclude that the foundation wall or floor is leaking. The cause may be condensation, particularly on warm summer days. Usually, adequate ventilation will prevent this from occurring. In houses with a crawl space, moisture or dampness may develop if the space is not adequately ventilated.

During your inspection, look for telltale signs of water in basement areas: discolored, stained, or cracked walls; excessive dampness; or the presence of sump pumps. Also check the walls for black mold or for a white powdery sustance called efflorescence. Look for rust or water stains on wood, plaster walls, under stairs, and in the furnace casing.

ELECTRICAL SYSTEM

Many older homes do not have a large enough electric service or enough convenience outlets. Most newer homes are adequately wired to take care of the various modern appliances and other electrical appliances in common use. However, if you intend to add a large appliance, such as a freezer or dryer or central air conditioning, consult an electrical contractor to determine whether additional wiring is necessary. Be sure that at least 150 amperes at 110/220 volts are available at the electric panel for a six to eight room house. If electric heating equipment is used, then 200 amperes or more are required.

Large appliances and power tools operate better and more safely on separate circuits.

Old knob and tube wiring must be inspected carefully. It is often old and the installation has a tendency to crack near light fixtures. Old light switches stick and often there are not enough electrical outlets and too many outlets are on the same circuit. This results in overfused lines. Determine if you have aluminum wiring and have this system checked by an expert for malfunctioning.

HEATING SYSTEMS

These include warm air systems with ducts and outlets, hot water pipe and radiator types, steam, and radiant pipe or panel types. These may be gas, oil, electric, or coal fired. Many systems have compact units of much smaller size than those of some years ago. The main concern is that the particular system has proper capacity for comfort and economy. A free or nominally priced inspection of the heating system often is available from fuel suppliers or a utility company. The major causes of poor heating are insufficient insulation and an inadequate or poorly functioning heating system. The condition of the furnace is often reflected in its appearance and by its age. An old boiler encased in asbestos probably is a potential trouble maker. An adequate clean furnace without rust may require minor repairs but usually has lots of good life left.

AIR CONDITIONING

The compressor is the heart of this system and the manufacturer warranty is over in five years. Most homeowners do not annually maintain this system and the compressor fails soon after the fifth year. A simple test procedure can evaluate the condition and future life. Determination of the proper size of the central air conditioning system is difficult for the home buyer. For a rule of thumb, a well insulated house without a basement, with a living area of 1,400 square feet requires a capacity of about 36,000 BTU/hour in the mid-Atlantic states. A larger house with less insulation will require more. Check the duct work and see that there is an adequate return system to provide good circulation.

AIR AND WATER TREATMENT SYSTEMS

This includes humidifiers, dehumidifiers, ventilating fans, and water treatment systems. Good maintenance and cleaning determine future operation and life. Our experience is that the homeowner neglects these items; they may need replacement or extensive maintenance.

PLUMBING

There are two plumbing systems in your house. One provides water for household uses and the other drains water from all home fixtures and carries it to a public sewer system or to a private disposal system. The plumbing system in a newer home will usually give you no trouble other than a dripping faucet or failure of the toilet supply valve to shut off. If your house is over 25 years old, then you can expect plumbing problems such as leaking and clogging of pipes with rust and mineral deposits.

In older homes, galvanized and brass piping will mean you can look forward to eventual replacement because of clogging and joint leaks. Prior homeowners may have replaced part of the system with copper plumbing and the dissimilar metals cause excessive corrosion. You can spot leaks by a visual inspection, and low water pressure can be seen when you flush toilets with a faucet open. Plumbing repairs are costly, so inspect closely.

BATHROOM PROBLEMS

A three-bedroom house with at least one full bath and one lavatory is now substandard. Examine the location of the wall switch for the light in the bathroom. Be sure that this switch is located so that you cannot reach it while standing in the bathtub. Inspect the tile and bathtub for proper installation and chipping. The principal area where cracked, loose, or leaking bathroom tiles occur is around the tub or shower area. New waterproof grouting help eliminate this.

Shower cabinets are an expensive cause of trouble. If you have a tile floor over a lead pan, they start to leak after ten years. Look closely at the tile and the tile floor. Are there any hairline cracks? On the ceiling below, are there signs of water stains? Does the ceiling appear to have been patched? Look closely at the light fixture for rust. In some cases, the leaks can be corrected by caulking.

HOT WATER HEATERS

Inadequate hot water is a common complaint. A hot water heater over seven years old is ready for replacement. Undersized hot water heaters will produce insufficient hot water. Capacities of hot water heaters range from 30 to 80 gallons. For a family of five, and with the usual appliances such as washer and dishwasher, a minimum of 50 gallons is suggested. The rate of heat recovery after complete hot water usage is important. If the heater is of the quick recovery type, 50 gallons may not be required. Electric heaters having a 60-gallon tank and two heating elements, both of which are rated at 4,500 watts, are considered quick recovery heaters. Some homes have instantaneous hot water heaters as an integral part of the heating boiler, but these are often unsatisfactory.

WATER WELLS

If the water is from a well, the odds are that it is adequate. Here again, the town health officer can help you. At the least, you should have a potability test on the water, and in problem areas, a capacity test. Deep artesian wells, if properly installed, do not cause problems to homeowners. You must remember that excessive usage may cause the well to temporarily run dry, so don't run the water all day to water the lawn—leave that to the rain. If the water is very hard or has a heavy ferrous content, you may wish to consider a water softener. Get a well log that will show the depth and g.p.m. of flow, and get the name of the well digger. Pumps usually require replacement approximately every ten years.

PRIVATE SEWAGE SYSTEMS

If you are buying a house that is located where there are public sewers, you will have little to worry about. If there are no public sewers, you will probably have a septic tank. Ask the homeowner to show you where it is located on your lot. Inquire about size or capacity in gallons, and locate the tank manhole and the absorption field. Check to see if the system is functioning properly. About 50% of septic systems don't operate properly. Either the toilets are slow to flush or there is a bleeding in the yard near the leaching fields or seepage pit. You can check these problems by flushing toilets and sinks and by closely examining all areas over and adjacent to the field soil absorption system. Look for wet, soggy spots, areas of dead grass surrounded by healthy grass, discolored or "sudsy" liquid and mold growth. These conditions usually indicate a failing soil absorption system or, in a few cases, a clogged septic tank. Permanent correction or repair of such failing systems is extremely difficult. On older properties, you should get advice from the health department or from people familiar with the neighborhood to find out whether septic tank systems in the area work properly. Ask how often the system has been pumped. Proper maintenance procedure calls for the septic tank to be inspected and pumped every few years.

FIREPLACE AND CHIMNEY

Chimney cleaning is needed every three to five years—particularly if you have oil heat. Check the flue for leaks and check the chimney for cracks and loose masonry. Be sure your fireplace damper is operational. Check the flue for cleanliness. Be sure the fireplace brickwork and mortar are sound. A proper draft requires a chimney at least 20 feet off the fireplace hearth. Shorter chimneys may cause smoking. That's why so few fireplaces are used.

WOOD INFESTATION AND DECAY

If your home is financed and it is in a termite-prone area, the bank requires a termite inspection and treatment if infestation is found. Periodic inspection should be made at least every six months if you live where termites are common. The existence of termites or infestation in older slab or basement houses is difficult to detect because contact with the soil is usually direct and tubes are not evident. Inspection by professional exterminators is essential in such cases. Termites work fairly quickly but if they are caught in time the damage is slight. You might get the termite bulletin distributed by the County Agricultural Agent to give you background on this pest and its control.

Wood rot is caused by poor ventilation, old termite damage, wet wood, and wood touching the ground. It can usually be found at the fascia around gutters, at the ridge of roofs, around porch post and floors, on outside decks, and where wood touches the ground. It can easily be detected by poking the wood with a sharp instrument like an ice pick. The only remedy is to cut out the rot and replace it with sound wood. Then remove the conditions that caused the rot.

CONDENSATION AND MOISTURE PROBLEMS

Wherever there is too much moisture in the warm air inside the house and it comes in contact with cold surfaces such as window panes, cold water pipes, and toilet tanks, condensation will occur.

Condensation and the resulting formation of water which is damaging to structural members often occurs when the temperature of materials falls well below 32°. It also occurs when the temperature of these parts is not that low, but water vapor from cooking, shower baths, washers, and dryers condenses on their surface. Sometimes condensation occurs in insulation, causing it to become wet and useless. Condensation often occurs in the attic, principally because of easy pathways for moisture to migrate from the living quarters or because of inadequate ventilation. Check to see that you have open louvers in the attic. It is very important that these louvers be left open throughout the year. In houses with a crawl space, vent openings are installed for the same purpose of providing needed air circulation. Closing up the ventilation areas can produce excessive condensation, and the resulting moisture may cause rapid deterioration of structural parts. The signs of condensation are excessive mold, delamination of plywood, and damp odors.

KITCHEN AND APPLIANCES

A kitchen has a useful life of about 15 to 20 years. Replacement is usually made because of poor storage, insufficient counter space, not enough window area, wasted wall space, poor traffic flow, poor layout of major work areas, and old appliances.

When you buy your home, certain items of equipment for the kitchen may be included in the purchase price. Make sure you know exactly what you are supposed to get and have it in writing. Examine these pieces of equipment to be certain they operate properly.

INSULATION AND ENERGY-SAVING METHODS

Infiltration of outside air into the house is responsible for as much as one-third of the loss of heat in the winter and of cooling in the summer. The amount depends on the number of cracks under doors, between building-frame members, and the application of caulking around window and door frames. Heat transmission losses through ceilings, walls, windows, and floors is the largest cause of heat waste in the winter and loss of cooling in the summer. The most effective method of lowering these losses is to use insulation. Insulation keeps surface temperatures of walls, floors, and ceilings at an even level. Applying insulation may produce water vapor condensation in house walls unless a vapor barrier is installed on the side of the wall that is warm under winter conditions. If condensation is allowed to form in this way, it may peel paint, dampen insulation, and cause rot. A vapor barrier on the warm side of insulated walls, therefore, is essential in cold climates. Chapter 30 contains a complete checklist on ways to reduce energy use in your home. This is important because energy costs will rise considerably over the next few years.

MAKING THE FINAL DECISION

After you have completely examined the house, listed any repairs necessary, and considered the intangibles, then you are ready to evaluate your findings. You are buying the property "as is" and you must live *in* as well as with your mistakes. So negotiate beforehand. The age of a house should not necessarily limit your choice. While older homes may require more repair work, many have received excellent care from previous long-time owners and will compare favorably with newer structures. If the foundation and frame are in reasonable condition, the repair and replacement items do not appear excessive, and the cost of buying and renovating the house does not exceed the fair market value of houses in the area, then it is a sound investment.

Few home buyers make a full-time business of checking house construction. If you have doubts about the soundness of the house you have selected, obtain an expert appraisal of the property to establish its value and point out deficiencies. In many cities, there are reputable inspection firms that will examine the home and give you a detailed report. If you must call in experts, first check their reputations and beware of unscrupulous operators who may justify their fees by exaggerating flaws which they may want to repair at inflated costs. If it appears that repairs and improvements are needed, be sure to secure estimates of the cost of the work and find out who will pay for it—you or the seller.

SUMMARY

When you become the owner of a used or new home, you agree in your mortgage to keep the property in good condition. Why sacrifice to buy an expensive house and then allow it to lose value through your neglect? Regularly put aside an amount for annual upkeep, allowing for the fact that maintenance costs will vary from year to year.

A house is a complicated mechanism and you can't expect to know how to keep everything in good working order. If you are handy with tools, you may be able to do some of the repair and improvement work. But don't tamper with expensive equipment and appliances unless you are sure that you know what you are doing. When the plumbing, electric, or heating system needs more than minor repair, it's time to call in an expert. Remember that preventive maintenance, while time consuming and sometimes costly, is worth the trouble and expense. A house is a major investment. If cared for properly, it will repay you with years of comfort and increase in value.

Part I. Summary
Checklist for Home Buying and Inspection

INTRODUCTION

The first five chapters have introduced you to buying a home and discussed the common problems you may encounter. The purpose of this summary is to present in convenient checklist form the steps discussed in Part I. Further inspection details are explained in Part II.

Buying a house is a serious, costly business and you should get expert advice. Once you've established your need, the next step is to decide on a neighborhood and evaluate homes available in your price range. Previously owned houses are generally sold in the "as is" condition. The time for inspection and noting defects for correction by the seller is during the contract negotiation. Repair or replacement items should be noted in the contract, along with who is responsible for them and at what dollar value.

The following checklist will help you systematically evaluate potential houses and assess their relative merits. However, not all items will apply to all houses you may wish to consider, so don't necessarily eliminate a house if it doesn't rate "yes" on all counts. The checklist is a guide to the items you should consider, but it is not all inclusive. Therefore, read each chapter, and add checkpoints to the list to fit your particular needs. Happy hunting!

INFORMATION CHECKLIST

Following is a list of information you will need when the time comes to make your credit, mortgage, and insurance arrangements and to take care of other aspects of your relocation.

( ) Checking accounts: bank names, addresses, and account numbers.

( ) Savings accounts: bank names, addresses, and account numbers.

( ) Other savings: value of your savings in U.S. Savings Bonds, other savings, and retirement plans (Keogh, etc.).

( ) Current value of stocks and bonds you own.

( ) Charge accounts: names and addresses of firms that extend you credit.

( ) Real estate holdings.

( ) Automobiles: year, make, and models of autos currently owned.

( ) Annual income from salary and bonuses.

( ) Sources of income beyond your regular salary.

( ) Other indebtedness not included above.

( ) Your will: check with your attorney to assure that it is legally acceptable in your new state.

Expert advice can be a big help in your preliminary planning. Discuss the extent of the services and fees of whomever you consult.

( ) Are the services of a relocation firm available through your company?

( ) Select a reputable broker and discuss his services.

( ) Find a home inspector-engineer to evaluate the condition of structural, electrical, and mechanical components of the house you select.

( ) Shop for financing.

( ) Find a local real estate lawyer.

( ) Discuss insurance coverage with an agent.

( ) Discuss the services of an appraiser.

PRELIMINARY PLANNING

( ) Prepare your housing needs.

( ) Decide to rent or buy.

( ) How much house can you afford?

( ) Estimate the downpayment you can afford.

( ) List the possible costs of homeownership.

( ) Decide whether it will be a new or used home.

( ) Discuss house style to fit the housing needs of your family.

( ) Post 1900
( ) Post World War I
( ) Post World War II
( ) Town house
( ) Ranch
( ) Colonial
( ) Split
( ) Bungalow
( ) Bi-level
( ) Tudor
( ) Condominium
( ) Row house

STARTING THE SEARCH

You will be wise to find out as much as you can about different areas and neighborhoods before you decide on one. Look at enough neighborhoods to get a feeling about them; ask questions of responsible persons who know the answers; locate the zoning map and study it; shop in the stores; visit the schools; note the commuting time.

( ) Where should you buy? ( ) City. ( ) Suburbs. ( ) Rural.
( ) Discuss potential areas (towns) with a relocation expert.
( ) Visit municipal offices and ask questions of officials.
  ( ) Zoning officer
  ( ) Building inspector
  ( ) Sanitarian
  ( ) Tax assessor
( ) Select a broker who covers the areas you're interested in.
( ) Select two or three neighborhoods or sections to view to see if they fit your needs.
  ( ) Is the neighborhood attractive and well maintained?
  ( ) Do the homes complement one another in design and color?
  ( ) Is the zoning character and quality of the neighborhood likely to remain unchanged?

( ) Is the neighborhood free from danger of flooding?

( ) Are there people in your age and interest group?

( ) Are there children in the same age group as yours?

( ) Are there sidewalks, curbs, gutters, and paved and lighted streets?

( ) Is the tax level of the community consistent with the services provided and consistent with what you can afford to pay? How does it compare with nearby areas?

( ) Will special assessments be levied in the near future?

( ) Is the neighborhood conveniently located with respect to schools, parks, transportation, and other services?

( ) Must the children use a school bus?

( ) Are utilities installed or available?

( ) Is there refuse collection? Cost?

( ) Are there any signs of neighborhood decline?

( ) Are there any nuisances that, when too close to a house, will decrease its value, such as highways, stores, offices, gas stations, etc.

VIEWING HOUSES

You will probably visit many homes before deciding to make an offer. Be sure to bring with you: a camera, flashlight, clipboard, graph paper, tape measure, and pencil. Prepare a quick House Fact Summary Sheet to be able to quickly compare alternatives. The following can be photocopied and placed on graph paper. Draw columns for the different houses.

QUESTIONS FOR THE HOMEOWNER AND OTHERS

When you've narrowed your selection to one or two houses, you are ready to ask more detailed questions of the owner.

( ) How much is the house assessed for?

( ) When was the house last assessed?

( ) How much are the annual taxes and the tax rate per year?

( ) Are there any easement or zoning restrictions?

( ) What is the total energy cost per year? Ask to see the bills.

House Fact Summary Sheet

	House A	House B	House C
Date			
Address			
Owner			
Telephone			
Realtor			
Telephone			
House Style			
MLS Fact Sheet			
Instant Photo Taken			
House Style			
Age			
Asking Price			
Occupancy Date			
School Location			
Distance to Work			
Zoning Changes			
Mortgage Assumable			
Mortgage Data			
Property Taxes			
Assessments			
Garbage Pickup/Cost			
Electricity Cost			
Heat Costs			
Water Tax			
Sewer Tax			

( ) What are the insurance costs for the house and the family car?

( ) Are there any extra municipal costs or a tax for garbage, water, water softeners, pools, etc.?

( ) What repairs or replacements were done within the last five years and what were the approximate costs?

( ) When was the house last inspected for termites and what was the result of treatment and repairs? Ask to see the report.

( ) Go to the city building department and ask to review the file on the property. Note variances, restrictions, non-conforming use, any code violations, septic or well problems, the need for a Certificate of Occupancy or a Minimum Property Code Inspection, and the need for flood insurance.

LOOK AT THE HOME

You have narrowed your selection to one or two houses. Be absolutely sure you check everything. A little bit of extra time spent now may save you a lot of time and money after settlement. If you have doubts about the soundness of the house you have selected, obtain an expert assessment of the condition of the property to point out deficiencies. However, if a professional is not available to you, consider the following in the examination of the house.

( ) Is the house the right size for your family? Is the design simple?

( ) Is the house suitable for the type of living and entertaining you enjoy?

( ) Will the house continue to meet your needs and be attractive to you during the next five years?

( ) Is there an entry or foyer space at the front door, with a guest closet?

( ) Is there a clothes closet near the family or service entrance?

( ) Is a blueprint of the house available?

( ) Is the living room separated visually from the front door and situated to avoid cross traffic?

( ) Is there adequate wall space for alternate furniture arrangements?

( ) Is the family room located best for your family's needs and activities?

( ) Are the bedrooms located best for your family and separated from living and working areas for privacy?

( ) Are floor coverings, wall treatments, countertops, and light fixtures in harmony and complementary in colors?

( ) Is there enough glass and ventilation area in all rooms?

( ) Is there good switch-controlled lighting near the entrance in all rooms?

( ) Are all stairways well-lighted, with a handrail on at least one side?

( ) Do you like the colors and surface characteristics of permanently installed materials, such as ceramic tile and brick?

( ) Are there enough bedrooms of sufficient size to meet your needs?

( ) Is there at least four feet of clothes closet rod space for each member of your family?

( ) Do clothes closets and general shelf storage have a minimum depth of 24 inches?

( ) Is there sufficient dry, well-ventilated dead storage area in the basement, garage, or elsewhere for your family's needs?

( ) Is there a mud room?

NEGOTIATING

Depending on local conditions, you may have to negotiate a price prior to and subject to a home inspection, termite inspection, and appraisal.

( ) Do you have a list of all closing costs?

( ) Do you have the annual house operating costs?

( ) Has the realtor provided comparables?

( ) Do you need a professional appraisal?

( ) Has the home inspector provided you with the cost of repairs?

( ) Have you decided what downpayment you can afford? What mortgage you can carry and obtain?

( ) Has the realtor given you an idea of what price the buyer will accept?

( ) Decide on your offer and how high you are willing to go. Discuss this with your lawyer.

( ) Give the realtor earnest money and get a written agreement guaranteeing the return of your deposit if your offer is not accepted within five days.

THE CONTRACT

Once your offer is accepted, then you and the seller are ready to go into contract.

( ) Have your lawyer prepare the contract and the condition of sale.

( ) Give acceptable percent of sale price deposit.

INSPECTING THE HOUSE

The most important part of buying a resale house is knowing what you are getting into. This checklist is designed to help you focus on some of the crucial physical factors before you are carried away by some superficial aspect such as a window or carpeting. This list is not designed to take the place of a professional home inspector, but it will help you eliminate those homes in too bad a shape. It will also help you direct questions to the inspector. Don't be shy about following the checklist and running equipment in the home you want to make an offer on. Bring old clothes if you intend to crawl in dirty places. Better to find out the condition beforehand when you can do something about it.

Tools.

( ) Do you have tools with you? You will need a flashlight, a long screw driver, a small level, a clipboard, a small magnet, a plumbline, a pen-knife, binoculars, and a copy of this checklist.

Grounds and Landscaping.   The poor location and orientation of a house on its lot substantially detracts from its livability. Unfortunately, the vast majority of existing houses are not located or oriented the best possible way. Therefore, be sure to check the following items.

( ) Is the lot graded so rain water will drain away from the house and property?

( ) What is the condition of the landscaping?

( ) Is the house oriented so that the living areas face east or south?

( ) If the living areas face west, is there proper sun control (overhangs, trees)?

( ) Is the view from the house pleasant and likely to remain so?

( ) Does the lot have attractive, well-cared for trees?

( ) Is automobile access and driveway to the lot simple, and safe?

( ) Are the walks logically located, placed only where needed, and adequate in width?

( ) Are platforms at entry doors at least five feet in their smallest dimension and flush or slightly below the threshold?

( ) Is there sufficient space for additions, and will additions be legally permissible?

Foundation. The house is supported by the foundation wall that rests on footings located below the grade.

( ) Is there a basement or is the house on a crawl space or slab?

( ) Are there any signs of major settlement cracks—not normal hairline cracks?

( ) Is the plaster coat sound? Is the mortar sound?

( ) Are the walls vertical and square?

( ) Is there an entrance from the garage to the basement?

( ) Are there enough windows in the basement for light and air?

( ) Are the basement walls and floors free of cracks, bulges, and signs of seepage? (Hairline cracks are not uncommon or objectionable on basement floors.)

( ) Is the basement usable as additional living space?

( ) In an older home, is there a dug cellar with wood sills resting on the ground (bad for rot and infestation)?

( ) Are the structural members sound?

Exterior Structure. This includes the siding and structure up to the roof.

( ) Are all walls plumb and square?

( ) Is the siding material in good condition, with no bulges?

( ) Do all doors and windows line up squarely in their frames with no dry rot?

( ) Are all the soffits and trim work on securely and free of rot?

( ) Is the paint in good condition?

( ) Are all joints caulked and weather-stripped?

( ) On masonry walls, is the mortar secure?

( ) What is the condition of porches, decks, and detached structures?

Roofs. A sound, tight roof is the first line of defense against water penetration. Use binoculars to get a close-up view.

( ) What is the condition and age of the roof surface?

( ) How many layers of roof coverings are there?

( ) Inspect all pitched and flat roofs up close to determine the condition of the backing.

( ) Are the flashings around chimneys, vents, and valleys in good condition, with no splits or holes?

( ) Does the ridge of the roof sag? Is the roof surface wavy?

( ) Are the gutters and leaders connected securely and in good repair?

( ) Do downspouts discharge where they won't cause problems such as icing or flooding?

( ) Is the attic well ventilated? (Most houses should have openings beneath the eaves and at the peak of the gable walls.)

( ) Is the attic structure free of sag and split wood?

Exterior Appurtenances.   This includes detached structures, walks, patios, driveways, garages, and sheds.

( ) Is the surface of walks, driveway, and patios in good condition? Free of cracks, settlement, and spalling? Is there good drainage? (Some towns and insurance carriers require all surface hazards to be corrected before insurance is issued.)

( ) Does the garage have at least one pedestrian door in addition to the garage door? Do all doors and closures operate?

( ) Are there signs of infestation in the garage?

( ) Are the walls, roof, and floor sound in the garage or shed?

( ) Have a pool service company check out the pool structure and surface plus all equipment.

Basement and Crawl Space Condition.

( ) Is the space dry and free of signs of previous water or flooding condition?

( ) Are the walls plumb and square?

( ) Are there any signs of sagging floors, rotted support posts, or jury-rigged props to shore up weak flooring?

( ) Are there any condensation problems?

( ) Is there a workable sump pump?

Electric Service.

( ) What is the size of the incoming service and circuit box?

( ) Does the wiring in the cellar appear to be neatly installed?

( ) Is there aluminum wiring? What is the municipality requirement of aluminum wire?

( ) Is the old knob and tube wiring in good condition?

( ) Are there ample interior and exterior switches and outlets?

( ) Are there ten or more 115-volt circuits?

( ) Are there enough 230-volt electrical outlets for such items as clothes dryers, range, air conditioner, etc.?

( ) Are there enough electrical outlets for each room? Are all plug-in outlets of the grounded type?

( ) Can utility meters be read from the outside?

Heating and Air Conditioning.

( ) What is the age and type of system? Was it originally designed to burn coal?

( ) Do all systems operate satisfactorily? Test also on a summer day.

( ) Are they free of rust, leaks, and signs of age and misuse?

( ) What is the annual energy bill?

( ) Are there enough registers, radiators, or baseboards in each room?

( ) Is the system adequate and efficient? (Check to see if the type of fuel used and the heating system are most economical for the area.)

( ) Are there leaks around the radiators?

( ) Call the utility or oil company to check the system.

Air and Water Treatment Systems.

( ) Does the humidifier operate?

( ) Is the water softening equipment operable, rented?

( ) Does the dehumidifier operate?

( ) Is there an electronic precipitator and cleaner?

Plumbing.

( ) What are the types of water, vent, and sewage pipes used?

( ) Is the water supply from the city or from a well or cistern? Plan to have the well water tested.

( ) If the house is not served by a public water system, is the water supply adequate for your needs and safe to drink?

( ) Is water pressure adequate?

( ) Is the drainage satisfactory?

( ) Is there a city sewer or private sewer system? Have the septics been serviced recently?

( ) Are there any shower, tile, or bathroom leaks? Look carefully at all ceilings for leaks.

( ) Is the water heater adequate for your needs? (Thirty gallon tanks are usually too small for the average family.)

( ) Is there at least a half-bath on the same floor as the kitchen and near the family or play areas?

( ) Are bathrooms located so you cannot look into them from living areas?

( ) Are bathroom fixtures in good condition?

Fireplace and Chimney.

( ) Are all surfaces in sound condition?

( ) Is the chimney high enough to give a good draft? If in doubt, start a paper fire in the fireplace.

( ) Are all exterior surfaces sound?

( ) Is there a clean-out door?

Termites and Rot.

( ) Are there any signs of wood infestation by termites, ants, or beetles?

( ) Are there signs of wood rot and decay?

( ) Is there adequate protection against decay and termites? (Make sure exterior wood is not in contact with the soil. Check provisions for termite protection. Before buying a house, request a termite inspection.)

( ) Is there vegetation too close to the house?

( ) Are there any signs of rot or infestation in the cornices or attic beams?

Condensation and Moisture.

( ) Are there signs of excessive moisture in the attic, cellar, crawl space, or around windows?

( ) Does the house have a moldy odor?

Kitchen and Dining Area.

( ) Is the kitchen arranged so traffic does not go through the work area?

( ) Does work flow conveniently from one work center to another in the kitchen?

( ) Are there sufficient cabinets and counter space in the kitchen?

( ) Is there space in the kitchen for the appliances you now own or may want to buy later?

( ) Does the house have the type of eating areas you want?

( ) Does the kitchen connect directly with dining and service areas?

( ) Can the whole family eat together comfortably in the dining area?

( ) Try all appliances to see if they work: stove, refrigerator, dishwasher, disposal, washer, dryer.

Insulation.

( ) Is the house adequately insulated? (Three inches of insulation in exterior walls and six inches in the ceiling between living area and attic are minimums.)

( ) Are the weather-stripping, caulking, and window putty in good condition?

( ) Does the house have a properly installed vapor barrier on the warm sides of the exterior walls and ceilings? (Paint problems on the exterior may be due to lack of a proper vapor barrier.)

( ) Is the house exterior protected by an adequate coat of paint and free of obvious paint problems? (Avoid homes with a history of paint problems, even if new siding has been applied over the old.)

Security.

( ) Are all windows and doors secure?

( ) Is there a smoke alarm?

( ) Plan to change all locks.

Final Inspection.   One or two days prior to closing, plan to make a final inspection to be sure all equipment is still in operating condition.

( ) From the owner get the names of all reputable professional and service people they have used.

( ) Get copies of warranties and instruction booklets for all appliances and equipment.

( ) Get the names of all municipal services.

( ) Make sure you receive a termite certificate and Residential Use Permit (Certificate of Occupancy—C.O.), if required.

( ) Get the forwarding address of the seller.

SUMMARY

Keep in mind when house hunting that there is no such thing as the perfect house. There are, however, certain factors that need to be considered from the point of view of your personal needs and the resale value of any house you are considering. Many sellers have warranty contracts but there are numerous items that are excluded if not noticed prior to settlement (scratched mirrors, chipped and marred tiles and porcelain, etc.), so take notice and list any and all discrepancies you find. Inspect again prior to settlement, to make sure that the condition of the property has not changed substantially since the contract was signed.

Part II and Part III contain specific chapters on the components, parts, and systems in the house. Read these to get a greater depth of understanding of the items in the checklist.

PART II.
EVALUATING YOUR HOME'S SYSTEMS

6.
Grounds and Landscaping

INTRODUCTION

Your property must serve the needs of your family in many ways. Convenience, location, municipal services, and privacy are all important. The physical aspects of the site have a great impact on how well the site serves your needs. A poor selection could result in periodic flooding, excess ground water, poor percolation for a private sewer system, and poor soil for landscaping.

This chapter discusses site preparation and landscaping for a new house. If you are buying a resale home, then note the problems of privacy and excess water.

SITE PREPARATION: INFORMATION AND PROBLEMS

In starting the job, the site designer should first determine the restraints that apply to the property. These restraints can be natural or legal in nature or a combination of the two. Steep slopes, generally those over 12%, are difficult to walk on and to maintain lawns on. They are subject to soil erosion and can be difficult to use for on-site private sewage disposal systems. In some states, steep slopes will creep or slide down the hill, taking the house with them. This is especially true of fill land.

In northern states, the slopes that slant toward the north will retain ice and snow longer on sidewalks and driveways than will south slopes. A garden on a south slope will generally produce a better crop than one placed on a northern slope. The prevailing and changing wind direction should influence both house and site design. Strong fall, winter, and spring winds from the northwest influence the construction of outdoor facilities as well as affect the heating of the home.

The bearing soil must support the foundation of your house. Be sure to check the local building department for the minimum required footing size called for by your community code. When rain falls, part of it soaks into the ground and the rest runs off. You should determine the type of soil you have and the effect the neighboring land cover will have on the run-off on your land. A soil that consists mostly of sand or gravel soaks up most of the rainfall, while a tight, sticky clay soil soaks up very little. An impervious ground cover, such as concrete, causes almost 100% of the rain to run off. A clay soil with no cover causes more water to run off than that same soil with a heavy grass covering.

In general, the ideal soil for most uses is one that is more than five feet deep, moderately permeable to water, free from flooding or high water tables and level to gently sloping. Such soils will generally support both buildings and growing plants. When selecting a site, ask yourself the following questions. Will the soil support my house without settling and cracking? What about the water table and the soil permeability? Can I dig a basement and keep it dry, or will it flood under certain conditions? Can I use a septic system, or does the soil absorb moisture so slowly that the effluent will come to the surface and cause a serious health hazard? Is the lot in a flood plain and subject to flooding from nearby waterways during a heavy storm? Is the lot on a hillside subject to slippage or severe soil erosion? Will the soil support grass, flowers, shrubs, and trees, or is it "fill" or raw subsoil that needs added topsoil or special fertilizer and special care? Are certain parts of the lot best for certain uses, such as a swimming pool or a vegetable or flower garden?

Legal restraints also influence the siting of residences. Local laws such as zoning ordinances, building codes, housing codes, health ordinances, sanitation codes, flood plain regulations, and deed restrictions all have to be considered. Zoning ordinances frequently establish front, side, and rear yard setback requirements as well as limitations on the height of buildings. Other restrictions deal with the types and heights of fences, hedges, gardens, and free-standing walls.

Building codes generally will involve the structural design, performance standards, and specifications for the construction of buildings. Housing codes set forth minimum design standards for various types of dwellings and minimum property maintenance standards which must be met. Many codes call for the inspection of resale homes for adherence to the new ordinance.

Health and sanitation codes influence site design where private or on-site wells are used for water supply and where septic systems are used for sanitary waste disposal. State and federal codes establish minimum distances that must separate these two systems and set design standards and materials specifications for both wells and septic systems. Distance requirements also apply to facilities on neighboring lots. Check with your local sanitarian for information on local acceptable practices.

Site problems can and do exist. The cost of a home site where the soils are favorable usually is the same as the cost of land where there are serious limitations. Be sure to check out possible soil problems before you buy. Many municipalities will not let you build if the soil is poor, so check with the municipal building inspector for information on soil conditions.

If you plan to pave a carport floor, garage floor, or driveway in an area with cold winters, be sure to put in a proper stone base and foundation, or the frost will play havoc with the surface, pushing the surface and structures resting on it upward, and causing cracks and settlement; then, when the soil thaws in the spring, the surfaces get soft and a driveway or street can become rough and impassable.

A soil that is excessively drained will make it difficult to establish and maintain a lawn. It will require a lot of water and this can be expensive. In some communities, water shortages have resulted in bans on lawn sprinkling. Soils that have rock and ledge are difficult to build on. Utility lines must enter from the street underground. Blasting and digging through rock in order to install a utility service can be costly and troublesome.

Certain types of clay soil have a tendency to expand considerably when they become wet. These soils, when placed as backfill along basement walls, are generally dry; but when they become wet, large pressures are exerted laterally against the basement wall. This pressure results in large cracks in the walls and structure and can cause uneven settling. Soils that shrink and swell a great deal with changes in their moisture content will cause sidewalks to crack and heave up. In some areas, it is necessary to water the soil at the foundation to prevent structural damage in dry seasons.

Local flooding conditions can develop in any terrain if the rainfall is excessive. Flat areas are difficult to evaluate from a flooding standpoint, as relatively small amounts of rainfall can cause streams to overtop their banks and spread water out for miles. Check your local authorities for flood plain data and the availability of flood insurance. Check also with neighbors who will be familiar with local conditions. Homes on the side of hills or built on fill soil can be in danger if grading precautions are not taken.

When building a new home, study the area carefully to determine if a high water table exists, if seeps or springs are present, or if shallow rock formations will prevent drainage. A check of adjacent road cuts or utility excavations can give an indication of potential problems. Subsurface water problems are frequently hard to identify until a prolonged wet season occurs. Then wet basements, inoperative septic fields, standing water, and drowned out trees, lawn, and shrubs make it all too clear that a real problem exists. So check carefully: the signs are there and the information is available.

If your home will require a private sanitary sewer, take note of the fact that many soils are too impermeable or too water-logged to properly dispose of the septic tank effluent. Some soils are too permeable and allow the effluent to travel large distances without adequate filtration, polluting ground water. If your home will have both a well and a septic tank and you have a very rapidly permeable soil, it would be a good idea to discuss this matter of filtration with a soil surveyor. (See also Chapters 21 and 22.)

Erosion of the soil can be very costly since it can cause serious foundation and stability problems. The rate of erosion is determined by soil type, cover, and slope and the rainfall patterns. Soils that contain a high percentage of sand are more readily eroded than are heavy clay soils. Bare ground is more readily eroded than if it is protected by grass and trees. When water cannot enter the soil, it must travel over the surface, causing greater flows, more erosion, and perhaps flooding. The homeowner who has steeply sloping land soon finds that erosion damage can be very severe unless the area is protected. Sediment, the by-product of erosion, creates problems on your lot and in locations far removed from it. It is also costly to remove.

The best control for erosion is vegetation. Establishing a quick temporary ground cover during construction keeps your topsoil in place. During cold weather, a mulch can be spread to prevent the erosion. Swales, diversions, and concrete waterways can be used to divert water run-off and control erosion. If a development above your property is producing large quantities of water and silt, the town should require the builder to install a basin or settling area to collect the water and sediment. These can usually be installed in the path of a swale or by excavating a basin alongside a stream.

Site plans and house plans should be developed simultaneously by professional help. All major features of a house plan should be reviewed in light of the impact on the site plan, and vice versa. Many times, hillsides are bulldozed level to build houses where two- or three-step hillside houses should have been built. It is better to select a site with minimum building disadvantages than to try to correct troublesome and costly problems after construction has already begun.

Once you have selected a lot with the proper soil, hold grading to a minimum. When grading is necessary, stockpile the topsoil. Soil excavated from the basement can be spread, and after grading, the topsoil can be put back on the surface. This will save you many hours of work and much frustration.

Drainage problems around your existing home are usually more expensive to correct than those on a site under construction. Chapter 13 discusses ways to correct cellar water problems. Foundation grading is important and this involves eliminating all areas where water can pond. This is done by sloping the yard away from the foundation and draining water from low spots. Storm sewers provide an excellent way of handling surface run-off, but the sewers may not do their job if large volumes of subsurface water enter footing drains. There are many instances where the storm drains back-up into the basement for this reason.

If you must build a house on wet soils, then you should not have a basement at all. This is true if you depend on a sump pump to remove the water from the drains. Sump pumps have a tendency to break down and ruin your basement. Some soils require footing drains both inside and outside the footing for dry basements. On some soils, it is very helpful to put the basement floor at a shallower depth than on well-drained soils. It is much easier to build a dry basement on some wet soils if the basement floor is placed only two or three feet below the existing soil surface instead of four to six feet as is often done.

LANDSCAPING THE PROPERTY

Landscaping means creating a plan to make the best use of the space available in an attractive way. It means shaping the land to make the most of the site's natural advantages. It means building such necessary structures as fences, walls, and patios. Finally, it means selecting trees, shrubs, and plants that best fit the design.

You should consider hiring a professional to lay out a complete coordinated plan. This plan should include the shape of the land, tree plantings, and a blending of bushes and flowers to fit the house and property. It is important to start with a plan. Then, as money is available, parts of the plan can be accomplished. If you want to do it yourself, go to the Agricultural Extension Agent, where you can obtain helpful booklets and advice in developing a landscaping plan. Work out the design on paper. It is amazing how ideas will develop and mistakes will show up on a plan. Be sure to include in the plan the public area, the living area, and the service area.

New housing developments provide so little indoor space that it is necessary to use the space around the home as an extension of the home into the landscape. The trend toward outdoor living has increased interest in this area. If possible, locate the outdoor living area where you can see it from the major living areas in the house. This way it can be enjoyed as fully from inside your house as from outside.

The utilities and service areas should be screened by a fence. The amount of available space will determine the extent of the screening for this particular area. A well-designed fence can be a basic part of the landscape, and its placement, function, and design can serve to emphasize the landscaping.

The relative acidity or alkalinity, texture, humus content, and drainage of the soil should be investigated. Your agricultural agent or state university can help. Soils that are extremely acid or alkaline can stunt growth. A very heavy clay soil will drain poorly and keep needed air from the plant roots. For easy maintenance, it is best to choose plants that will tolerate your particular soil condition. Local experts can help you make these choices.

SUMMARY

Each family's needs are different. Include in your site and landscaping plans only those family interests that will make the living space, both inside and out, most livable and useful for your family. It is certainly not necessary for you to complete your total design all at once. Your first job is to put on paper what your landscape development will include and what parts are to be completed first. Then, as money is available to finish different sections, these sections will fit into the total picture. Completing the entire plan could take five years or more. Professional help will assist you in producing a balanced, proportioned look over the years.

7.
Foundation and Basement

INTRODUCTION

A foundation consists of the footings and walls and serves several purposes. The foundation supports the dead weight of the building and other vertical live loads such as people, furniture, and snow; it stabilizes the house against horizontal forces such as wind; and it serves as a retaining wall that supports the earth fill around the house. The foundation walls provide an enclosure for a crawl space, basement, or cellar wall, and may also enclose livable usable space.

Good design will produce a foundation free of settlement and a basement that is light and dry. This chapter discusses problems, maintenance, and inspection of foundations and basements.

TECHNICAL INFORMATION

The parts of a foundation include the construction below grade (footings, cellar, or basement walls) and the walls above grade. The footings distribute the weight of the building over a sufficient area of virgin ground or pilings so the foundation walls will stand properly. Footings are usually twice the width of the foundation wall and one width deep. They are usually constructed of concrete; however, in the past, wood, whole trees, and stone or rubble have been used. Some older houses and outbuildings have been constructed without footings and these will show settlement. Your town code will specify footing sizes for local soil conditions.

The foundation bed may be composed of solid rock, sand, gravel, or unconsolidated sand or clay. Rock, sand, or gravel materials are the most reliable beds for footings. Unconsolidated sand and clay, though found in many sections of the country, are not as desirable because they are subject to sliding and settling. Pilings and piers are used to support the building in poor soil bearing areas. Soil tests should always be taken if the soil condition is unknown.

The foundation walls may be made of wood, stone, brick, poured concrete, or masonry blocks. They should be made moisture-proof with either a membrane of waterproof material or a parge coating of portland cement mortar. The waterproof material can consist of plastic sheeting or a sandwich of standard roofing felt, joined and covered to prevent water from penetrating the wall material and leaving the basement or cellar walls damp and subject to deterioration.

The most common foundation is the continuous wall that could be built of stone, clay tile, block, brick, or concrete and set on concrete footings. Recently, treated wood, metal, and other materials have been used. Continuous walls are used to support heavy loads or to enclose a crawl space, cellar, or basement. Pilasters or vertical wall shorings are used to support long runs of walls. The code will call for at least one pilaster for every 40 feet of wall. If the soil is poor, pilings may be driven to support the footings. A step foundation is a continuous wall of variable height. It is used on steep grades or for houses with partial basements. If you are buying a new home, check if a ten-year structural warranty is available.

The pier foundation consists of a series of piers that support the house. They are generally masonry, but sometimes they are made of other materials. The pole or post foundation is a special kind of pier foundation built of pressure-treated wood. It is often used on steep terrain where there is considerable variation in the height of the piers and where a regular masonry pier might bend and break. The beams that support the house are placed between the piers of a pier foundation and the house is built on this structure.

The slab on ground foundation is a special foundation that floats on top of the soil and serves as the floor of the house. The slab is thickened under all of the walls to support their heavy loads. All slab floors are not slab foundations but are simply concrete floors. A separate footing and foundation supports the wall loads, and the concrete floor is supported by a bed of gravel and the footing. Insulation and moisture barriers are essential in this slab construction.

A grade beam foundation is a pressure-treated wood or reinforced concrete beam which is submerged to a depth of about eight inches below grade. It may be supported on a stone fill or on underground piers which extend into the ground below the frost line. The grade beam is especially useful in dry climates or well-drained soils where the house can be built close to the ground.

A foundation or basement wall is often called upon to be a decorative surface, equipped with all the conveniences found in other walls. Basement walls can be insulated and finished in several different ways. Your lumber yard dealer can suggest several methods. After insulation is installed, panel board or other wall finishes can be attached to the insulation or studs with a good grade panel adhesive. Adhesive can likewise be used to attach baseboard and moldings. Electrical outlets may be surface mounted or wires may be counter-sunk into the insulation or through the studs. Another way is to use furring strips or studs on your basement wall and then attach a panel board to the strips. Always use a moisture barrier.

The basement floor is usually made of three inches of concrete poured on a bed of gravel. Footing drains, sump pumps, and good roof and site drainage should keep your crawl space or cellar dry. (See Chapter 13 for further suggestions.)

PROBLEMS AND SOLUTIONS

A foundation should be checked regularly for proper elevation and alignment. Complete foundation failure is a rare occurrence but some settling or horizontal displacement may occur. The use of eight-inch masonry walls below grade has caused some buckling or bowing of walls. Standard practice formerly called for 12-inch walls below grade, but the new code allows for eight-inch block. *Check carefully.* The common causes of foundation movement are inadequate footings, poor soil, overloading the structure, excessive ground water, frost heaving, adjacent excavation, and earth tremors.

Foundation movement may show up as cracked walls, damaged framings, sloping floors, sticking doors, and windows that won't open. Vertical or diagonal hairline cracks are to be expected, but once you see horizontal or vertical cracks over 5/16 inch, you may have a problem. Corrective action may be to underpin or replace a wall, and to pipe away excessive ground water. Material deterioration can be corrected by troweling on a new surface once the cause is corrected. Active cracks can be sealed.

In summer months and wet climates, moisture in basement air is particularly troublesome. If humid air comes in contact with the cooler wall or floor surface, it will condense. This is called condensation or sweating and can cause growth of mold and fungi and be quite objectionable. The problem generally goes away in the winter months when the heat is on, but there are exceptions. For example, even in the winter, moisture is produced by extensive cooking and by frequent use of hot showers. Another problem is moisture from the soil soaking through the basement wall and evaporating into the air. These conditions are correctable by ventilation and good drainage.

Basement humidity can be dealt with by dehumidifiers that will remove many quarts of moisture per day from the air. For dehumidification to be effective, the basement doors and windows should be kept closed.

Another way to deal with moisture is to eliminate cold surfaces in the basement or house. This can be done through insulation. Floors may be covered with felt paper or tile and walls may be insulated and finished. You must provide a vapor barrier to prevent moisture in the air from flowing through the insulation to the cold surfaces where it will condense under the insulation. A plastic film, some paints, and several other materials are effective vapor barriers.

Ventilation should be used when the problem can't be handled by insulation, or when periods of high moisture production are of short duration. In the winter, ventilation can remove excess moisture from the basement or crawl space. Ventilation becomes extremely important if moisture is being produced here. But ventilation brings in cold air and exhausts warm air, so excessive ventilation will carry off a good deal of heat. Heating the crawl space and insulating the foundation wall can eliminate the need for vents, and probably reduce total heat loss from the house. During the summer, crawl space ventilation is necessary.

Another problem is moisture that flows out of the soil into the basement either through the wall or the floor. This can be prevented by providing the house with gutters and downspouts to carry roof rain water away from the foundation wall. Slope the grade away from the house on all sides of the foundation to drain rain water and prevent ponding. Using swales or open drainage ditches will carry off surface water. Back-filling behind the foundation wall with porous fill and providing drain tile at the base of the footing below the basement floor level will drain moisture away from the house. Parging the outside of the foundation wall will prevent moisture coming in contact with the wall from soaking into or through it. Waterproof paints and coating should be used over the parging to increase moisture resistance.

One effective method of removing ground water is to dig down on the outside of the wall and install a drain field at the footings. Then parge and paint the foundation wall and back-fill with a coarse aggregate, such as cinders, gravel, sand, or stone. If the drain field can't be emptied by gravity, install a sump pump to carry the moisture away from the bottom of the foundation wall. In older homes, the drain pipe is installed below the concrete floor at the inside footings and the pipes terminate at a sump hole—about two feet square and one to two feet deep—in the basement floor, using a gravity drain or a sump pump to carry the moisture away.

Several patching and plastering materials have been developed for sealing cracks on the inside of basement walls. Most are effective. Those that are good will stop the flow in one place, but the moisture will simply back up and find a new flow path. If you can be satisfied with a wet wall, some systems have been developed to keep the floor dry by collecting the water at the base of the wall and carrying it to a drain or sump. Using this same collection system, one can reduce the wall moisture by drilling a series of holes near the base of the wall, just above the collection system. This causes the moisture to flow through the wall at a lower level to the sump.

Concrete floor slabs can be protected from moisture by a gravel fill and drain tile below the floor level. A plastic vapor barrier placed over the gravel fill and under the concrete floor is another aid in keeping soil moisture from flowing through the floor into the basement. The basement temperature can be maintained by installing a proper size heating system. But if you are going to heat economically, the foundation or basement wall must be of reasonably tight construction to prevent warm air from escaping through cracks. Most people will also want a well-insulated basement wall for maximum economy and comfort. Since concrete is a good heat conductor, you must take special care when concrete slabs are installed vertically down the inside of the foundation wall, or between the floor slab and the foundation wall and then horizontally under the slab. This is important to prevent the floor near the walls from freezing and forming ice crystals.

Foundations acting as retaining walls must be designed to prevent overturning or breakage. Breakage may be prevented by reinforcing rods or by making the wall thicker on the bottom. Overturning may be prevented by making the wall thicker, tying the wall to anchors in the soil (dead men), or counter-balancing the wall. Retaining walls are usually poorly designed in residential construction and many are in a state of collapse.

Holes in the foundation walls are common in older houses. These holes may be caused by missing stone, bricks, or blocks. Holes and cracks in a wall are undesirable because they make an easy entry for moisture and indicate the possibility of further structural deterioration. These holes should not be confused with ventilation vents in the wall that permit air movement and prevent moisture entrapment.

Some northern states have a five foot or deeper frost level. If the foundation walls are not thick enough (at least 12 inches below grade), the lateral frost pressure will force the foundation masonry wall off the first block. Be very careful, as it is easy to miss this problem, and it is very expensive to repair, since the entire wall must usually be replaced or at least reinforced. If you are building, then consider tying the wall to the footing with reinforcing rods.

MAINTENANCE

Severe structural foundation problems rarely occur, but when they do, they are expensive to repair. Periodically check the walls for dampness, moisture, stains, and signs of settlement such as bowing and cracks. If you feel the settlement is dynamic, then glue a plate of glass over the crack and watch for breakage. If the glass breaks, have the condition corrected. Plug any leaks (usually caused by defective mortar joints). Cement-water paints and cement grouts, available commercially, are sometimes effective for damp-proofing, if the leaks are small and the water is not under pressure.

Untreated wood posts rot rapidly at the ground line. Replace them with treated posts or with masonry piers. Exposed wood usually deteriorates at fastener joints first and causes metal fasteners to loosen. Remove loose spikes and driftbolts. Treat the holes and affected areas with a preservative. Plug the holes with wood dowels or with tar. Replace the spikes or bolts in new locations. Cut away sections of unsound sills and replace them with plank patches. If the whole timber has weakened, replace it.

Where the soil under the footing is eroded but the foundation wall is not damaged, ram a mixture of damp sandy clay and portland cement under the footing: this will provide a firm, secure bearing. Then bank soil against the foundation, high enough for protection from frost. Slope the soil to divert surface and roof water, and then pave or sod the banked soil to protect it from wind erosion. If you feel your settlement or moisture problem is excessive, call in an engineer or home inspector to advise you.

INSPECTION

If you are building or buying a resale house, take a little extra care and save yourself the enormous problems that are common to poorly installed footings and foundations.

When purchasing a house, check the exterior foundation carefully. Check the type and size of the wall structure and material. The wall should rise ten inches above grade. The width should be not less than eight inches above grade and twelve inches below grade. Are there any cracks? Longitudinal cracks mean bowing of the wall and excessive lateral pressure. Vertical and diagonal cracks indicate footing settlement. To be serious, the crack must be open at least 5/16 inch. Try to determine if it is stabile.

Is the wall at the bottom of a hill? If so, sight the exterior wall to see if there is any movement inward. Are there pilasters supporting the wall? Are there any holes in the walls? Is the grading satisfactory and is the roof drainage system adequate?

What is the condition of the exterior cement plaster coat? Check piers and support posts for porches, decks, and chimneys. Frequently, insufficient attention is given to the porch or deck footings, with the result that the structure settles and pulls away.

Check the condition of the interior foundation walls. Hairline cracks over 1/16 inch require some attention: patch them. How deep is the frost line? Observe the first block to see if the wall is pushed off this block. The cause is usually deep frost, too small a block, or the wall being on the side of a hill. Check the condition of the cement floor slab for settlement and cracks. Check chimney footings, especially the arch that supports the hearth.

Sight down the wall to see if it is bowed in. A longitudinal crack may be seen about three feet off the floor. This is usually caused by too small a wall width, deep frost, wet earth pressure, or carelessness during the back-filling operation. Check footings of all lally columns, pilasters, piers for cracks at the floor level. Beware of telescoping columns and jury rigs that were added under high traffic floors.

Check for problems of moisture, poor drainage, and sump pump usage.

In older homes, check carefully the condition of rubble stone or brick foundations, wood tree supports, wood infestation, and moisture problems.

Check all crawl spaces thoroughly, especially for signs of mold, fungi, and infestation. Check the vent screens, and look for signs of poor ventilation.

SUMMARY

House settlement can usually be traced to poor footings and foundation wall design. Minor cracking can be expected from temperature changes and the drying out of wood framing. When major foundation settlement does occur, and this is rare, the repair expense is large because it involves underpinning or a new wall. Water penetration is the next major problem, but 99.9% of the time it is correctable for little money. (See Chapter 13.) If you expect to rehabilitate an older house, it must not have foundation or structure problems, as the cost to correct these conditions is great.

8.
Structural Soundness and Settlement

INTRODUCTION

This chapter covers problems in the structure above the top of the basement wall. Structural faults that affect the beauty and possibly the safety of your home are often minor and easily remedied. An understanding of some common problems will be invaluable to you in the selection and maintenance of your home. Chapter 10 discusses exterior siding, windows, and doors, and Chapter 11 discusses exterior appurtenances and their structural soundness.

Structural members include walls, beams, girders, joists, roof rafters, columns, sill plates, posts, chimneys, trusses, slabs, lintels, headers, windows, doors, studs, sheathing, and floors. These members are subject to rot, decay, wood-destroying insects, and settlement like sagging and deflection. This chapter discusses structural soundness and settlement of these members.

TECHNICAL INFORMATION AND PROBLEMS

A potential homeowner should understand the nature of construction materials and realize that they will shrink to some degree. Shrinkage occurs in masonry during the setting or curing period after installation. Initial shrinkage in masonry material varies widely, depending upon the mixes and on curing conditions. It occurs in lumber as it is seasoned or as the moisture content is reduced.

Lumber used in construction should have a moisture content of less than 19%. It should be allowed to dry or season over an extended period. Lumber installed with a high moisture content will dry in place, then shrink, and possibly twist so that cracks develop in finished walls, ceilings, and floors. Many parts of the country use green lumber in the entire house with little settlement. Problems occur when green and kiln-dried lumber are mixed.

Basement girders are supported by the foundation walls and intermediate columns made of steel, wood, or masonry. Most house girders are wood; usually 2×8's, 2×10's, or even 2×12's. And in older houses, you'll see wood, brick, or even stone columns propping up these girders. In some homes, steel I-beams, girders supported on steel lally columns, are used.

If your home is old, your inspection for girders may turn up one that is badly sagging. If so, it can be supported with a steel telescoping jack column on a new footing poured over well-tamped gravel. Be very careful in removing settlement as this procedure can cause further damage. Once you've got the girders spotted, go upstairs and determine which bearing partitions are placed over them. If your house has a second floor, you'll find the bearing walls almost directly over the walls on the first floor. Bearing partitions act as intermediate supports within exterior walls. It's easy to identify such partitions if you know what to look for. Some homes have no bearing partitions; these one-story homes, with trussed roofs, have the entire weight of the roof supported by the outside walls.

Many do-it-yourselfers want to remove walls to make rooms larger for new uses. Before you do this, be sure to determine if the wall is a load-bearing partition or just a stud wall called a partition wall. A man in New Jersey who wanted to put a pool table in his cellar playroom removed the two steel columns that were in the way. He had plenty of room to play pool, but in a few days, the floors began to settle and doors would not close. The house nearly collapsed. This type of thing happens again and again, so be sure you know what you're removing. In older homes, many people want to make a bedroom larger. This can be done, but you must know how to support the ceiling above the wall you plan to remove.

Though the bearing partition should never be removed, openings can be cut through it, or existing openings can be widened. The main point to remember is that if you cut through the bearing walls you must transfer the stress taken by the removed studs over to other studs. If the gap is no wider than a standard door or window, you can settle for a header consisting of a pair of 2×4's set on edge, supported in turn by double studs on each side. If the width of the opening is to be greater than a door width, 2 × 6's should be used across the top. Heavier bridging will be required for a first floor opening in a bearing partition that supports both the second floor and roof. Before you begin cutting into a bearing wall, erect a temporary support on the opposite side of the wall to take the weight until you get the opening framed.

Interior walls are either plastered or covered with such materials as plasterboard, plywood, wood paneling, tile, or glazed faced masonry. Ceilings are usually plastered or covered with plasterboard or acoustical materials. Good construction practice dictates that a house be designed and built so that wood shrinkage is evenly distributed in the inside and outside walls. This should reduce plaster cracking to a minimum. Plaster walls and ceilings that crack because of wood or concrete shrinkage are unsightly but do not present a structural hazard. Usually these cracks are not large enough to cause damage. They contrast to the cracks that develop in foundations from uneven distribution of house loads over footings, from footings of inadequate size, or from unstable soil conditions. Cracks which develop in basement or foundation walls or in exterior masonry walls usually indicate structural deficiencies of some kind but are patchable.

If you have a choice, avoid buying a house with large structural cracks. Minor hairline cracks and holes can be patched, but a new wall covering should be applied if large cracks and holes are numerous, if the surface is generally uneven and bulging, or if the plaster is loose in spots. The same general rule applies to ceilings. Obtain professional advice from a builder, architect, or engineer to determine the cause of the cracking and the steps to prevent further damage. Stresses that cause plaster damage should be investigated and corrected before repairs are made to the plastered surfaces themselves.

Structural cracks are easy to identify because they are usually large and well-defined, extending across the surface and through the plaster. They will develop the first year and, in most cases, can be successfully and permanently repaired. Before repairs are initiated, the cause of the failure should be determined and precautions taken to prevent recurrence of the failure. Structural cracks may extend diagonally from the corners of door and window openings, run vertically in corners where walls join, run horizontally along the junction of walls and ceilings, or occur in walls where two unlike materials join.

Loose plaster is noticed by bulging and cracking of large areas of the plaster surface. The problem can be determined by lightly tapping the surface with a screw driver and listening for a dull unfirm sound. Loose plaster may result from excessive moisture caused by leaks in the roof, seepage through an exterior wall, plumbing leaks, or heavy condensation. In some cases, the plaster may bulge or sag but continue to hang in this condition quite a long time before falling. Occasionally, moisture causes the fastenings holding the lath to the structural frame to corrode, permitting both the lath and plaster to bulge or sag. Before repairing damaged plaster, it is necessary to locate and eliminate any source of moisture.

Paints are not indestructible and coatings properly applied will gradually deteriorate and fail. If repainting is not done in time, disintegration of the paint will take place, followed ultimately by deterioration of the under surface.

Floors should be strong, firm, level, and easy to care for. In checking wood floors, look for buckling or cupping of boards that can result from high moisture content of the boards or wetting of the floor. Notice if the boards are separated due to shrinkage. If the floor is generally smooth and without excessive separation between boards, refinishing may put it in good condition. Be sure there is enough thickness left in the flooring to permit standing. Most flooring cannot be sanded more than two or three times. If floors have wide cracks or are too thin to sand, some type of new flooring will have to be added.

Floors with resilient tile should be examined for loose tile, cracks between tiles, broken corners, and chipped edges. Look to see if any ridges or unevenness in the underlayment are showing through. Replacement of any tile in a room may necessitate replacing the flooring in the whole room because tiles change color with age and new tile will not match the old. Always put down a new base of ⅛-inch plywood to support the new tile properly.

MAINTENANCE

The wood frame and structure are subject to rot, decay, wood-destroying insects, weathering, and normal general settlement. Keep the rain water away from the foundation by proper grading and roof drainage. Check all window and door rain caps to see that they shed water. Correct any rot or decay and eliminate the causes. Keep all painted surfaces properly covered. Tuckpoint all mortar joints as needed. Keep a good finish on all floors, walls, and ceilings. Consult the preventive maintenance checklist in Chapter 33 for further helpful checkpoints. A well-maintained structure will bring a higher sales price.

INSPECTION

Most homes will show signs of normal minor settlement and this usually occurs in the early years. Today, houses are built according to strict local, state, or national codes. And the great majority of homes are structurally sound. However, a lot depends on the accuracy and competency of the code inspector. Your main objective is to find any indication of settling or structural unsoundness. In some cases, you cannot inspect the structural component because it is covered. If so, look for cracks, shrinkage, and settling.

The tools you need for inspection are a flashlight; a long, sharp screw driver for probing; a level; and a ruler. The structural members to be probed were discussed in the introduction.

While outside the house, observe that the ridge and eaves are straight and that the walls are plump. After a house is a few years old, you can often detect visual signs of defective framing. One sign is bulging exterior walls—best seen by standing at each corner of the house and sighting along the wall. Stand back from the house and look at the ridge line. If it sags in the middle, the rafters may need knee walls for support. This occurs often on bi-level and low pitch roofs.

Window sills that are not level are a sign of settling or defective framing. A careful inspection should include the opening and closing of every window. Sticking windows may be a sign of settling or defective framing.

Check the header over all openings for proper support.

Another sign of trouble is a large crack developing on the outside of the house between the chimney and the exterior wall. A crack running outward from the upper corners of window and door frames is another bad sign. Check all doors: have the bottom or the sides been planed to allow free movement after sagging of the frame caused them to jam?

Is there tremor or shaking of floors when you jump in the middle of a room? Sagging and sloping floors, which may be detected visually or by use of a level, may be a sign of defective framing or may be caused by weak or defective floors.

Cracks in the walls are not conclusive evidence of framing problems, since all houses settle unless built upon solid rock. These cracks should be of concern only when accompanied by some of the other signs of settlement. If you suspect the house has defective framing, get professional advice to confirm your opinion. Check all ceilings and walls for quality of the paint and wall coverings.

Check for crumbling concrete and cracks in walls and slab floors. Check masonry for loose and cracked joints. Check bricks for soundness of the surface and the mortar joints. Moisture is the cause of much trouble.

Check for absence of building paper beneath roofing, finish flooring, and siding. Check the condition of the sheathing. Sometimes gypsum board is used and regular nails will not hold, causing the siding to pull away when it gets wet.

Check for mold build-up and delamination of plywood in the attic and crawl space. This is caused by poor ventilation.

While in the cellar, probe all sill plates, girders, and floor joists for signs of rot, decay, or wood-destroying insects. Note any sag or deflection in girders or joists. Is there a vertical steel lally column or support post or pier under the main girder every seven or eight feet? (The span can be longer under steel girders.) Is there rot at the bottom of wood posts? Is there diagonal or solid bridging between the floor joists? Are the sill plates bolted to the foundation? Are there double floor joists under all bearing walls? Are all floor openings doubled and properly supported? Are there adequate foundation support pilasters?

Check the foundation and cellar floor and slab for cracks and signs of settlement. Check for signs of condensation and water problems.

Check for decay and damaged members in all crawl spaces—a bad area for termite problems.

Jack posts may be found under dining rooms, where they are used to stiffen a springy floor or to carry heavy loads. Be sure there is a steel plate under the post to distribute the load over a larger area.

If you notice that a floor squeaks, look for undersized floor joists or sagging joists that pull away from the subfloor. Small wedges or construction mastic squeezed into the joists may stop the squeaking.

A major cause of settlement is the framing of floor joists around stair openings. Often, this will continue to the third floor. The only solution is to arrest it by proper supports in the cellar.

Rot and wood-destroying insects can cause excessive sill damage and uneven frame settlement. These problems are correctable by jacking up the building, and installing new wood after treating the infestation.

SUMMARY

Structure settlement can usually be traced to poor footings and foundation design, normal material shrinkage, and improper framing. Minor cracks can be expected from temperature changes and the drying out of the wood framing. When major settlement does occur, the repair bill can be large. Minor settlement of floors and walls can be corrected by jacking up the settled area, but this must be done over a period of time to avoid further damage. If you feel that settlement is occurring, then adhere a piece of glass over the crack with epoxy. If the glass breaks, you know the settlement is continuing and corrective action is necessary.

The best thing you can do about a house with a defective frame is not to buy it. If you still like the home, then seek the advice of an engineer or competent contractor to determine what may be done to arrest the problem.

9.
Roofs, Gutters, Leaders, and Flashings

INTRODUCTION

Most of us clean, fix, and paint those parts of a house that show the most need, but the roof gets little attention as long as it sheds water. Your roof receives the hardest wear of any part of the exterior structure. It suffers wear and tear from beating rain, sleet, wind, and hot sun, and in some areas, by alternate freezing and thawing temperatures. As a result, it can and does develop leaks. Leaking roof systems are a source of major home buyer complaints, so inspect thoroughly before you buy. Leaks or potential leaks are easy to spot, as well as the true condition of the roof surface.

This chapter will introduce you to the major components of the roofing system: i.e., the roof, flashings, gutters, and downspouts. An understanding of these components will enable you to inspect and maintain your roof satisfactorily.

TECHNICAL INFORMATION

The life of your roof and the kind of maintenance that it will need depends mostly on the materials from which it is made. The type of roofing to be employed is somewhat dictated by the style of the roof. For pitched roofs, several types of covering are used—wood shingle, composition asphalt shingle, metal, rigid asbestos, slate, and tile. These are called multiple unit systems. Roof surfaces are measured in squares; that is, 10 feet by 10 feet, or 100 square feet, is called one square.

Pitched Roofs. The most common roofing material is asphalt. It is low in cost, resilient, and a good noise insulator. You can buy it in rolls or as shingles. It may also be found in several weights. It may be either plain or surfaced with mineral granules which reduce erosion by slowing the flow of water across the shingles and shielding the asphalt from direct rays of the sun by reflection. The sun causes the asphalt to become brittle and easily damaged or eroded. Asphalt roll roofing for flat roofs will usually last five to ten years.

Asphalt shingles, also called composition shingles, are widely used for roof covering because of their moderate cost, light weight, and durability. In shingles, the asphalt is overlapped to give a total roofing weight of about 240 pounds per 100 square feet. The shingles are composed of asphalt-saturated felt coated with asphalt and are surfaced with mineral granules on the weather side. Asphalt shingled roofs allow moisture to escape from attics in vapor form. They are available as single shingles or in strips of several units, in a wide variety of colors and patterns. Asphalt shingles are designed to last 15 to 20 years.

Asbestos shingles cost about twice as much as asphalt. The shingles are very brittle and can break if walked on. They are designed to last the life of the house. Asbestos-cement shingles are made of asbestos fiber and portland cement. They are strong, durable, and fire-resistant. They are available in a wide variety of colors and surface textures. Moss tends to grow on these shingles and can cause capillary leaks. Asbestos roofs cannot be roofed over.

Slate is considered a deluxe roof and will last the life of the house if maintained. Slate shingles are very expensive, but they make an attractive, durable, and fire-resistant covering. They are available in different grades and in various colors. Slates are very heavy (700 to 900 pounds per square) and require strong roof framing. Some dark slates fade to a lighter gray on exposure. Certain green slates may become buff or brown after a few months' exposure. This change is sometimes considered desirable and it has no effect on the quality of the slate. Slate roofs need periodic maintenance of the shingles to correct broken or slipped slates.

Wood shingles or shakes are quite popular where satisfactory species of wood are available. They are light in weight, attractive, and provide a well-insulated roof. Their economy will vary in relation to the cost of wood and labor. Wood shake makes a virtually lifetime roof if maintained with a preservative every five to seven years. Many owners do not do this and find the roof leaking in 15 years.

Metal roofing is more expensive than asphalt, but aluminum and steel are stronger and capable of spanning relatively long distances without support. You don't need a solid deck under metal. Thus, overall cost of the metal roof plus the sheathing may be less than asphalt. Aluminum reflects sun rays, providing a cool attic. Be careful to use special nails with aluminum. Steel nails in contact with aluminum will cause rapid deterioration. Copper is quite expensive, but some builders use it for decorative effect. Copper roofing is generally thin and a relatively solid deck is needed to support it.

Ternemetal is another metal roofing material which was widely used in the past. It is a soft, steel-coated metal with a lead and tin alloy which can be crimped and bent easily. It has wide use for irregular roof shapes, but has decreased in popularity because of its high labor requirement and the special tools needed. Ternemetals are strong and a relatively solid sheathing should be used under them.

Flat Roofs. Flat roofs or roofs with low pitch require roofing which depends on water-tightness properties rather than their water-shedding ability. Built-up roofs and flat seam metal roofing are examples of water-tight membrane roofing systems. Built-up roofing consists of several layers of light weight felt, lapped and cemented together with a bituminous material and covered with a layer of small-sized gravel or slag. The roofing, if maintained, is long-lived and low in cost. It has high fire-resistance, although it will burn freely once ignited. Until it is about 20 years old, this type of roof need not be replaced if it springs a leak; just patch the hole with roofing cement, which will hold for several years. Poor flashing installation is a major cause of failure and leaks.

Metal roofing laid with locked or soldered joints can be used on low-pitched roofs with little danger of leakage. One common type often found in inner city townhouses is the ternemetal or tin roof. If kept painted, it can last the life of the house.

INSTALLATION FACTORS

Once you have selected roofing, a change in the type of material may be quite expensive. Select carefully and keep the following in mind: roofing materials vary widely in price. Cost in roofing, however, involves more than the cost of materials. Labor, decking, scaffolding, and other factors make up a large part of the cost. Good quality, long-lived roofing should be used on permanent buildings, even though the first cost is high. If maintenance, repair, and replacement are considered, low quality roofing can be more expensive in the long run.

Roofing materials vary in fire-resistance. Slate, asbestos-cement shingles, and metal roofings are the most fire-resistant. Remember that metal roofs melt at relatively low temperatures and are easily damaged in the presence of fire. Others, such as asphalt shingles and roll roofing, provide satisfactory protection, if they are of good quality and are kept in good condition.

Color is an extremely important part of your roofing system. With proper planning, you can make maximum use of a dark roof as a heat collector and a part of your heating system in the winter, but in the summer, when cooling is required, the excess heat is not needed or wanted. A light-colored roof which will reflect the sun's rays would be most favorable during summer, but obviously a bi-annual roof color change would be too expensive. Attic ventilation to divert the excess summer heat would be more realistic if you choose the dark-colored roof for its winter benefits. With light-colored roofs, excessive winter heat loss may be controlled by extra layers of overhead insulation.

If the slope of a roof is less than three inches on twelve inches, then asphalt shingles may leak due to capillary action. In these situations, membrane roofs are used.

Roofing materials vary in weight. If the roofing is too heavy for the framing, sagging may occur. A roof that sags is unsightly and hard to keep repaired. If you install a second roof, then add collar beams or knee walls.

Along seacoasts, the air is saturated with salt; around industrial works, it may be polluted with fumes. The salt and fumes may corrode galvanized or aluminum roofings and shorten their life. Steel roofing, even though galvanized, is particularly susceptible to such corrosion. If used, it must be kept well-painted.

If you live near a chemical or other plant which emits gaseous compounds, you should check with your local building officials before using roofing materials or coatings which may react chemically with such gases to cause deterioration.

Flashings.   Leaking flashings are the major cause of supposed roof leaks. Flashings are used where the roof intersects with other structures, such as walls, chimneys, and dormers, and in the valleys where two roof slopes intersect. Flashing materials provide protection from water penetration at these points. These materials are usually of galvanized sheet iron, copper, aluminum, zinc alloy, or flashing felt. When properly installed, they prevent water from penetrating the roof. Flashings should be sealed with roofing cement periodically because as the building settles, the flashing materials separate and rain water can enter.

Gutters and Downspouts. Roof drainage systems are needed to control the disposal of water from the roof. Unless the home is designed with large overhangs to dispose of the water, gutters should be installed to prevent damage to exterior walls and foundation and dampness in the basement. The gutter runs along the eave of the roof and the downspouts or leader pipes carry the water to the ground.

Gutters and downspouts are needed in those areas that have a high rainfall, especially where cold temperatures accompany high rainfall. Such drainage equipment will reduce erosion and protect walkways and stairs from unwanted water. In cold climates, gutters can reduce the problems of frozen stairs and walkways. They prevent the formation of water holes around buildings and damp conditions around foundations; they also reduce maintenance cost.

Gutters may be made of wood built in as part of the cornice and lined with metal. This type is called a New England gutter and tends to leak unless periodically sealed. Gutters also may be metal troughs hung along the eaves facia board. Downspouts must be large enough to remove water from the gutters satisfactorily. One downspout every 30 feet is needed.

MAINTENANCE

In the long run, the most efficient protection against weather damage to your home is a periodic preventive maintenance plan. Below are some general guidelines for maintenance of the roofing system.

Keep trees trimmed to prevent scuffing by branches, or damage by falling limbs. Keep climbing roses and vines trimmed back.

Keep gutters, downspouts, and roof surfaces clear of fallen leaves, twigs, and other litter so that water will drain freely and not back up. This should be done three or four times a year.

Be careful when installing guy wires and television antennas.

The slope of your roof should be steep enough to permit rain water and melted snow to run off without collecting on it. Check the roof—or have it checked, if there is danger of falling—once or twice a year to make sure it is in good condition. Many roof lives can be extended by five to ten years if small problems are attended to quickly.

Replace warped, split wood shingles and deteriorated composition shingles with the same kind of shingle or a piece of rust-resistant metal. In an emergency, make a temporary repair with metal cut from a tin can. If metal is used, paint it on both sides. Slip it under the shingle in the course above. Be careful not to dislodge sound shingles. This can also be done to slates. Do not walk on roofing shingles; it is dangerous and can damage the shingles. When it is necessary for workmen to go on the roof, they should use walk boards, ladders, or other suitable protection.

When removing snow or ice from a valley or roof area, be careful not to damage the roof with the tools being used. Be careful not to slip.

Moss, which can grow on any kind of roof, especially if it is in a damp, shaded location, is mostly commonly seen on wood and asbestos shingles. To kill it, scrape it off, taking pains not to damage the roofing. Then spray or brush a preservative such as Woodlife or Pentaseal on a wood roof. Treat other roofs with 1/2 ounce of sodium arsenite in 10 gallons of water. Be very careful not to get any of these solutions on plants. Retreat the roof when moss starts to grow again.

Flat asphalt roofs require periodic resurfacing. A built-up roof can be maintained for years with a conscientious program of inspection, repair, and recoating. The roof should be inspected every year by a reputable roofing contractor. The roofer will pay particular attention to flashings, roof penetration, and distressed areas such as blisters and cracks. If the roof is not maintained, it will start to leak within five years. Metal roofs should be painted periodically.

Reroofing.   All roofs have to be replaced in time. If the roof is worn badly in the tabs or suffering from old age, then limited repairs won't help. A roof tends to wear uniformly and even the best roofing materials will eventually succumb to continued exposure to sun, wind, rain, hail, and temperature change. Many an asphalt roof was installed over an old wood roof and although the asphalt has worn, the roof rarely leaks. When you plan to reroof an old building, consider laying the new covering over the old. The municipality usually allows up to two resurfaces. This is not always possible or desirable but there are advantages. The old roofing will provide additional insulation; you can lay the new roofing without exposing the interior of the building or the sheathing to the weather; and you avoid the labor, expense, and mess of removing the old covering, which can be up to 40 to 50% of the cost of the new roof.

Gutters and Downspouts.   If gutters and downspouts are not securely in place and free of leaves and branches, water may back up under the eaves of the house and seep down inside the walls. Never allow water from a downspout to pour directly onto the roof below. Direct the downspout to the gutter which drains the lower roof or run a leader to the ground. Gutters need periodic adjustment due to settlement and rain or snow loads.

Flashings.   Water may also enter the house if the flashing is not sound and properly fastened. Inspect and seal the flashings annually. This is very important, as 99% of roof leaks are due to faulty flashings.

INSPECTING FOR PROBLEMS

Roof.   For maximum service and protection, the roof should be installed properly and kept in good repair. Improper installation and poor maintenance can result in leaks or other trouble and shorten the life of the roofing. A leaking roof is discovered by water stains in the attic or on ceilings or outright leakage into the house. When this happens it's too late to prevent the damage. Your house is a candidate for a leaking roof if the roof is over 15 years old and particularly if it is black. Black roofs absorb the heat of the sun more readily then light-colored roofs and therefore age quickly. A standard roof shingle has a 15-year life expectancy, and some development houses need roofs after ten years.

You don't have to get on a roof to check its condition. Climbing up on a roof is not only dangerous but can damage the roof. You can take a hint from home inspection experts, who check roofs with field glasses or place a ladder against the roof and observe the shingles up close.

Check the general roof surface for cracks, blistered surfaces, curled or missing shingles, and dull, flat, or faded color.

Check the roof for patches of dark gray or black where granules have worn off, leaving the paper surface exposed. Also check gutters and the area around downspouts for concentrations of loose granules. Large amounts of loose granules are the best indication that the roof has lost its ability to withstand further sun, wind, and moisture.

Look for loose and missing nails or nail heads that have torn the shingle or are no longer tight against the shingle. Too often, shingles are nailed too high or with too few nails. The wind can then easily crack or blow the shingle off the roof.

Check valleys carefully. Be especially aware of these critical areas. Look for torn or worn spots. Leaks caused by a faulty valley can appear anywhere and should be corrected at once.

Look for signs of leaks where roof attachments have been nailed to the roof. A TV antenna anchored to a vent without proper guy wires will vibrate and loosen caulking around the flashing.

Next go into the attic, and with your flashlight, look at the floor or insulation surface. Beginning leaks show up as little dust splatters or as stains on the chimney brickwork. Look for white salts (efflorescence) which indicate leaks.

Most homeowners lack the skills to apply a new roof or do extensive repair work, but they are capable of patching leaky spots until permanent repairs can be made. Take care when making such repairs; do not attempt to walk on a steep roof without a rope or a ladder hooked to the ridge of the roof. Many accidents occur on roofs, so use a roofer.

Most types of flat roofs can be coated or painted to extend their life. Coatings have even been developed to extend the life of asphalt and aluminum. If flat roofs are painted or recoated at proper intervals, the base materials will not deteriorate or wear away and the life of the roof can be extended almost indefinitely. Coatings are not effective on pitched asphalt shingle roofs, although contractors will try to sell you on their merits.

Gutters and Downspouts.   Problems with gutters and downspouts can lead to leakage and paint erosion. The causes of drainage systems problems are varied and can include inadequate size of gutters and downspouts; gutters not sloped properly; too few downspouts; hanger or strap spacing too great; failure to provide expansion joints; and failure to pipe the downspout drains away from the foundation, causing blockage. The drainage system should have wire netting or strainers to prevent debris and leaves from clogging the system.

Periodically inspect the system. If possible, do it in the rain. Look for sagging rain gutters, rusted out areas, blockage caused by leaves or debris, broken joints or broken elbows, and improper drainage at the corners of the house or lack of proper splash boxes. Defective rain gutters or leaders almost always cause damp or wet basements. If the gutters are defective, make a mental note to check the basement later for water problems.

Flashing.   Poorly applied flashings open and allow water to penetrate the roof surface. Occasionally, metal flashing may warp and draw out of the groove or joint in the vertical surface where it was embedded when installed. Flashing can be torn loose by wind force. If valley flashing is too narrow, back-up water may find its way under roofing materials. This readily occurs when valleys become dammed with snow and ice. The approximate location of flashing leaks is often indicated by wet spots on interior walls or ceilings.

Inspect the metal flashings, caulking, and areas around stacks once a year to see if they have loosened. Mortar may have fallen out of the joint where the flashing is embedded in the masonry and repointing may be needed. Flashing cement and similar sealing compounds are effective in sealing such cracks. If there are rust signs on exposed metal, it should be cleaned with a wire brush and painted with a good metal paint, or sealed with fiberglass and roofing cement.

SUMMARY

Understanding the materials, problems and maintenance of your roofing system will greatly lessen your need for repairs. You can be assured of an efficient, leak-free roof if only you invest a little time in practicing the suggestions outlined in this chapter. If you are buying a resale house and the roof and drainage system is aging, then you have a home improvement expense that will fall due. Most important, new owners always redecorate, so don't spoil all this redecoration effort by missing a leak or a potential leak situation.

10.
Exterior Surfaces, Windows, and Doors

INTRODUCTION

This chapter discusses the maintenance and inspection of house siding, exterior windows and doors, and chimneys. The major problems for these elements are caused by exposure to the weather and the resulting rot and decay caused by poor maintenance. The exterior inspection is a visual examination that can be easily done by observing the building and using field glasses to view high places. Consider a sharp probe to check for rotted areas. When in doubt, get up on a ladder to check the condition of eaves, rakes, and soffits, especially on older homes. Structural problems and settlement are discussed in Chapter 8.

TECHNICAL INFORMATION

Exterior walls are made of a wide variety of materials, including wood shingles, clapboard and plywood, concrete and masonry, aluminum, enamel coated steel, and mineral products like asbestos shingles and asbestos-cement sheets. No one wall material is right for all possible circumstances. Siding differs in quality, ease of installation, cost, and permanence. Actual selection for new or old homes should be based on individual taste and cost considerations.

Wood Siding. Wood clapboard siding is available in most parts of the country and its in-place cost is generally lower than that of masonry. Disadvantages lie primarily in the need for painting or staining every few years, higher fire insurance rates, and susceptibility to termites and weather. The use of pre-primed materials is recommended because they have built-in protection during the construction phase. They can be easily painted, and generally you have fewer problems with them.

A good looking siding is the result of an annual inspection and maintenance. Painting should be done very five to eight years, but be sure to spot and scrape weak areas in between paint jobs. All exterior surfaces should be cleaned each year. If there is mildew, scrub the surface with a chlorine bleach and with trisodium phosphate. Wash down thoroughly. If there is stubborn dirt on the sills or on the siding, clean with a stiff brush. Remember to always start at the bottom to avoid unsightly streaks on the siding as dirty water washes over dirty siding. To prevent termite damage, be sure that all siding is at least 12 inches from the ground. To keep walls watertight, inspect caulked joints each summer. Scrape out loose caulking and replace it with vinyl caulking. Siding will tend to pull away from its support if it is not nailed properly. When this happens, remove the nail and replace with a new nail.

Wood Shingles. Sidewall shingles and shakes may be left untreated if the change in color caused by weathering is considered attractive. Sidewalls weather to various shades. Those who wish to exercise some control over the appearance of their walls can apply clear wood preservatives, which inhibit rapid changing color. Available also are the semi-transparent penetrating stains that come in a variety of colors and materials. Wood shingles can be a distinct fire hazard. For this reason, wood shingles are outlawed in many municipalities for both the roof and sidewall.

Hardboard Shingles. Advantages of hardboard siding lie in its reasonable cost and availability. It is relatively easy to work with. Disadvantages closely follow those of wood siding. They include the need for paint and susceptibility to termites and weather. Hardboard siding may require more maintenance through the years than most other materials. Be careful of moisture entering the end joints.

Asbestos-Cement Siding. Asbestos-cement siding will not need painting if you keep it clean. This siding will need a periodic cleaning with a detergent and a stiff brush. Aluminum windows tend to stain this material, and to prevent this, be sure the weep holes in the storm windows are open. To remove stain, scrub with an abrasive household cleanser. If the stain persists, then brush on an aluminum cleaner and wash the siding thoroughly.

Masonry Siding.   Generally, masonry materials are the most expensive because cost of the materials is higher and the labor time is increased. Basically, you have three options: stone, brick, or stucco. Each has its own design characteristics.

Brick and stone require virtually no maintenance. They carry a quality image unmatched by other materials. Disadvantages of brick and stone primarily center on initial cost and the skilled workmen needed. Concrete block shares many advantages of brick and stone and is lower in initial cost. Disadvantages include a relatively limited selection for residential use, an unfinished look which may not be aesthetically pleasing in all applications, and a possible need for painting.

Stucco.   Stucco siding is found on many older homes. The disadvantages of stucco are its sensitivity to climate changes, its tendency to crack, and the need for skilled craftsmen.

Aluminum Siding.   Aluminum siding is often less expensive than wood sidings and will normally withstand intense sunlight, snow, ice, sleet, and salt spray, and remain impervious to blistering, crazing, flaking, and peeling. It comes in a variety of colors and repainting should not be required for 15 to 20 years. The siding finish has been designed to gradually release microscopic particles of pigments in the form of a light powder. This controlled chalking is the best way for exposed surfaces to age. It also provides a self-cleaning feature which helps eliminate loose surface dirt during normal rainfall. It is only reasonable to expect your aluminum siding to become soiled and require cleaning every few years.

Periodic flushing of the siding with your garden hose will greatly reduce the labor involved in washing. Siding may become soiled by tree sap, insecticides, or fumes. When this happens, the use of warm water and ordinary household detergents applied with a soft cloth will do an excellent job. One-third cup of a mild detergent per gallon of water is recommended. Care should be exercised not to use undue pressure, as this has a tendency to create glossy spots. To minimize streaking, wash the house from bottom to top. Immediately rinse surfaces thoroughly with a garden hose. If stains cannot be removed using normal household detergents, request a special siding cleaner from your aluminum siding contractor or directly from your siding manufacturer. Do not use abrasive or solvent type cleaners or paint removers. These materials may soften or actually remove your siding finish.

The most common aluminum siding repair consists of filling dents and holes, and these are easy to fix with plastic aluminum. Clean the metal, apply the plastic aluminum, and when dry, coat with touch-up paint.

Vinyl Siding.   Advantages of vinyl siding are somewhat similar to those of aluminum. However, vinyl siding won't fade or rust and tends to resist dents. Disadvantages are the possibility of cracking in low temperatures and the difficulty of installation. Also, the fire resistance of vinyl siding is less than that of aluminum or masonry.

WINDOWS AND DOORS

There are seven types of windows now in use: double-hung, horizontal-sliding, casement, awning, jalousie, top-hinges, and bottom hinges. All wood windows are subject to deterioration by the weather and by termites. Problems with windows, such as sticking, slipping, and binding, can usually be corrected by making minor adjustments. The trouble lies most often with the opening-closing mechanism. When a modern double-hung or horizontal-sliding window becomes difficult to slide in its channel, lack of lubrication and a buildup of dirt in the channels are the most common problems.

Older double-hung windows are controlled by sash weights and cords. The problem here is that a sash cord may break. To repair one, pry off the stop strip with a broad-bladed putty knife. This allows you to remove the window from the channel. Pull the broken piece of sash cord from the channel and disconnect it from the window. Then replace it with a new chain. Check with your hardware store for spring-acting fixtures that replace the sash cord.

Wooden doors and window frames tend to swell and shrink with climate changes. Sometimes a warped door will straighten in hot, dry weather. If this occurs, paint the sides and edges of the door to keep it from warping again. A door that sticks from swelling can be planed down, but if planed too much, it will never fit properly if the wood later shrinks. In new homes, ask the builder to adjust any windows or doors that do not open and shut properly.

Storms.   Aluminum storm windows present other problems. Screws that hold storm sash to the house can loosen, allowing cold air to enter into the house. Tighten all screws and replace any that are missing.

Aluminum windows may become difficult to slide up and down. This is corrected by spraying channels with silicone lubricant or by rubbing paraffin into the channels. Open and close the window several times to distribute lubrication over the entire channel. Latch locks that bind should be dabbed with a drop of lightweight household oil. Keep all rain water weep holes open (there should be two—one at each end). If your aluminum sash doesn't have weep holes, then put them in; they will prevent water from leaking into the house and ruining the wallpaper.

INSPECTION

Siding.   The useful life of exterior cedar or redwood siding is the life of the house. Plywood, pine, and other soft wood or pressed woods start deteriorating in five to ten years. Rot and decay are major problem areas, so be on the lookout during your inspection.

The main problems with siding and trim stem from excessive moisture, which can enter from either inside or outside the siding. One of the main contributors to the problem is the lack of roof overhang or drip caps at eaves and windows, allowing rain to run down the face of the wall. Moisture may also enter from the inside if there is no vapor barrier causing moisture to condense within the wall.

Look for spaces between horizontal siding boards by standing very close and sighting along the wall. Some cracks can be caulked, but a general looseness may indicate new siding is required. If the boards are not badly warped, renailing may solve the problem. Check siding for decay where two boards are butted end to end, at corners, and around window and door frames.

Good shingle siding appears as a perfect pattern, whereas worn shingles have a ragged appearance, and close examination will show individual shingles to be broken, warped, and upturned. New sidings will be required if shingles are badly weathered or worn.

Insulated sheathing board makes a poor nailing base, so check the sheathing. Sometimes gypsum board or pressed board is used and the nails will not hold, causing the siding to pull away. This is a major problem. Sheathing can be seen in the attic and it is usually black or brown rather than the normal plywood color.

Check painted surfaces for paint failure. Go to a paint store and get a trouble-shooting pictorial guide for paint failures and their causes. This way you can prevent further failures. Finish failures may be caused by poor paints, improper application of good paints, poor surface preparation, excessive moisture, or incompatible successive coatings. Excessive peeling may require complete removal of the paint. Since this can be very expensive, re-siding should be considered as an alternative.

Check masonry siding for loose and cracked joints, settlement, or the absence of ties. Check siding for damage and decay, especially behind trees and shrubs.

Check all wooden parts with a probe, particularly near the ground, for decay or rot and termites. Siding should be 12 inches off the ground to protect it. Check siding for missing units, settling, need of stain and preservative, and need of a cleaning (especially aluminum or vinyl). Check also for mildew. Check for use of plasterboard or fiber board on exterior surfaces, as these materials absorb water and rot quickly. Check weatherstripping for damage and tightness of fit. Check caulking at doors, windows, and all openings and joints between dissimilar materials.

Check attached decks and porches for rotted members. Be aware that, in many cases, insufficient or no footings were used, causing the structure to tend to pull away from the main house. Test for rot and termites. Check the entrance canopy and its flashing.

Check the condition of the cellar areaway. Be on the lookout for crumbling concrete and cracks in walls and slab floors. Observe the exterior for signs of settlement.

Check concrete walls for cracks, spalling, broken areas, settlement, exposed reinforcing, for termite tubes.

Check masonry surfaces for eroded or sandy mortar, mortar cracking and pulling away from brick or concrete masonry units, efflorescence, settlement or expansion cracks, termite tubes to wood surfaces, and soft, spalling, or cracked bricks.

Check parapet walls for loose coping stones, eroded or sandy mortar joints, expansion cracks, and defective cap flashings.

Wood Trim Parts. The major problems are rot, settlement, and peeling of paint. Trim is usually pine and if wet will rot quickly. Note capillary action off roofing materials near fascia board. Note if there are rain caps on windows and overhangs that will prevent water running down siding and trim. Are all trim parts caulked and secure?

Wood decay is caused by wood-rotting fungi that grow in damp wood. Fungi attack wood members in contact with damp masonry foundations, moist ground, or standing water, and water pipes that accumulate condensation or on which moisture condenses. Poor ventilation around the wood hastens the process of decay. Wood decay is indicated by a damp, musty odor, crumbling of the wood, the presence of fine reddish-brown powder under the building, and a hollow sound when the timber is tapped. Corrective actions taken to alleviate wood decay include the spraying of infested areas with a wood preservative and eliminating the source of moisture. Some fascia and eave rot is almost always present with internal and old wood gutters. Check for soffit ventilation vents, especially with hip roofs and large overhangs.

Windows.   Decay and poor maintenance cause windows to deteriorate. Storm windows help protect prime windows. Check storms to see if they are single, double, or triple track units, and note their condition. Are the weep holes open to drain water? Are the units fitted properly, caulked, and weatherstripped? What is the extent of corrosion? Try random windows and doors for ease of operation. Check the condition of exterior sills and frames. Check for rot at top of casement windows. Check for broken seals on thermopane windows (note fogging).

Chimneys.   See Chapter 23 for a more detailed checklist. Check the edge and condition of the cap with field glasses. Look for efflorescence, indicating leaks through bricks or mortar. Check height and position relation to ridge of roof and adjoining roof. Is there a need for rain caps or down draft deflectors?

The most obvious defect to look for in chimneys is cracks in the masonry or loose mortar. Such cracks are usually the result of foundation settlement or the attachment of television antennas or other items that put undue stress on the chimney. These cracks are a particular hazard if the flue does not have a fireproof lining. The chimney should be supported on its own footing, not by the framework of the house. Look in the attic to see that ceiling and roof framing are no closer than two inches to the chimney.

See if there is a ceramic flue, metal, or brick lining, and check the condition. Is there a separate flue for the fireplace and oil burning equipment? Two gas units can use the same flue, if certain precautions are taken. What is the condition of the flashing? Have any bricks fallen into the chimney? Are animals building nests? Does the unit need cleaning?

SUMMARY

Regular preventive maintenance is necessary to protect the surface of siding, wood trim, windows, and doors. Moisture and weathering can wear the protective coatings and cause rapid decay. Wood-destroying insects can cause additional damage. It is possible, through periodic inspection, to catch these conditions before they go too far and require extensive replacement. Use the preventive maintenance plan described in Chapter 33.

11.
Exterior Appurtenances and Driveways

INTRODUCTION

Exterior appurtenances are the structures apart from the house. They include detached garages, porches, stairs, decks, walks, patios, retaining walls, fences, areaways, and driveways. In this chapter, we will look at each item completely before going on to the next appurtenance. Weathering, excessive moisture, wood insects, poor installation, and no maintenance are the causes of appurtenance problems.

TECHNICAL INFORMATION

Detached Garages.   Detached garages were usually placed at the rear property of older homes. Attached garages, which became a popular part of the home in the fifties, are discussed in Chapter 8. The detached garage is usually small and in some cases may have a front extension and door to accommodate the larger cars of today.

Detached garages tend to be a problem, so check them thoroughly; repairs can be expensive. There is usually termite damage or rot in the sill because the sill plate is close to the ground and subject to excessive moisture. Many owners do not maintain the roofing and siding and this causes leaks that result in decay. Many rear walls have been pushed out by a driver who failed to stop in time. With patience, the wall can be jacked back in place. It was common practice to install inadequate footings that caused settlement. Cracks in the garage floor are a result of a poor stone base, and the cracks probably began many years ago. Check the older swing-out doors for ease of operation and for signs of rot. Check all structural components. Many times, there are no collar beams or tie ceiling joists and, as a result, the building can tilt to one side. Check for proper dainage at the foundation, as moisture produces rot and termites.

If you do have structural problems or rot at the sill, it may not pay to do any major repairs. Get an estimate of repair as well as a quote on adding a garage attached to the house.

A garage or carport is an extravagance in today's concept of house planning if it only serves as a shelter for an automobile. The garage should be designed to be multi-purposed: it should provide a convenient storage area for garden equipment, bicycles, and bulk storage; a utility area for laundry equipment; a workshop area; and terrace space for porch or outdoor living. Size the garage to handle two cars. Consider two single doors for greater convenience and the additional clearance between cars for easier access. Automatic electric door operators are available for most doors and they are convenient. One service door is recommended to the house, and another door to the side or rear yard. At least one window is desirable for light and ventilation. If the roof is high enough, a storage attic should be constructed with a pull-down stairway.

The building code requires that the wall between the house and attached garage should have a one-hour fire rating. This is typically 5/8-inch gypsum board. The wall should be insulated and should not contain plumbing that can freeze. Raise the foundation walls at least six inches above the floor to protect the sill from dampness. If the driveway slopes toward the house, be certain to put a large trench drain along the front of the garage apron to prevent water from entering the garage. If possible, put a drain in the center of the garage floor and pipe it to a drywell or slope the floor toward the driveway to remove the water. In cold climates, the garage should be heated to keep the temperature above freezing. To prevent gas fumes from entering the house, return air ducts should not be used. If your driveway is on a steep slope, why not consider an electric or hot water snow melting system embedded in your driveway?

The best choice of a garage door from an operational standpoint is the one-piece canopy-type door or a one-piece door mounted on tracks. Sectional doors are least desirable because of maintenance problems. The reasons that an overhead garage door will fail to operate properly include incorrect adjustment, loose hardware, binding, and friction. An extension-spring door has springs along both horizontal tracks. A torsion-spring door has a torsion spring wrapped around a shaft that extends across the top of the door. The door is equipped with cables that wind on winchlike drums attached to the same shaft on which the torsion spring rides. Examine the springs for cracks and rust. Spray a light machine oil over the spring surface to retard corrosion. About every 15 years, the springs will require replacement.

Porches, Stairways, and Deck.   One of the parts of a house most vulnerable to decay and insect attack is the porch. Since it is open to the weather, windblown rain or snow can easily raise the moisture content of wood members to conditions for promoting growth of wood-destroying organisms. Steps are often placed in contact with soil. The life of many wood members is determined by how they are protected from rot. Some pine decks fail in five years. Redwood, if wet, will deteriorate.

Check all wood members for decay and insect damage. Give particular attention to the base of posts or any place where two members join and water might get into the joint. Decay often occurs where posts are not raised above the porch floor to allow air to dry out the base of the post. It may be worthwhile to replace a few members, but the porch that is in a generally deteriorated condition should be completely rebuilt or removed. Be sure to inspect under the porch. Look for termites, rot, settlement, and deteriorated floor boards. Use your screw driver to probe. On enclosed porches, check out all windows and structure for rot due to roof leakage. Check for adequate ventilation and proper floorboard spacing. Check the stability of supports on the deck. Check the deck's railings for stability. Are additional supports needed? Examine the deck's structure carefully. Some do-it-yourselfers have installed undersized girders and supports.

Walks and Patios.   Failure of walks and driveways are due to insufficient base course, tree roots, poor drainage, frost heave, and weathering. Some units will fail in a few years if not installed properly and cared for. Check heave due to frost and tree roots. Note municipal codes or insurance company practices that may require correction of hazardous walk conditions. Check all curbs, gutters, and manholes for cracks, breaks, misalignments, damaged tops, inadequate expansion, and crown. Check drainage for obstructed ditches, improper grading, and shoulder protection. Check spalling of the surface caused by inadequate expansion joints. Check all cracks. Interior corner cracking is indicative of a poor base support or overloading. Longitudinal cracks are caused by improper joint spacing, inferior coarse aggregate in the concrete mix, or poor subgrade support and overloading.

Fences. Here again, weathering, moisture, and insects are the causes of failure. Check fences for discontinuity, looseness, vertical and horizontal misalignment, and erosion that would permit entry. Check metal posts for rust corrosion; loose, bent, leaning, broken, or missing or mechanically damaged posts; and the settlement of concrete foundations. Check metal gates for misalignment and difficult opening and closing. Check wood posts and gates for loose, leaning, splintered, broken, or missing or mechanically damaged posts. Check wood gates for loose, broken, splintered, rotted, or missing parts; misalignment; difficult opening and closing; loose, missing, or broken stops, checks, rollers, hinges, latches and locks.

Retaining Walls. Many walls fail because of inadequate footings, no weep holes for drainage, and insufficient wall thickness. Check structural inadequacy and poor physical condition of deadman anchors and other attachments and fastenings. Check embankment slopes and areas behind walls for erosion, settlement, or slippage resulting from improper drainage, lack of full sod or vegetation coverage, and damage from burrowing animals. Grade properly to keep water draining away. If the wall is leaning, it may pay to remove it and build a new one. Many building materials can be used.

Driveways. Concrete driveways should be at least four inches thick with expansion joints required every ten feet. Additional joints are required where the driveway joins the garage, slab, or sidewalk. Concrete stains badly but otherwise provides a good surface if the driveway is well-built. Staining from autos can be prevented if the driveway has two narrow wheel strips with grass between. Air-entrained concrete should be used in cold climates, as it is more resistant to frost action than standard concrete.

Asphalt paving or blacktop is rarely a satisfactory driveway because paving contractors take short cuts that result in cracking and breakup of the surface. The only way to prevent this is to insist that the contractor build the driveway in conformance with specifications that are available from the Asphalt Institute, the municipal building department, or your architect.

Another driveway surface is brick laid in concrete or brick laid on crushed stone. The first is more durable and easier to snow plow, but the second is easier to repair.

Gravel is usually an unacceptable surface, although it is usually the cheapest. Many suburban homes use gravel but it is difficult to snow plow, rain water is not shed easily, and the surface needs continual leveling.

Building a New Driveway. Get a good set of specifications and have the contractor give you a quote and install the driveway according to these specs. Check on all municipal ordinances covering the number, size, and placement of driveway approaches and also regulating the street or rear alley where these may be located. Get the necessary permits.

Most driveways are made of bituminous pavement or concrete, although there are other acceptable paving materials used in local areas. You can have a more attractive driveway today as a result of improved asphalt techniques and new surface treatments. Consider the five planning factors in building your driveway and the result will be years of trouble-free usage. You'll have a good driveway if you take adequate precautions.

The first part of the plan is taking care of the subgrade. The subgrade can be soil of any kind—hard or soft, strong or weak. To "proof-roll," run a heavy piece of equipment over the area where the driveway is to be built, and observe the result. Rutting in the wheel path means the subgrade is weak, and a reasonably thick pavement is needed. In some cases, where the subgrade is very soft, the contractor will remove 12 to 18 inches of soft subgrade and replace it with suitably strong material, such as stone, slag, or bank-run gravel.

A base course, four inches thick, should be part of every driveway (step two). This is made up of compacted good quality stone, slag, or gravel, and is required even if the sub-base course is excellent. An asphalt should be applied after the base course is at the correct thickness.

The third factor is good drainage. Water under a pavement is harmful. The contractor should slope or crown the asphalt pavement by not less than a quarter inch to the foot. Water drainage from downspouts should be piped well away from pavement edges. If the soil is wet or the rains are heavy, then drains should be installed and the run-off piped away.

A good wearing surface (fourth factor) laid on the base course should vary from two to three inches thick and should be properly compacted. Unless a curbing is used, the base course must be wider than this top layer to prevent edge cracking. The pavement should slope at least two inches per ten feet of driveway for drainage.

The last step is to avoid placing the pavement when construction conditions are unfavorable. Water on the area to be paved should signal the suspension of paving operations until the surface is dry. In cool weather, the asphalt mixture should be brought to the site in insulated-covered trucks and used immediately.

The Asphalt Institute is today recommending Full-Depth Asphalt, in which a minimum of four inches of asphalt mixtures are laid directly on the subgrade or improved subgrade and properly compacted. The pavement thickness should be determined by the contractor. The Asphalt Institute does not rule out the consideration of the older method described above. Discuss both methods with the contractors when getting your bid.

Driveway Maintenance. Periodic inspection of your driveway will help in eliminating some costly repair jobs. During your inspection, consider the following points carefully: Are the edges ragged? Does the base layer fail to extend beyond the top surface? Is the base layer thin and inadequate instead of four inches thick? Are there soft spots in the wearing surface after a rain? Is the surface a series of hills and valleys? Has your car left tire ruts in the surface? When it rains, go out and observe the water running off the driveway. If you are lower than the street, does the street water flow down the driveway? If so, then you'll need a burm at the top of the driveway. Does water collect in spots? If so, then patch the area or install drains and pipe it to a lower spot or dry well. Most problems are repaired at a minimum expense. For maximum benefits, perform all seasonal maintenance, such as cracks and joint-filling, at the proper time and according to best practice.

SUMMARY

Exterior appurtenances tend to be neglected by the homeowner until it becomes necessary to replace the entire unit because it is unsafe or has deteriorated so it can't be used adequately. Repairs are generally easy to do and usually involve simple patching, while replacements tend to be expensive. Use the preventive maintenance checklist in Chapter 33 to aid you in your periodic maintenance.

12.
Swimming Pools

INTRODUCTION

If the house you are considering has a pool, don't let it scare you off. I bought a resale home with a 20 × 40 foot in-ground pool, and it has turned into a pleasure for the entire family. There is some work to any household equipment, but if you plan the maintenance, you should have a wholesome family activity.

There are now over two million in-ground residential swimming pools in the United States, and the figure is growing. In addition, another three million American families own above-ground pools large enough to swim in. Both above- and in-ground pools are not within the range of the average family's budget, although installed prices do vary throughout the country.

This chapter will introduce you to some of the basic elements of maintaining and inspecting your own pool. Much more detailed and specific information is available to you from the manufacturer or installer of the pool in the home you plan to buy.

TECHNICAL INFORMATION

Pools come in a variety of shapes, sizes, and materials. In most areas of the United States, a pool will add little to the value of your property. You can ordinarily expect to recover only a small part of its cost when you sell your house. In addition, you could wind up biding your time until a buyer who wants your house *and* a pool comes along. Check with your broker, as pool value varies in different parts of the United

States. Think of a pool not primarily as an investment, but as a place for fun and exercise and an added bonus in a resale home.

The size and depth of a pool will be dictated by your location, lot size, soil condition, local ordinances, and installation cost. Pools deep enough for diving are more expensive because the added depth means more reinforcing, and a larger pump and filtration system are needed for the greater volume of water.

A pool will increase your property taxes. Check with the tax assessor on the assessed valuation percentage used. Insurance coverage for liability is usually included in your homeowner's insurance policy premium, but check with your agent for the maximum coverage. Local laws will require four-foot high well-maintained fencing around the pool to prevent accidents.

In-ground pools can be constructed of concrete, of fiberglass, or of aluminum framing with a vinyl liner. Concrete pools are made by spraying concrete into a reinforcing grid, by pouring concrete into forms, or by using masonry blocks and a cement waterproof coating. Cement pools can last indefinitely if installed properly and maintained regularly.

Vinyl liner pools use a waterproof liner that fits against a wall framework of aluminum, steel, concrete, or cement blocks and rest on a sand, concrete, or vermiculite bottom. The liners have a ten year warranty and will usually need replacement after that time.

Fiberglass pools are lighter in weight than all-concrete pools. One kind comes as a single unit like a bathtub; another has a poured concrete floor and fiberglass walls that are bolted together and sealed. Fiberglass reequires no paint, because colors can be incorporated into the material by the manufacturer. It has a life of over 20 years.

The decking around the pool must be graded away from the pool so that dirty water cannot flow into it. Because of the chemicals in the water, it is best if this water is kept out of the garden. Well-placed drains can take this as well as rain water to a sewer. The deck need not be a slab of concrete. It can be made of cement block laid on a bed of sand. The main objective is to have drains to take care of excess water and not allow this water to undermine the sides of the pool.

Above-ground pools are popular because they are relatively low in cost, usually don't add to the real estate tax property assessment, are relatively portable, and have the built-in safety feature of being about four feet higher than ground level. These pools, usually four feet deep, range from circular ones 12 feet in diameter to rectangular ones 20 feet wide by 40 feet long. Models can be assembled on a week-end and are available in stores. Pool walls are galvanized steel or aluminum and hold the water in a plastic liner. The floor is sand. There are special filters and skimmers for above-ground pools to keep water sanitary and free of debris. Best of all, maintenance is low and above-ground pools can be taken apart if you move, which keeps them free of taxes in many communities. A good quality above-ground pool will last for at least five years if properly cared for.

Pool Equipment.   In addition to equipment such as ladders and diving boards, the swimming pool has a skimmer, a filtration system, and, as an option, an automatic cleaning system. The types of filters most generally used are sand, diatomaceous earth (DE), and a cartridge filter like that on a vacuum cleaner. The sand filter is a simple vat through which the water passes, leaving behind dirt particles. The DE filter uses inexpensive minute diatomes (microscopic sea creatures) spread over a membrane inside the filter tank. As the water passes through, these "creatures" trap the equally microscopic dirt particles. The cartridge filter contains fibrous material which traps the dirt particles as water passes through it. Once the filter material gets dirty, it is necessary to clean it by backwashing the filtration system.

Allow at least two or three hours a week if you intend to clean the pool yourself. A built-in fully automatic cleaning system will save you time, but will add 10 to 15% to the total construction cost of the pool. It can also be inconvenient to remove the hoses. Portable cleaning systems are also available and may be installed on already constructed pools. Both automatic and portable (operated by a garden hose) cleaning systems work on the principle that the agitation of water keeps dirt and algae from adhering to the walls and bottom of the pool, thus making it easier for the filter to process them out.

Pools must be chemically tested daily. Pool water increases in acidity due to acids used in chlorine to stabilize it. There is also natural chemical decomposition. To maintain the correct balance, chemicals should usually be added daily. Inexpensive and simple test kits are available to determine how much chemical to add each time. Heavy traffic in the pool requires careful attention to the pool's pH or acid/alkalinity count. The ideal pH range for a pool is 7.2 to 7.6. Easy-to-use chemicals may be employed to restore the desired balance if the pool becomes too acidic or alkaline. Follow directions carefully in both the use and storage of chemicals.

The chore of daily chlorine additions may be avoided by purchase of an automatic chemical dispenser. Safe and easy to use, it may be electrically timed to dispense chemicals when the pool is not in use. The filter need not be used 24 hours a day and can be put on a timer. Algaecides and chlorine are used to kill algae, to retard the growth of bacteria, and to oxidize the dirt particles not processed out by the filter. Backwashing will be necessary when the flow from the filter and the pressure gauge reading decreases.

Many areas of the country require heated water for swimming during a full season. Both gas and oil heaters are expensive to operate. Simple solar heaters do a good job. There are also solar pool covers that do a fair job of raising the water temperature. Be sure the sun rays are not shaded by trees off the pool during the 10 AM to 4 PM time slot.

Building the Pool.   If you don't have a pool but are considering one, then be prepared to do some research before deciding on the type of pool and the contractor who will do the job. Poor deals and sharp practices by some pool salespersons have given many homeowners headaches. Before you buy, take the steps listed below.

1. Talk with pool owners to get an estimate of installation, annual pool maintenance, and parts replacement costs.

2. Get bids from three contractors. When you're ready to buy, be sure there is a written contract specifying material grades, colors, prices, makes of equipment, details of financing, and who is responsible for each part of the installation. The contractor should belong to the National Swimming Pool Institute, have access to the group's model contract, and be obliged to follow their code of ethics.

3. Sign only with an established contractor whose reputation is known in the community. Check up on him at the local Better Business Bureau, at his bank, and from homeowners who are his past customers.

4. Be sure the guarantee for workmanship and equipment is for at least one year. Vinyl liners usually come with a ten-year warranty. The price should be a firm one with no escape clauses. Some contractors will want a price escalation if there is an unusual excavation problem. Be careful.

PROBLEMS

The major problems with pools deal with the regular care of water and equipment. Pumps, filters, and piping will need periodic care and lubrication and the correction of any leaks. Pumps should be protected from rain and the elements. Keep the manual that comes with the pool handy and follow maintenance instructions.

Water testing should be done daily to check the pH and chlorine content. At the beginning of each season, have your chemical supplier check the pool for stabilizer. This makes the chlorine work more effectively.

As the summer progresses, adults and youngsters will be spending more time than ever in the pool, and everyone will be perspiring. Besides perspiration, suntan oil, hair sprays, skin creams, and other foreign substances will be carried into the water. High temperatures of midsummer promote the growth of algae. Also, prolonged hot weather cuts down the efficiency of water sanitizers. Finally, the increased frequency of thunderstorms in midsummer creates a great deal of ammonia in the air, which is then carried into the pool by rain, and ammonia is a direct enemy of the sanitizing action of the chlorine you add to your pool. So check the water condition daily, and keep chlorine and pH levels on the high side.

Summer winds blow dust and plant pollen into the water, and bathers around the pool apron and yard track dirt into the pool. This foreign matter reduces the effectiveness of your sanitizer. The symptoms of these problems are seen as green or black algae patches on the water's surface, discoloration of the water, and an unpleasant odor. The cure is to give the pool water a shock treatment or superchlorination with chlorine tablets or granules. Follow the directions on the chemical container and then vacuum the dead algae away. Before you shock or superchlorinate poor water, always *check the pH factor* of the water. Bring the water up to the ideal pH factor, 7.2 to 7.6, and then shock the pool. The best time to treat is in the evening, since this allows the chlorine to do its work quietly in calm waters. The next morning, take another pH reading. Keep everyone out of the pool until it drops to a safe level. A pool cover is recommended whenever the pool is not in use for long periods of time.

Pool accidents can be prevented by proper attention to pool safety rules and checks on equipment. It is a good idea to keep a first-aid kit on hand. Both family members and guests should adhere to a posted set of rules available at pool stores. Simple reminders of "no running" and "no swimming alone" are needed by everyone. If yours is an above-ground pool, keep the ladder up when the pool is not in use. Keep the pool area well lighted and the fences locked. Diving boards and water slides are potentially dangerous. Be sure your board is well dampened to prevent high dives. For water slides, a feet first position is recommended. Caution everyone against sliding or diving onto other swimmers. Don't buy a diving board too big for the depth of your pool.

Pool lights and other area wiring should be checked annually, as should ground protective devices. Equipment should conform to the National Electric Code. Keep all radios and appliances well away from the pool area. Instruct everyone not to bring glass objects into the pool area.

MAINTENANCE

Maintenance must be continuous. Water must be warmed in most areas of the country, and this can be done by solar heat or fuel heaters. The pool water must be circulated through filtration media to keep it clean, and chemicals must be added to purify the water.

This section discusses opening your pool, maintaining it, and closing it for the winter.

Opening Your Pool. Your local pool company will be glad to do this for you. The price will be about $100, or you can do it yourself as given below.

Clean the water and leaves off the cover and then remove and store it.

Brush the sides of the pool; then vacuum and backwash.

Bring water up to ½ of the skimmer box.

Put in proper amounts of algaecide and shock.

Wait 24 hours and adjust the pH level. Add chemicals to put the algae into solution.

Wait 24 to 48 hours and then backwash. Vacuum the pool and again backwash.

Adjust chemical content to acceptable levels.

Daily Maintenance. Check the pH and chlorine content of the water, then follow this simple checklist when cleaning your pool.

Skim the pool's surface with a standard leaf skimmer.
Brush down pool walls and tile with a stiff-bristled brush.
Clean the skimmer's basket and hair-lint strainer.
Vacuum the pool bottom (as needed).
Clean the filter (when sufficient dirt has accumulated and the recirculation flow has decreased).
Hose clean the pool deck.

Winterizing Your Pool.   It is very important to properly winterize your swimming pool in order to protect pool and water, as well as the equipment and accessories. Failure to take these precautions will result in unnecessary expense and labor in the spring when the pool is opened for use. It can also cause delay in using the pool when warm weather returns. Your instruction manual will provide details for winterizing your particular pool. Clean the pool, backwash, then put on a heavy duty vinyl pool cover (it will cut down on maintenance time and expenses). If it freezes in your area, then the pool water level must be dropped and all equipment drained and covered.

INSPECTION

If you are purchasing a home with a swimming pool or merely want to inspect your own, the following check points will prove useful. If in doubt, always call in a local manufacturer, because structural problems are expensive.

Check concrete for cracks, breaks, spalling, exposed reinforcing, and settlement.

Check tile for settled, chipped, cracked, loose, and missing pieces. Check for defective mortar joints.

Check expansion joints for leakage.

Check wall and floor finishes for roughness and dirt.

Check depth markers and lane strips for legibility.

Check and test springboards for cracks, rot decay, breaks, splintering, and other damage. Check for loose or missing fastenings and the absence of nonslip coverings.

Observe and test ladders for rust or corrosion of metal parts. Check loose, missing, broken, or rotted wooden parts. Check misalignment of diving towers.

Check other metal accessories for rust, corrosion, broken or missing parts, and other damage.

Check other wooden parts for cracks, breaks, splintering, loose joints or fastenings, rot, insect, other damage.

Check main drains for sediment, rust, and proper drainage.

Check gutter drains for obstructions. This includes drains in the walks.

Check walls for stains from corroded fittings.

Check fences, barricades, dividing walls, and footings for settlement or other damage.

Check painted surfaces for blistering, checking, cracking, scaling, wrinkling, flaking, peeling, rust, corrosion, or the complete absence of paint.

Check plastic liners for fading, patches, age, rips, and condition. Is the liner secure along the rim to prevent water from undermining it?

Check all walks for settlement and cracks. Walks along the perimeter of the pool should slope away so excess water will not wash down the sides and erode the bottom of the liner.

SUMMARY

A home swimming pool, carefully selected to suit your needs and pocketbook, with the proper equipment and maintenance, can give you many hours of family fun and healthful exercise at reasonable cost. But it must be maintained to protect your investment. If the house you are buying has a pool, then get professional help to inspect it.

If the pool is winterized, arrange with your lawyer to set aside money to fix any problem that is found when the pool is inspected and run in the summer.

13.
Solving Wet Basement, Wet Crawl Space, and Wet Slab Problems

INTRODUCTION

The most miserable homeowners are often those with water problems: wet basements or crawl spaces. Tired from buck-passing sessions with contractors, builders, or former owners, they are left with a problem that is both uncomfortable and unhealthy. But if you are buying a house with a damp or wet basement, don't despair. It may be possible to correct the situation.

Based on years of inspecting, I find that 90% of all wet and damp basement problems can be solved with minimum effort and expense. By following the outlined recommended solutions, you can have a bright, dry basement and gain a useful storage, workshop, or recreation room. Wet basement problems can be as slight as the occasional damp spot after a rain to as extreme as flooded property.

TECHNICAL INFORMATION

Danger Signals. There are a number of danger signals that could indicate that your basement has a water problem. Check for the following carefully.

Damp spots on the walls.

Cracked walls in the basement and crawl space.

Cracked floors.

White salts (efflorescence) on the walls.

Peeling paint.

Rotted or warped paneling.

Stains on the sheetrock or structural framing members.

Fungus.
Rust, mold, and mildew.
Insects and bugs.
A musty or mildew odor.

PROBLEMS AND CAUSES OF WATER

Get to know your basement as well as you know your living room. After discovering a danger signal, your first step is to find the cause. The most common causes of seepage in basement walls and floors are given below.

The original workmanship may have been poor.

The house may have settled, causing cracks to appear in either the floors or the walls, allowing water to enter.

Rain water funneled down leaders exits at the foundation, causing surface water build-up and water seepage into the basement or crawl space via cracks, or through the wall or window wells.

Areaway drains are clogged and the areaway is not covered.

The property is flat or slopes toward the house, permitting surface water (rain or melting snow) to collect and drain down against the outside basement walls. Water leaks through cracks or other openings in the wall or may pass through the block and mortar, leaving wet wall surfaces or standing water on the floor.

There are no gutters or leaders (or defective ones) to handle the roof water. The free-falling water forms puddles and erodes the soil near the foundation wall. Water leaks or enters by capillary action.

Condensation (or sweating) of atmospheric moisture occurs on cool surfaces—walls, floors, cold water pipes—in the basement, leaving puddles of water.

Leaking plumbing or other sources of moisture increase the humidity of the basement air and produce condensation.

Dense shrubbery and other plantings close to the house prevent good ventilation.

Poor mortar joints in either concrete or cinder blocks (or cracks in concrete walls) or where the floor meets the foundation wall allow water to penetrate from the outside.

The subsurface or ground water level (water table) is close to the underside of the slab or floor. (A water table can be defined as the upper surface of ground water of the level below which the soil is saturated with water. This level may fluctuate by several feet throughout the year depending on the soil, landscape, and weather conditions. In many areas of the United States, especially where the annual rainfall is 20 inches or more, the seasonal high water table is two to five feet below the ground surface. The water table is higher than the basement floor. Water leaks in again by capillary action causing flooding and sometimes failure of the footings or foundation wall. Frost heaving is another problem, but since it is a structural matter it is not covered in this chapter.)

On many sites, natural springs and seeps occur because of existing soil, rock, and landscape characteristics. Water may flow throughout the year or only seasonally, during periods of heavy rainfall or spring thaws. Water may flow into or around your house if it is constructed over or near a spring or seep.

On some properties, surface waters will pond on your lawn or driveway. The cause is usually poor grading.

Some soils have slow permeability. If the soil at your homesite has a dense layer, especially a layer of clay, the flow of water through the soil may be restricted and water may pond on your lawn.

After finding the cause of the unwanted water, you must decide if you can repair it yourself or if you need professional assistance. If you decide on using a contractor, be sure to get at least three quotes on the same set of specifications and insist on a transferable guarantee in writing. A thorough understanding of the problems will help you converse intelligently with contractors about solutions and costs.

SOLUTIONS TO MINOR PROBLEMS

Unfortunately, drying up the basement can be a hit or miss proposition. You can get help from local building suppliers, county or municipal authorities, or your soil or water conservation district office, which may be able to provide more information about planning and installing specific drainage measures around your home.

Start with the inexpensive remedies and work up to the expensive ones, stopping when the water condition is corrected.

Correct the Grade.   First see that the ground around your foundation is graded to run the rain water away from the house. Raise the level of the soil adjacent to the walls to a slope of three inches per foot for a distance of three feet (that's a 15° angle). Look for areas which show signs of pooled water or erosion along the foundation wall and pack soil in there. Be sure, however, there is a place for the water to go. If you find an erosion hole near the house, it's a sure bet where the water is coming from. A small load of top soil costs under $50 and a typical job for material and labor by a landscaper could run from $200 to $500, depending on the amount of shrubbery to be removed. But don't despair; probably with a minimal effort, you can do the job for nothing.

Unclog Gutter Systems.   Make sure your gutter system is not clogged and leaking. Clogged gutters dump water right next to the foundation, gouging out ditches in the process. Check to be sure all downspouts are clear and terminate onto a splash block. If possible, pipe downspouts to a storm sewer, to the street, or to a low spot on the property well away from the house. Dry wells tend to clog up and should be avoided unless you intend to install an effective leaching field. See your building supply dealer for instructions in the use of orangeburg or plastic underground pipes.

Plant Sod.   Next, encourage a good stand of grass and grade the lot to direct the water away from the building and toward the street. Sod is a quick way to get a strong turf to reduce erosion of the soil. Raise or cover window wells. If you have window wells, raise their level and place stones or bricks around them to help prevent water from running in. Be certain that window wells are cleaned, are of proper height, and have plastic covers to shed water. You might even want to consider buying plexiglass window well covers from your hardware dealer or building supply. They're expensive but could solve your problem. In addition, they keep leaves and dirt from gathering at the bottom of the well and rotting out your windows. Areaways should have a workable drain and be covered. Always anticipate the excessive rainfall and maintain the correct drainage pattern.

Install a Dehumidifier.   Hook up a dehumidifier over or into a basement or crawl space floor drain. You should run the unit from May until October. This will control the moisture in the air of the basement area. If possible, obtain a dehumidifier with an automatic shut-off feature to prevent water overflow when the unit's reservoir is full. Of course, it is good to ventilate the area, but rarely can this be done conveniently.

NOTE. If the water has stopped after any of the above steps, then prepare the walls to receive a good waterproof paint. Seal up all joints, cracks, and holes with a waterproof caulk. Patch large broken-out areas with mortar. Ready mix mortar in small quantities can be obtained from the hardware store. The paint will not hold back water but it will contain the dampness. A variety of commercial compounds are available for dampproofing the walls. First, prepare the surfaces by thoroughly cleaning off all paint, mold, efflorescence salts, and dirt. If you don't, the paint will not adhere. Your job is now done. If you decide to panel the wall, use a vapor barrier insulation and set the stud wall at least an inch away from the basement wall.

SOLUTIONS TO CHRONIC PROBLEMS

The above outlined steps will correct most typical wet basement problems. However, if you live on the side of a hill, or where there is ponding of surface water, or where the soil has slow permeability, the area is marshy, or rains have raised the water table, then you may have to go further with your plans.

Excessive Runoff. To control excessive runoff, especially if you are on the side of a hill, develop a thick turf, add more trees, prepare contour planting, terrace the slopes to slow down the runoff, and/or dig a swale around the house about ten feet away. These procedures will channel the water into the soil and provide a runoff away from the house. A landscaper can quote on this work. It can be expensive due to the labor involved, and for this reason, many people decide to do the work themselves.

Ponding.   For ponding, you can install small diversions or ditches to channel off the water. These are usually located near property lines in back or alongside of houses. For low flows of surface water, you can install a surface inlet leading to a subsurface drain. The drain outlet can empty into the street gutters or storm sewers if permitted by local building codes. You should grade your yard so the surface water drains away from the house. A minimum grade of one foot in 100 feet is generally adequate. When filling in low areas, use the most permeable soil available. Save the top soil to spread over the new fill and establish a turf.

Dense Soil.   If your soil has a dense layer near the surface, you can dig a small trench through the layer and fill it with sand, gravel, or other coarse material to improve permeability in a small, low-lying wet spot. For larger wet areas, you can install subsurface drains four to six inches in diameter at a depth of three to five feet. The drains should be packed with a porous material like sand or gravel.

High Water Table. If the water table is high, you may find that floor level open drains at the foundation are needed to direct the water to a sump pump. Cost varies from $300 to $600. You can also install drains around the inside wall under the basement floor and pipe them to a sump pump. Lowering the water table under a basement floor should be done with caution. On some soils, especially slow draining silts and clays, unequal settlement may crack the wall and floors.

If the water table problem is extreme, then the outside of the foundation must be dug up. To do this, the exterior walls are sealed with an impervious substance and drain tile is installed with the discharge to a lower spot on the property or to a sump pump. In some cases, it is not possible to dig up the outside of the foundation wall; then, the same job must be done on the inside.

Flooding Due to Location.   If your home is in a flood plain of a nearby creek or stream, it may be flooded during periods of heavy rains or rapid snowmelt. Usually, community-wide measures such as diking and deepening the channel take long in coming. Before buying a home on a flood plain, check with your county or state flood commission to see what plans are in the works for correcting the problem. Talk with the town engineer.

In a very few cases, it may be necessary to have the drain tile discharge into a cement tank away from the foundation and then have the water drain or be pumped into the street, a storm sewer, or a leaching field. This condition exists in old stream beds and on property bordering flooded areas.

In upland areas, flooding can occur if your home is in the path of a natural drainage system. In housing developments, natural drainageways are often altered or blocked. If man made sewers are not installed to carry away the seasonal flow of water, then nearby homes can be flooded, often without warning. The homeowners can and should exert pressure on the municipality to correct the condition.

IMPORTANT. In no case should you deal with the contractor who proposes to pump a sealant into the ground at the foundation or into your block walls. This approach is virtually useless. Some municipalities have branded this practice a fraud.

MAINTENANCE AND INSPECTION

As a homeowner, you should periodically inspect your property during rain storms and winter-spring thaws. Look for puddles at the foundation, low spots on the lawn, water surging down the hill, and effective roof drainage. Every few years, check the grade at the foundation, as soil has a tendency to settle each year. Clean the gutters and leaders and inspect all joints and seams at least twice a year as the seasons change. Clean all underground drains and keep screens cleaned on all inlets and outlets.

If you are a home buyer, then become familiar with the wet basement danger signals discussed earlier. Once you've discovered the signal, then look for the possible causes. When in doubt, get professional help, and check with neighbors and town officials for problems peculiar to the area. Each section of the country experiences different soil and environment conditions. Don't assume anything.

SUMMARY

The problem of wet basements, wet crawl spaces, and damp slabs has become even more acute with the growth of the suburbs. New buildings and roads have taken away natural drainage areas that once absorbed the rain. The results are floods, excess street water, and poorly drained soil. This environmental deficiency, in conjunction with poor roof drainage systems and inadequate site grading, has caused a rash of unnecessary wet basements, and in more drastic cases, water flowing through the first floor or basement of the home.

If you are moving into a new area, be sure to check with the town engineer or building inspector to discover the flood areas and any other local problems. Also, speak with neighbors within a few blocks radius to see what water problems, if any, they are experiencing.

If you are already in a house with a water problem, analyze the situation and the causes discussed in this guide. Then start with the inexpensive solution methods first. Solving water problems is an important step for your own safety and physical comfort. Even more important, water problems can affect the sales price of your home and the ability to sell it quickly. Home buyers are quickly turned-off by water problems in a potential home. Remember, maintaining your basement is a form of preventive maintenance and, as such, requires attention on a periodic planned basis.

14.
Electrical System

INTRODUCTION

Your electrical system serves an important function in your home. If the system is not properly designed, installed, and maintained, it can be a safety and fire hazard as well as a great source of irritation to you, the homeowner. Some knowledge of the electrical system will help you when you contract for electrical work and plan for future maintenance.

This chapter covers the maintenance and inspection of your electrical system. Electric wiring is a mystery to most people. Yet with a little basic knowledge, it is easy to test and examine. All major changes to the system or the correction of malfunctions should be done by a licensed electrician. If you have aluminum wiring installed prior to 1974, then you should have an electrician periodically check all switches, convenience outlets, and major appliance connections.

TECHNICAL INFORMATION

Electrical power is fed to your home through service lines from the utility pole to the weatherhead on your house, through the meter to a distribution panel. Three wires indicate 110-220 volts, while two wires indicate only 110-volt service. The amperage is based on wire size and is usually shown on the distribution panel or the main disconnect circuit breaker. The minimum a home should have today is 110/220 volts and 150 amps.

The main service entrance of wires and load center in most homes can be found in the garage, basement, or utility area of the home nearest the point of entry of the electric service. A grounding conductor is used to connect the wiring system to a grounding electrode, such as a cold water pipe or a driven ground rod. This provides a positive ground for equipment attached to the wiring system.

Protective devices built into home electric systems for safety and convenience are of two approved types, circuit breakers and fuses. Both give acceptable protection for the wiring system. Their purpose is to limit the current flow in case of a fault and to prevent overheating of the wiring. Fuses are marked with the number of amperes they will carry and are of two types: *plug fuses*, which screw into position, and *cartridge fuses*, which are held in place by spring clips. *Circuit breakers* are thermally operated switches which automatically open after there is an excessive surge of current. Another type of unit is the magnetic circuit breaker, which contains an electromagnet that releases the contact when current is excessive.

The procedure used to restore interrupted service is simple. A blown fuse must be replaced with a new one of the same capacity. Circuit breaker resetting requires operation of a toggle handle to restore the circuit connection. Replacing a fuse or resetting the circuit breaker should be done only after the cause of interruption has been removed. Use only the proper size fuse or circuit breaker to protect the wire in the circuits; generally a 15 amp fuse or circuit breaker with a number 14 wire, and a 20 amp fuse or circuit breaker with a number 12 wire. Beware if you see 20, 25, or 30 amp fuses in lighting circuits. It means an overloaded circuit.

The volt is the unit used in measuring electrical pressure. It is similar to pounds per square inch of water pressure. The ampere is the unit used to measure electrical rate of flow and is similar to the flow of water in gallons per minute. Resistance is measured by ohms. It is the property of materials to oppose the flow of current. The larger the wire (or pipe), the more current (water) it can carry.

There are two general types of circuits that conduct the flow of electricity: two-wire and three-wire. A two-wire service consists of two wires; one black, designating a hot wire, and one white, denoting a neutral or ground. The two-wire system is simply two sides of one circuit carrying 115 or 120 volts. In a three-wire system, two wires are hot and one is neutral. One of the hot wires is black, another red, and the neutral is white. With a three-wire system, the voltage can carry 220 to 240 volts. Electrical wiring varies with diameter, which governs the load-carrying capacity of the wire. Wire sizes are 18, 16, 14, 12,

10, 8, 6, 4, 2, 00, and 0000. As the gauge decreases, the amperage capacity increases. House wiring should never be less than 14 gauge, which can carry up to 15 amperes.

Several types of wire are used in a home. The most common is type NM (non-metallic) cable, usually referred to as "Romex," which is used in dry locations. Type NMC is non-metallic cable for corrosive or damp locations. Type AC (armored cable, also called BX) has a metal armor spiralled around the wires, and is required for home wiring in some areas. Type UF (underground feeder) is meant for burial underground. Cable is stamped with the type number and the number of wires, and the size of the wire is stamped every foot or two on the outside cover. In older homes, knob and tube wiring was used with fabric coverings and friction tape joints. These should be replaced when the service is updated.

The minimum lighting in a house is 3 watts to square foot of building area. The location of outlets is important. Receptacle outlets on 15- or 20-ampere branch circuits must be spaced no more than 12 feet apart, so that no point on the wall measured along the floorline will be more than 6 feet from an outlet. For safety, wall outlets should be grounded. Grounding-type outlets permit the connection of parallel-blade, two-wire plugs used on appliances as well as three-wire plugs which connect devices that must be grounded. Weatherproof outlets are desirable on the exterior front and rear walls of the house. Additional weatherproof outlets may be needed on outside walls of the house for patios or porches. Three-way and four-way switches are needed to control lights from two or more locations.

Timer switches for both inside and outside lights will turn lights on and off at pre-set times. They allow you to return home to a lighted house and discourage burglars while you are away. Photoelectric cells do a similar job of turning lights on at dusk and off at dawn.

Lighting circuits may also be controlled by low voltage switching systems. In these, the actual switching is done by a relay operated by a 24-volt circuit and controlled by low-voltage switches. Any number of switches to control the same light outlet can be easily and inexpensively added to the circuit. The use of master switches allows control of many lighting outlets from several different locations. Maintenance tends to be high on these units and parts may be hard to obtain.

When purchasing appliance cords, it may not be necessary to have a full-length cord if the appliance is used on the kitchen counter. You can buy short coiled cords that will retract like telephone cords to avoid cord clutter on the kitchen counter. Electrical cords and fittings used outdoors should be of the non-metallic type, weatherproofed and properly grounded. Permanent, outdoor weatherproof receptacles can be installed for plugging in outdoor lighting. If fixtures are intended for outdoor use, they will carry the UL label and a statement of their purpose.

PROBLEMS AND MAINTENANCE

Many electrical maintenance and repair jobs around a home do not justify calling an electrician but can be done by the homeowner if care is taken to understand what is involved. Learn the location of the fuse box or circuit breaker in your house. These are the protection devices in your electrical system. When an outlet or switch fails to work, it often indicates a blown fuse or a tripped circuit breaker. Before you install a new fuse or set the breaker, locate the cause of the failure and correct it. Some typical causes of failure are too many appliances plugged in at once, a short circuit resulting from a defective switch, a worn appliance cord, a defective plug connection, a defective appliance, and starting an air conditioner or motor on an overloaded circuit. Starting a motor can take twice as much current as running a motor and can overload a circuit. If there is a short circuit in the inaccessible wiring system, it is good practice to call an electrician.

Should the power go off completely (this rarely happens), check to see if neighboring houses have power. If not, there may be trouble in your outside service line. Call the power company and report the failure. If neighboring homes have power, then either your main breaker or fuse may have failed. Reset the breaker or replace the cartridge fuse.

Light switches wear out eventually and can be replaced if care is given to put things together in the same way as they came apart. Always secure the power to the circuit by tripping the circuit breaker. Receptacles also wear out and can be replaced. Bending the prongs of a loose-fitting plug is only a temporary solution and could cause overheating of the plug. Probably more electrical problems originate in plugs and cords than anywhere else. Cords should be checked periodically to be sure they are in good condition. To check a cord, after disconnecting it, pull the length of the cord around your finger, watching for cracks, worn spots, or a point where it bends too easily, indicating a broken wire. When replacing cords, be sure you get the size and type of cord suitable for the light or appliance.

Aluminum wiring was used in many houses built between 1964 and 1974. Some problems have been associated with it, and a number of towns have now outlawed its use. The problem is that the aluminum wiring was installed with improper outlets that resulted in loose connections. This is signaled by flickering lights and is not difficult to correct. If you buy a house with aluminum wiring, you should have an electrician check the switches, outlets, and connections and correct them, if necessary. Call your municipal electrical inspector to see what the town is recommending.

If your house is over 25 years old and the wiring has never been updated, you probably need a major rewiring. The symptoms of inadequate wiring are dimming or flickering of lights when appliances go on, appliances heating up when operating, fuses blowing or circuit breakers tripping too often, the television picture shrinking when an appliance goes on, outlets and switches seeming scarce when you need them, an outlet that looks like an octopus of cords, and common usage of extension cords around the house. Rewiring an older house can include new service entrance wires, a new breaker panel, adding new circuits, or replacing old knob and tube wiring. When installing new wiring, electrical contractors are required by code to bring your entire electrical system up to minimum safety standards. Your job is to recognize the deficiencies and call the electrician to install a safe system. Electrical wiring costs are usually quoted on a per outlet basis and include the wire, junction boxes, and installation.

A safe wiring system offers protection against electrical shock and fire. It should deliver satisfactory voltage to each outlet, and include enough circuits, outlets, receptacles, switches, and over-current devices to meet at least the minimum code standard of safety and basic standards of comfort and convenience. When purchasing electric parts, be sure they carry the label of Underwriters' Laboratories. The UL label means that the cord or device has met minimum safety requirements for the purpose intended. Of course, it could still be unsafe if improperly used, so when in doubt, call an electrician.

Safety is the prime objective when operating your electrical appliances. DO NOT handle wires or plug in appliances when your hands are wet or when you are standing on a wet floor. Electric switches or outlets should not be placed within reach of the shower or tub in the bathroom. The wiring system should conform with the requirements of the National Electrical Code, local building codes, and the utility company furnishing the power. Compliance with provisions of these codes should result in an installation reasonably free from hazard if properly maintained.

Equipment grounding must be provided for appliances and outlets in damp or moist areas, and the 1975 National Electrical Code requires grounding-type receptacles throughout the house in new construction. Receptacles on the outside of buildings require a weatherproof box and cover. They usually have spring loaded covers with rubber gaskets to keep moisture out. A recent requirement of the code for dwelling-houses is that kitchen, bathroom, and outdoor receptacles should have a "Ground-Fault Interrupter." The GFI is a device which will sense the fact that current is going to ground and shut off the power before a person is injured. The GFI's are available as portable, plug-in units, as separate devices in a metal box, and as part of a circuit breaker for mounting in a breaker box. The GFI does not protect from all kinds of shock, such as shock from grasping one wire in each hand, but since shocks usually involve current flow to ground, it will protect against most of them. Each GFI has a test button. When pressed, it simulates a current flow to ground, so you can check periodically to be sure the GFI is working.

INSPECTION

If your home is over 15 years old and has less than a 150-amp, 110/220-volt service, then you may need an upgrading of your electrical system. Homes built in the 1930's commonly had as little as 30-amp, 110-volt service, scarcely enough for lighting and a few small appliances. Even 60-amp service adds only enough power to accommodate an electric range and a hot-water heater. For the last 15 years, 100-amp service was the minimum and even with that, you had little or no margin on which to operate the new portable appliances and central air conditioning.

Look outside for three wires in a single casing coming into the house from the utility pole. This means 110/220 volts. Check the door of the service panel box and the fuses or circuit breakers for a tag noting the amperage. The amps may be stamped on the circuit breaker or cartridge fuse main disconnect. The minimum service today should be 150 amps, or over 200 amps if there is electric heat with other major electrical appliances. Homes built prior to 1970 may not have a main disconnect switch.

Feel the main circuit panel box. If it is hot, overloads are indicated. Check the type of wiring (aluminum or copper) and the size. The type and size of the wire is labeled every few feet on the surface of the covering. Is there one main panel box or are there many auxiliary boxes (indicating a need for new service and a large single circuit breaker box)?

Aluminum wire began to be used in 1964. To tell whether you have aluminum wiring, check for the AL symbol for aluminum on the cable insulation. The most common failing of aluminum wiring occurs at the terminal screws. If the house is wired with aluminum wire, have a licensed electrician or the fire or the electrical inspector check the circuits, particularly at the terminal connections. If they get loose, heat will be generated. Ask the owners if they experience any flickering lights. Note any odor of burning insulation. A warm receptacle faceplate or wall switch should alert you to a possible malfunction. Lamps that blink when you walk past them or static that crackles when you tap the outlet plate adjacent to an AM radio tuned to a weak station may indicate loose aluminum connections.

Check the number and amperage rating of the various electric circuits. Fuse boxes in older homes may be installed in unlikely places or on each floor so do a little hunting to find them all. The former owners may have replaced fuses with new ones of a higher amperage to avoid the inconvenience of constantly blown fuses. This is a very dangerous practice, since a fuse is a protection against circuit overload. Most older homes are wired with number 14 wire requiring 15-amp fuses—so be suspicious of any 20- or 30-amp fuses you find, especially if the home has never had any new circuits added. Look for new or used boxes of fuses, indicating problems or overload. If there appear to be problems, have an electrician evaluate the circuit.

Check the type and condition of wiring. Does it look old and frayed? Check the condition, especially in the attic where animals may gnaw on it. Knob and tube wire is old wire and you should plan for eventual replacement. Check the condition and fastening of the ground wire to the water pipe or ground rod. Is it all corroded and loose? Examine all grounded plug outlets with an inexpensive ground tester to be sure they are operating. Insert a male plug or test light in random outlets to test for malfunction. Note all missing or broken cover plates. Be sure major appliances are grounded. Check for broken sockets, broken insulation, frayed wires, and loose and broken fixtures. Test and operate all switches. Are they loose? Do the lights flicker? Try all three- and four-way switches. Do all exterior plugs work? Is there an adequate number of convenience outlets in each room and hall? Two is the minimum. Where there are no overhead lights, is there one receptacle outlet controlled by a light switch? Does the sump pump have a separate grounded circuit? Is there a wall switch in the bathroom away from the tub or shower? Many outlets on bathroom light fixtures are ungrounded. Check the condition of all lamp cords. Do you experience a slight tingling shock from handling or touching any appliances? This means a grounding problem. If there is an electric range oven, an electric hot water heater, a dryer, central air conditioning, and electric heat, there should be at least a 200-amp service. If only the first four are used, the house must have 150 amps.

Note any do-it-yourself wiring and look for the electrical inspection ticket, especially if home improvements were done. Insurance companies require all electrical work to be inspected. Pay particular attention to wiring in the attic for fraying or loose connections. Are there any octopus outlets or wiring? Are there ground fault interruptors on the pool circuit and outside circuits, and on bathroom and kitchen circuits? These are installed for safety.

After you move in, you may find you need a few more receptacles or an extra circuit to rid the place of octopus wiring plus tangled extension cords and blown fuses or breakers. You should make a circuit survey. To do this, turn on all the lights in the house and then go to the circuit box. Stand on a dry surface and disconnect one fuse or flip one circuit breaker to the "off" position. Then go through the house to see which lights have gone off and which outlets are dead by using an inexpensive circuit tester or small lamp. List all the dead lights and outlets on the circuit. Mark this on a chart at the circuit box. Repeat the procedure for each of the remaining circuits.

Next, decide what the load is in each circuit. to figure each circuit load, add up wattages of all the lamps and appliance that can be used on it at the same time. Wattages are marked on lamp bulbs and on the nameplates of most appliances. Where the power load is shown in amps instead of watts, multiply amps by volts to get watts. As a rule of thumb, the load is 16 amps on a 20-amp circuit and 12 amps on a 15-amp circuit.

In older homes, the original wiring was snaked through the gas lines. Check to be sure the gas lines are secured and capped. Many homeowners have not done this, creating a dangerous situation.

SUMMARY

Safety and convenience are the major factors in your home's electrical system. Have all malfunctions corrected immediately. If you have aluminum wiring, have the outlets checked periodically. If you need more outlets or switches, have this done by a licensed electrician. Don't overload any circuits. Avoid octopus outlets. Don't use long extension cords. Increase the incoming service and circuit box size if you have less than 100 amps. Secure all circuits before you work on a switch or outlet.

Examples of methods used to calculate required circuits, feeders, and main entrances may be found in the National Electrical Code, a copy of which may be purchased from the National Fire Protection Association, 60 Batterymarch Street, Boston, Mass. 02110. Other helpful guides may be obtained from the National Electrical Manufacturers Association, 155 East 44th Street, New York, N.Y. 10017, or from the Residential Group, Electric Energy Association, 90 Park Avenue, New York, N.Y. 10010. Check also for installation guides available in your general hardware store.

15.
Heating Systems

INTRODUCTION

You will find many variations of heating systems when you are inspecting resale homes. The method used to heat the house will depend on the age of the house, the popularity of the system when the house was built, and cost factors. Most replacement units use the same fuel and heat distribution system. With the cost of all fuels rising, it is important that total energy costs be considered over the life of the unit. Chapter 30 discusses energy-saving methods in the home.

Modern heating systems include forced warm air, hot water, heat pumps, and electric resistance units. The fuel used can be gas, oil, wood, or electricity. The last two units can only use electricity.

A heating system may also include air conditioning features (Chapter 16), humidifying units (Chapter 17), and special air treatment devices. This chapter examines the types of heating systems you may find, their maintenance and operating problems, and how to evaluate their condition.

TECHNICAL INFORMATION

Central Heating Units. Most homes in areas that experience fall and winter weather will have a central or a space heating system. In the southern part of the United States, there may be some form of self-contained heating for cool nights. In all but a few instances, homes will have a central heating system. Central heating systems are good investments and thermostats make their operation almost automatic.

A central heating system may include:

A fuel burner or means of burning or converting the fuel or energy, gas, oil, coal, wood, or electricity to "heat";

A furnace or boiler to transfer the heat to the air, water, or steam that is used to distribute the heat;

Ducts and pipes for heat distribution;

Room heating units, such as radiators, convectors, registers, baseboards, and diffusers; and

Controls, such as thermostats, dampers, blowers, or pumps.

When you move into a new house, consult the instruction manual that comes with the furnace. If you are moving into an older home, you may have difficulty obtaining information about the heating plant. Try to contact the last occupant or the person who last serviced the system. Oil burner service companies usually keep detailed records. Gas utility companies have service crews to help you in case of emergency. While it is unlikely that you will attempt to repair or service the system yourself, you should know what kind of boiler or furnace you have, how it operates, and what you must do to maintain it.

Fuels.   The fuels used for heating today are coal, oil, natural gas, propane, wood, and electricity. You may not have a choice if the fuel your present system uses is one of these types, since the system is usually designed for a specific fuel. However, if you are faced with replacement of the present system, you should analyze the cheapest fuel over the life of the unit. This could very well be a combination of solar heating and electric auxiliary heat.

Warm Air System.   Forced warm air furnaces using gas, oil, or electricity are the most common types of heat used in homes today. In some areas, wood burning furnaces are becoming popular as an inexpensive energy source. The furnace usually has a fan or blower that pushes the warmed air through ducts that may be run through the house to register outlets.

Forced warm air systems heat uniformly and respond rapidly to changes in temperature. The ductwork can also serve as an air conditioning system. This dual use of the ducts is the most economical installation. A satisfactory system will have the ducts on the outside walls with both high and low adjustable registers, and with a return register in each room. Central hall returns can give uneven heat. Warm air heat can be very dry and a humidifier should be considered (Chapter 17 discusses air treatment devices). If you are looking at a multiple family dwelling with forced air heat, the municipality will require one heating system to serve no more than one living unit apartment.

Gravity Warm Air.   Older homes may have a large "octopus" furnace that circulates air by heating it. Since warm air is lighter, it rises. There are usually very few outlet registers and one large return in the floor. Some of these units were modernized with blowers, and converted from coal to oil or gas. There are few of these left and if you see one, it is probably on borrowed time.

Hot Water Systems.   Hot water boilers with gravity feed are most frequently found in older houses, either with radiators or with copper or cast iron baseboard. A hot water system is generally considered the most satisfactory type of residential heat. There are very few moving parts, and the cast iron chamber will last over 30 years as long as it does not crack. One disadvantage is that a boiler becomes increasingly inefficient with age, and it may pay to replace it before it actually breaks down. Gravity boilers have an expansion tank that must be kept full of water on the top floor or attic.

Heating is fairly quick in the modern hot water boiler (often called a hydronic system). Boilers are small and the hot water is circulated through the heat distribution system by an electrically driven circulator pump. The system cost using baseboard convectors is higher than a good forced warm air system.

Three types of hot water piping systems are in widespread use today. The first system pipes hot water from one room's convectors to the next in a straight line and then returns to the boiler. The disadvantage of this system is a lack of control over the heat in an individual room's convector. The most heat is liberated at the first room in the line and the last room gets the least heat.

A second one-pipe system differs from the first in that the radiators or convectors do not circulate all the water through each convector. The convector takes the hot water from a main supply line through a regulator valve. The water leaving the convectors re-enters the supply lines. The water then circulates to the next convector and gets colder as it circulates.

The two-pipe system uses separate supply and return pipes. The supply pipe feeds each individual convector with water of the same temperature and returns it to the boiler, where it is reheated. This system is costlier as it requires larger diameter pipes. However, each individual convector can be controlled by a separate thermostat or adjustable valves, giving a better room heat. The water temperature varies from 150° to 200° F at a pressure of 12 pounds. Note the gauge on the boiler.

Steam Heat.   Steam heat is produced in a boiler that is similar to a hot water boiler except there is a gauge glass showing the water level. The heated water in the boiler boils, making steam heat that is forced by pressure through heat pipes into radiators throughout the house. Pressure is rarely over one pound. Steam heating systems are difficult to control, especially when only small amounts of heat are needed. They are found in very large and usually older homes. Generally, they are more expensive than other systems to install. The boiler can be used to heat hot water.

There are two piping systems for radiators. One is a single-pipe system in which steam rises, cools, turns into condensate, and flows back to the furnace to repeat the cycle. The one-piece gravity steam heating system is common in older homes. This, if properly installed, will provide adequate heat with no great response or control. It can be modernized by replacing standing radiators with baseboard convectors.

The two-pipe gravity steam system is more responsive. It requires the addition of traps and a return condensate line. The two-pipe system rarely was utilized except in more expensive homes. The system can be modified to a circulating hot water system, and the use of circulating pumps results in greater speed of heat distribution as well as good control.

Electric Heat.   Room electric resistance baseboard heating is one of the least expensive to install compared to other fuel systems with the advantage of individual room temperature control. Electric warm air furnaces need no vents and require no maintenance other than servicing the fan, motor, and filters. Electric heat has been more expensive to operate than other types of heat. However, with the rising cost of oil and gas, electric heat will become competitive. Before installing any electric heating units, make certain your wiring service entrance is sufficient. Existing homes generally do not have extra capacity for these units.

You should ask the present homeowner to see his electric bills for the past year or two to get an idea of what your costs will be and whether you can absorb them in your budget. Your local utility can give you typical costs for the house you will buy. Some utilities have low rates for electric heat.

Electric radiant cables in the ceiling are satisfactory for heating the entire house. But they are expensive to operate. They provide uniform temperatures and are noiseless. The heat is controlled by a wall thermostat in each room. Electric wall heaters with or without fans and with self-contained thermostats sometimes are used, but may not provide uniform temperatures except in small rooms.

Electric Heat Pumps. Electric heat pumps have been used in moderate climates (above 40° F) for some years, and are becoming increasingly cost effective even in colder areas. But you must check to see what the total electric energy bill is.

Heat pumps provide warm air heating through ducts in addition to cooling like conventional air conditioning systems. In winter, the heat pump absorbs heat from outside air and distributes it in the house. In summer, the system reverses and extracts heat from the inside of the house like a typical air conditioning unit. The heat pump's efficiency decreases when it is very cold outside, and it must usually be supplemented with expensive electric resistance heating. So check those operating costs.

Solar Heating and Hot Water Systems. The sun can be used to heat domestic hot water and provide central space heating. As more companies enter the market, the installed price will drop to be competitive with other fuel systems. Government tax incentives may accelerate this heat source but for now you must pay a premium. Average return on capital may be five to ten years.

The solar system provides two basic functions: capturing the sun's radiant energy, converting it into heat energy, and storing this heat in an insulated energy storage tank; and delivering the stored energy as needed to either the domestic hot water or heating system. The parts of the system which provide these two functions are referred to as the collection and delivery subsystems.

The key component in the collection subsystem is the collector, the basic function of which is to trap the sun's energy. The transparent cover plates made of glass or a suitable plastic material allow the rays of the sun to pass into the collector. Once inside the collector, the sun's rays are absorbed by a blackened metal absorber plate and transformed into heat energy. On sunny days, absorber plate temperatures can reach well over 200° F. Heat energy is removed from the collector by circulating a fluid through tubes in the absorber plate or by passing air over or under the absorber plate. The heat energy so removed is carried by means of insulated pipes or ducts to an insulated energy storage tank near or in the building.

The energy storage tank, which may be full of a liquid such as water, stores the heat so that it may be withdrawn upon demand. The transfer of energy to the storage tank is accomplished by means of a heat exchanger. Storage tanks and collectors are usually sized to enable the system to supply enough energy to support the building's heating and hot water requirements for a few consecutive cloudy days.

The delivery subsystem is divided into two parts: one for providing heat to the hot water tank and another for providing heat to the building heating system. When either the domestic hot water or the heating system requires heat, hot water from the energy storage tank is pumped to a heat exchanger in the domestic hot water tank or in the building ducts.

Air Treatment Devices.   A heating system may also include humidifying equipment and special air cleaning equipment. This is covered in Chapter 17.

Non-Central Heating Systems   (Self-Contained or Space Heaters). Non-central systems (self-contained) or room units may be placed within the space to be heated. These systems include heat pumps, electric resistance heating in the form of baseboard, convectors, panels, or embedded cables, or small units that combine many of the features of a central system. Supplementary heat is often used in additions, enclosed porches, and finished attics, rather than extending the main house system.

Size and Location of the Central System.   Get a reputable dealer to do a heat balance on the house and figure the correct size you need. Don't buy too small a furnace or boiler because of a lower price, as you will not get the quick heat desired at times. You may use more fuel each year and the heat exchanger may not last. On the other hand, too large a furnace is inefficient and may not provide even temperatures.

A cellar is the best place for the furnace. If a crawl space is available, then a horizontal type of furnace may be hung under the roof. There should be plenty of room to get to the furnace to service and repair it. Furnaces located in the main floor of the house may be noisier than basement installations. Be sure to insulate all exposed ducts and close all exterior space vents in the winter.

If you plan to build a house with a slab, you can form ducts into the concrete floor. Provide openings for registers along outside walls. This system gives a warm floor and satisfactory heating. Be sure you correctly grade the soil at the foundation or water will find its way into the floor ducts and produce an unhealthy environment.

Lowering Heating Costs.   Many of the things you do to effect improved climate control will not only improve comfort but will reduce heating costs. Chapter 30 covers energy savings methods in detail. These relating to heat include the following.

Properly insulate the house to get comfortable, uniform temperatures and low heating bills. In colder climates, more insulation is desirable, particularly in ceilings. In new construction, be sure to insulate around the perimeter of the concrete slab floors on grade.

Vapor barriers are essential in most areas of the country; otherwise, moisture passing through the walls and ceilings from inside to outside may condense. This will reduce insulative value, cause the insulation and structure to deteriorate, and leave bad odors.

Weatherstrip windows and doors and caulk cracks between the trim and the siding to reduce air leakage.

Seal all interior joints, even around light switches and electrical outlets, with special tape.

Cover the ground of a crawl space with a heavy plastic film vapor barrier to reduce transfer of moisture from the ground to the wood floor above. Add insulation between the crawl space ceiling joists.

In most climates, *storm doors and windows* are a must. Storm windows must fit tightly. If they leak air, the effectiveness is lost. In severe climates, triple-glazing is recommended. Storm windows can serve as one layer of glazing.

Install a *set-back thermostat* and use it regularly.

Tune up your system periodically.

Use the sun to the best advantage by opening all drapes and shades during the day.

Controls.   The central heating systems described above are operated by automatic controls which keep the house at an even temperature that regulates the heating system on and off. If the house has two or more zones, there will be that many thermostats. To conserve fuel, an automatic set-back thermostat should be used. There are also control devices that turn the fan on and off, activate the circulating pump or zone valves, cut off fuel if it does not ignite, and protect the boiler in case of low water or high temperature or pressure. These control devices need periodic inspection and maintenance by service personnel.

PROBLEMS

If the Unit Doesn't Operate . . . If the furnace or boiler doesn't operate, check the following before calling a service man.

Is the *thermostat* set correctly?

Is the *switch* bringing electricity to the unit turned on? (It is usually mounted on or near the furnace at the time of installation.)

Is a *fuse* blown or a circuit breaker open?

Is the air *filter* dirty or plugged? (This can cause the furnace safety controls to shut off the fuel.)

Is the *gas* "ON" at the meter? Do you have enough oil?

Is the *pilot* lit and burning cleanly?

Is the *manual gas valve* open at the furnace? Some installations also have a manual valve in the gas pipe just before it enters the furnace.

If the unit still doesn't operate, then call your service person.

Other Heating Problems.   After more than a decade of research, the experts have found that nearly every heating problem boils down to the following common troubles.

Little or no insulation, causing cold walls, chilly drafts, and discomfort that even the most expensive heating system cannot combat.

Dirt-clogged air filters, one of the biggest reasons for poor warm-air heating. (The house gets colder and colder as not enough heat gets to the rooms. The reason: the air filter is clogged with building dust.)

Sometimes the heating plant is too big or too small. As many as 80% of all houses get an improperly sized furnace. One reason is that many heating contractors persist in figuring the size needed by a fast rule of thumb, and scribbling a few figures on the back of an envelope. Another reason is that a skimpy furnace is used to save a few dollars. Still another is that many people believe in an oversized unit just to have reserve capacity. Your gas or oil company can aid you in sizing a new furnace.

Erratic heating can be caused by *an unbalanced heating system.* This is because many heating contractors omit the final adjustments necessary for apportioning the proper amount of heat to each room. The furnace blower, duct dampers, and room registers must be adjusted for good heat distribution.

Improper air-control settings occur when furnaces are not set according to the continuous air circulation (CAC) principle. Set your fan switch to the "ON" position, not the automatic position. The blower will now run continuously while the heat is turned on, when the thermostat calls for it. CAC keeps the air moving and prevents stagnant pockets of air from forming. It is especially needed in split-levels and bi-levels when the inlet register in lower rooms is at the ceiling, and there is only a central hall return.

Not enough warm air outlets in the right places will produce a chilly room. To help combat chilly downdrafts from cold window glass, the experts stress the great importance of proper heat discharge into a house. At least one warm air outlet should be located below a window at every outside wall.

Cold floors happen particularly in houses with a concrete slab floor and no basement. There are two preventatives: thick edge insulation around the concrete perimeter, and perimeter warm air ducts or radiators which supply heat directly to the critical house perimeter. Cold floors are also a problem in houses with a crawl space. Adequate floor insulation and a vapor barrier should help the cold floor.

A heating plant can be starved for oxygen. This occurs chiefly in new homes built so tightly that you cannot count on outside air leaking in around doors and windows. As a result, the system does not get enough oxygen to support combustion. Air must be made available to the heater. A small window opening or spring vent may be necessary.

Poor heating often occurs in split-level and bi-level houses. The biggest problem here is the lowest level room, usually a playroom or bedroom. It gets so cold that it is out-of-bounds in winter. It's a difficult problem because the floor and walls are generally below ground level, and the only heat supply is often a small duct discharging warm air into the room from ceiling level. The floor and lower wall surfaces are not properly heated. One solution is cutting down on the direct heat input to the high rooms; another possibility is the installation of a separate thermostat and zone controls to provide heat upstairs only when needed. One other solution is to provide heat at the floor level with adequate returns, using the CAC principle.

Finally, there are *cold ducts.* Supply ducts from the furnace to the house may pass through a cold space, and thereby lose so much heat that little warmth reaches rooms. This happens unless the supply ducts in such spaces are insulated.

Balancing the Forced Warm Air System.   There are five easy steps in balancing your forced warm air system.

Pick a typically cold day. Leave the thermostat at one setting for several hours. Of course, the blower should be on continuous operation (CAC) and all the dampers in ducts and registers should be wide open.

Check the temperature in each room. You can do this by "feel," but it is more effective if you use thermometers. If you use thermometers, lay them out together in one room so they can equalize. If there are differences in their readings, take this into account when measuring temperatures in the various rooms. Take the temperature in each room about two or three feet off the floor and near the center of the room. Doors to rooms should be left in their normal positions, closed or open. Let the system operate about 30 minutes before taking readings.

If you now find some rooms too warm, partially close dampers to outlets in these rooms. Do this one room at a time, It's best to start with the room that contains the thermostat if that room tends to overheat. Some hot air registers have a damper control inside the register and the cover must be removed to make an adjustment.

As air delivery is reduced at some outlets, it automatically increases at others. So after the air has been reduced to rooms that need less heat, allow the system to run for 30 minutes or more. Then check temperatures again; the formerly too-cool rooms will have become warmer.

Keep adjusting dampers until rooms reach the temperature balance you want. Fasten the damper in this position. Be sure to allow enough time for temperatures to stabilize after you make each adjustment. Also, check temperatures in each room every time, because as you cut delivery to one room, you can never be sure which other rooms will receive the resulting gain.

Hot water and steam systems can be controlled by adjusting valves or adjusting convector dampers at each unit.

MAINTENANCE

Periodic maintenance requires cleaning the burner, heating surfaces, ducts, and radiators; adjusting dampers; changing filters; and oiling the blower motor and fan. Many dealers have contracts available for periodic boiler or furnace inspection and maintenance. Ask your dealer about this.

Furnaces.   Check the condition of the smoke pipe for rust and good joint fittings. Permanent, cleanable filters (metal frame) or disposable filters (cardboard frame) should be cleaned or replaced periodically. Follow the manufacturer's instructions for removing dust and lint from the cleanable variety. Hardware and department stores sell the disposable kind. If you have a hammock filter, remove it, sliding the assembly out of the furnace. To change media, snap the holding frame open and remove old media; replace with same size 1-inch thick fiberglass. Air should enter the colored side of the media. Remember— always use papers to protect the floor when changing the filter. The blower access door must be in place while the furnace is running.

Relubricate motors periodically according to the manufacturer's instructions on each motor. A forced warm air system has an electric motor and a fan in the furnace enclosure. Some have permanently lubricated bearings, while others should be oiled at the beginning of the heating season and occasionally during the period when the furnace is in use. Motor, fan, and oil cups can be reached by removing the front or side panels of the furnace housing.

On belt drive blowers, check the belt annually for wear and proper tension. The belt should be as loose as possible without slippage. To adjust, loosen the nut on the blower motor mount, and slide the motor up or back. If the blower speed was altered for cooling, have your dealer readjust for heating.

It is important to maintain your humidifier and air conditioning condensate drain to prevent it from overflowing onto the heat exchanger, causing rust. Some heat exchangers have failed after only 10 years, when the normal life is 18 to 25 years.

Gas fired furnaces have pilot lights which most utility companies suggest be left burning constantly to prevent rust formation and condensation on heat exchanger surfaces. This practice also avoids delay in starting the system when cold weather comes. The furnace should also have a safety device to cut off the gas supply if the pilot light accidentally goes out.

Furnace cabinets are designed for minimum care. Simply wipe them off periodically with a damp cloth. A coat of wax will enhance the finish. If the unit rusts because of a wet basement, then correct the cause and paint the casing.

Boilers.   Most modern hot water heating boilers are the "closed" type, with a pump for forced circulation of heated water. The expansion tank permits heated water in the system to expand against a cushion of air in the tank without discharging water from the pressure relief valve. Occasionally, expansion tanks become "water-logged" and a small discharge of water from the relief valve occurs each time the system heats up. When this happens, the expansion tank should be drained and recharged with air. Occasionally, an accumulation of air in the top of a radiator unit will cause it to heat improperly. This can be corrected by opening the small valve near the top of the radiator to allow the air to be released and replaced by water.

The radiator and other valves of a steam or hot water heating system tend to leak as they get old. If the radiator leaks around the stem, it should be promptly attended to. Worn or insufficient packing inside the nut, or a loose packing nut at the base of the stem, may cause a leak. To remedy this, the nut should be tightened. If the leak does not stop, it will be necessary to repack the valve. Two forms of packing may be used to pack a valve stem: washers of different sizes and various sizes of packing cord. If washers are used, the valve handle should be removed by loosening the screw that holds it. After the handle is taken off, the packing can be removed from the stem. The new packing washers should be slipped over the stem. Remember, the new washers must be the right number and size to fill the packing space in the nut, or the valve will still leak. For a steam heating system, it is advisable to let the fires go out, or at least to have a very low head of steam, before starting to work on the valve. After the system is cool enough, the valve should be closed tightly and the packing nut unscrewed to permit the use of metallic packing compound. This packing compond is different from that used for the hot water system. A small screw driver can be used to put in the packing compound.

Other spots subject to leaks in both a steam or hot water system are the nipples that connect the pipe fittings to the valve. Periodic inspections will reveal possible leaks. Fixing these leaks is a job for a plumber.

Another fitting that leaks is the gauge glass on the steam system. This glass should be removed each year and cleaned. Usually, rust accumulates in the glass, making it impossible to see the water level. The packing gland nut is similar to that found on the radiator valve and should be packed in the way described above.

Many steam systems have an instantaneous hot water system

connected to the heating system. Watch the heating system for leaks. If you are in an area of hard water and you notice that the pressure out of the hot water faucet is low, the coils will have to be cleaned. This process is usually done with an acid.

On a steam system, drain the low water cut-off float each month to ensure smooth and safe operation.

INSPECTION AND EXPECTED LIFE

A quick visual inspection of the heating system will seldom show much beyond the type, age, and apparent care given the unit. The only way to check the adequacy of the system satisfactorily is by starting it up and checking the system's ability to raise the temperature in the house. If the system provides the desired degree of comfort in all rooms, check the furnace or boiler for overall condition. If you have a question or any doubts, seek professional help. All types of units require periodic preventive maintenance. Heating units have an average operating life and are costly to replace, so check or have the unit checked thoroughly.

General Comments. Call the utility company or the oil service company to check the system. Have them refer to their records on the maintenance given the system. Often, the service person has made condition notes. Find out the annual energy costs.

Check the BTU input rating. Discuss the adequacy of this with the homeowner and service company. A three-bedroom house with 2,000 square feet should have a 120,000-BTU input unit (as a rule of thumb).

With the system operating, *check for any loud or peculiar noises.* Note if all thermostats and zone valves operate.

Note any heavy oil or gas odors, indicating some leaks or improper ventilation.

Check the condition of the flue pipe as it enters the chimney. Note signs of rust or an improper seal.

Is there an exterior fresh air vent to the basement or utility room so warm interior air isn't used to support combustion?

Is the oil tank sound and free from rust, oil spills, and oil odors? Oil tanks start leaking after 20 years but can be repaired if not in the ground. Check the operation of all emergency shut-off switches. They are usually red and carefully marked.

Note signs of rust or leaks on the casing of the boiler or furnace. The cause may be leaks or a damp basement-utility room.

Forced Warm Air. When you are checking a forced air system, turn up the thermostat, listen to the furnace run to see if there are any unhealthy sounds, and check the forced air distribution at the registers all through the house. Oil and gas furnaces have an average operating life of 18 to 25 years. Look particularly for rust caused by leaking humidifiers or blocked air conditioning condensate lines. This can cause cracks in heat exchanges after eight or ten years.

Check the air flow from each register. Note the location of return registers and use a piece of paper to measure suction. Note black soot or dirt streaks around inlet registers, which could mean a cracked heat exchanger. Note the flame prior to and after the fan goes on. There should be no disturbance of the flame. If there is, it may mean a cracked heat exchanger. The service person can pin-point or verify cracks by a visual examination, by the use of odor-producing sprays, and by inspection mirrors.

Hot Water (Hydronic). You should look for a circulating pump attached to the boiler; without it (a gravity system), any radiators placed lower than the top of the boiler will not be effective. Any leaks or problems are usually quickly revealed when you turn up the thermostat and run the boiler for 15 to 30 minutes. The age of the house will usually indicate the age of the boiler. A steel or cast iron boiler normally lasts 18 to 25 years, but there are some cast iron units converted from coal that are still running after 50 years (they tend, however, to be inefficient).

Check the operation of all radiators, convectors, and baseboard units. Note any leaks at the boiler and at the heat distribution pipes. Note the condition of the fire box brickwork or coating.

Check all radiant heat surfaces for leakage or rust stains. Be sure the pressure remains steady, indicating no leaks. The gauge is on the top or the front of the boiler; it records both pressure or temperature.

Steam. Steam boilers indicate trouble by leaks (both exterior and interior), rusted casing, crumbling brickwork, panting for air, missing pipe and casing insulation, missing radiators, a broken pressure gauge, dirty water in the gauge glass, no low water alarm or automatic water feed, and noises. Boilers start to experience trouble after 18 years for steel boilers and after 25 years for cast iron boilers. There are coal-converted cast iron boilers going strong at 50 years, but these are the exceptions. Steam boilers should be serviced annually.

Electric.   Electric and hydronic baseboard units are usually trouble-free. Hydronic units need occasional bleeding and cleaning of dust off the surface. Check joints for leaks. Some heating systems have electric resistance burners that are trouble-free and will last as long as gas-fired units.

Heat Pump.   The compressor unit starts to experience trouble after ten years. Check these units as you would an air conditioning system. They are complicated and a service person with special tools is needed.

SUMMARY

Heating systems are controlled to operate automatically, but the unit must be on a schedule of regular maintenance to give trouble-free operation during the life of the components. Gas and oil units require yearly adjustments of the firing mechanism to give the highest efficiency. Filters must be changed, condensate lines kept free of dirt, and all moving parts lubricated. The thermostat should be kept clean. No obstructions should be in front of baseboards, radiators, or registers. Consult Chapter 30 for ways to reduce energy use. Get a setback thermostat, preferably the timer type, to lower the temperature at night and when you will be out of the house during the day. The key to a long system-life is periodic preventive maintenance done by service people. Periodic lubrication and cleaning can be done by the homeowner.

As a buyer or homeowner, you can visually check the age and condition of a heating system. The checkpoints discussed earlier should provide clues for when to call in specialized help. Don't let a problem go by for long before correcting it. Longer equipment life and lower operating cost will result if good preventive maintenance is the practice.

16.
Central Air Conditioning and Room Units

INTRODUCTION

Each year, more and more homeowners equip their homes with a summer air conditioning system. In some sections of the United States, a home must be air conditioned to be saleable. The benefits of summer cooling are clean, cool, and dehumidified air. With the installation of a cooling system, the windows can be kept closed, excluding dirt, dust, and other disagreeable elements. Babies, older people, those with heart ailments, and those affected by dust and pollen are helped with conditioned air. Less noise from the outside may be an additional benefit.

This chapter discusses your air conditioner and how to maintain it. With proper understanding and attention, your air conditioning unit will provide efficient cooling for many years.

TECHNICAL INFORMATION

How Air Conditioning Works. The basic physical principle involved in modern air conditioning is that a gas expanding under pressure absorbs heat while a gas condensing to a liquid releases heat. The major elements of an air conditioning unit are an evaporator coil and fan, a condenser coil and fan, a circulating refrigerant, and a compressor.

The refrigerant liquid, usually freon, passes through an expansion device into the evaporator coil and expands to a gas. In the process, it absorbs heat from the air forced over and through the evaporator coil. The cooled air is blown from the coil into an air collection chamber or plenum, from which it is distributed through ducts into the space to be air conditioned.

The gaseous refrigerant freon circulates from the evaporator coil to the compressor, where it is compressed back into a high pressure gas. It then passes into the condenser coil, where it usually transfers heat to the outdoor air and becomes a liquid. A fan forces air across the condenser coil, where it picks up the heat. Some condensers use water to cool the freon gas rather than air.

The process begins again when the liquid refrigerant circulates back to the expansion device. It can be seen that an air conditioning unit works by removing heat from the air inside the home, and releasing heat into the air outdoors. Heat pumps which both cool and heat homes work much the same way, but are reversible in winter.

Central Air Conditioning.   Central air conditioning involves the control of climate in the entire home or apartment and is a "system." It includes an air conditioning unit, sometimes more than one, plus a means of distributing conditioned air throughout the living space, usually by metal or fabric ducts. Central systems become an integral part of the home once they are installed. With proper maintenance, a central air conditioning system will last for many years.

There are two principal types of central systems. The most popular one is the split system. This places the evaporator coil and a fan inside the home, usually as part of a forced warm air heating system, while the condensing unit is located outside. This saves interior space and minimizes sound inside the house.

In the single package home system, all the elements of the air conditioning unit are combined into a single package and an air exhaust connection with the outdoors is provided. This system can use ducts to distribute the conditioned air.

Individual room air conditioners affect only one or two rooms of a dwelling-house. They are appliances and require little or no installation work. Some room units are portable so that they can be moved from one room to another. Room air conditioners mounted in windows are generally less expensive than central systems, but provide less uniform temperatures. They are noisier than well-designed central systems and shut out some light from the windows where they are installed. Keep in mind, though, that the house can be air conditioned initially with room air conditioners and additional units added as funds permit. The amount of cooling in various rooms with window units can be varied. As the cost of energy rises, it may be too expensive to cool an entire house and buyers will be forced to cool only selected rooms.

The units discussed thus far are of the electric compressor-cycle type which represents most of the units installed in the United States. There are other types, as well: the gas absorption cycle system, the chilled water system, and the evaporative cooling system. Since these represent specialized equipment, they are not covered here. The heat pump is an electric compressor cycle that is reversible in summer.

PROBLEMS AND SOLUTIONS

A summer cooling system should be operated in much the same fashion as a winter heating system. The house should be closed most of the time to retain the conditioned air. The unit should be controlled continually by a thermostat. If the house is left open until the indoor temperature becomes uncomfortable, it will take a considerable length of time before the cooling system can catch up and bring about a noticeable change in humidity and temperature. Opening the windows after sunset allows considerable amounts of humid air to enter the house, undoing all the work of the cooling system.

Possible problems you might encounter involve the following.

Improper cooling capacity. Since an air conditioner is responsive to temperature only, a unit that's too large would quickly cool your room and then shut off, leaving the humidity level high. You'd probably feel uncomfortable due to the excessive humidity. On the other hand, a unit that is too small simply would not be capable of cooling your room. Either way, the wrong cooling capacity means your air conditioner would be inefficient and expensive to operate.

Odor. Unusually tight houses can have odor problems in the summer. Odors from cooking, smoking, and living can accumulate more readily in the summer since natural ventilation is not good. Smoking is probably the most difficult odor to control. It is practically impossible to maintain a fresh indoor atmosphere in houses where smoking takes place. An electronic air cleaner will remove some of the smoke that passes through it, but it will not remove the odor. Occasionally, the house should be ventilated in the odor-producing areas like the kitchen, bathrooms, and utility room.

Ducts. In central systems, the best cooling occurs when each room has an inlet and a return register and when top floor rooms have ceiling inlets. If your second floor rooms get warm, consider ceiling height inlets and run the fan continuously.

Heat gain.   Use drapes, awnings, screens, and trees to help keep out the sun's rays.

INSTALLATION INSTRUCTIONS

To be assured of a quiet, comfortable, and dependable air conditioning system, you should be aware of some of the general installation recommendations suggested by manufacturers. Central air cooling units can be installed in some hot air systems, thus utilizing the same ducts for distributing cool air through the house. The ducts must be insulated. Hot air systems with small diameter delivery ducts are not fully satisfactory for air conditioning. The higher air velocities required for cooling need more power and create undesirable noise. Be sure all ducts are insulated, especially in attics. New forced-air cooling systems may be installed in the basement, hung from the ceiling in central halls if the ceiling heights permit, or placed in the attic. These installations require new ductwork, and be sure to put in adequate returns to promote good circulation.

Existing hot water systems with upright forced-air convectors in the rooms may be adapted for cooling by adding a chiller to cool the water pumped through the system. This is not too effective as a retrofit installation and is not recommended.

Correct location of the outdoor unit compressor condenser unit is important. The unit makes noise and although some types are quieter than others, it is essential that the unit be located so it will not disturb neighbors. Units should also be installed in the coolest location that is practical, preferably on the north side of the building or in the shade. The cooler the air entering the compressor, the more efficient it is. Landscaping can be used as a sound barrier and to shade the condenser. Be sure the foundation is level or it will reduce the compressor life.

Installation costs vary considerably, depending upon the temperature, exposure to the sun, the size and construction of the house, and labor rates. When purchasing a new air conditioning unit, don't buy a unit larger than needed to cool an area. Buying an oversize unit with the idea that it will be more efficient is a common misconception; not only will it cost more initially, it won't control the humidity properly because the compressor will be cycling on and off. Unlike heating systems, cooling systems work best slightly undersize. This is because a major benefit of cooling is dehumidification. In order to dehumidify the air passing over it, the evaporator must be kept cold, which means the compressor should run almost continuously for maximum comfort in hot weather.

To make sure you select the right window unit or central system, the cooling load should be calculated. For a window unit, get a Cooling Load Estimate Form from your dealer. For a central system, the dealer must come to measure the square footage and openings of your home. From this, he will size the proper unit.

The dealer should also check the location and size of the ductwork and recommend additional ducts and a large evaporator fan, if necessary. Be certain an electrician determines that the incoming electric service is sufficient to run the extra load.

MAINTENANCE

Room Units.   You can get the most effective use from your window air conditioner by proper purchasing and yearly maintenance. Operation and maintenance information can be obtained from the manufacturer. Different units need different service. In any event, the units should be inspected once or twice a year.

To maintain your air conditioners, the dust should be cleaned off all surfaces. If there are oil openings, a few drops of motor oil (non-detergent) is usually in order if the motor has been in service for some time and specific information is not available. Too much oil can be harmful, as it is messy and collects dust. Accumulations of dust interfere with normal motor operation and can cause overheating.

The fan belts should be inspected for wear and tension, although the mounting is usually such that the motor weight provides constant tension. Fan bearings should be checked for wear. Some require oiling and if they have become worn, it is usually difficult to maintain oil in them.

Servicing the air filter is probably the most important and most frequent maintenance requirement. Dust restricts air flow, thus reducing efficiency. Most systems have disposable filters, although washable filters are available.

Many people look on a window air conditioner as one of man's foolproof inventions. Simply stick it in the window, plug it in, and sit back to enjoy the cool air. You can do that, of course, but in the process you'll lose a lot of the side benefits of air conditioning, and you will add to your electricity bill every month during the cooling season. If you already have a room air conditioner, then you know that weatherized window units need to be taken out of the window during the wintertime. If your window units have been stored all winter, then the unit must be placed upright on a perfectly level surface for a period of at least 24 hours to allow the oil in the sealed system to drain back into the compressor. If manufacturer's instructions call for other oiling, this is the time to do it.

It's always wise to test-run the unit on the floor. Make sure that the fan runs, that the compressor starts, and that cooling occurs. If the unit runs but does not cool, it usually means that it has lost its refrigerant. Call your dealer. Every three or four years you should have the unit checked by a professional.

Central Air Conditioning.   Central air conditioning does not require a burdensome amount of maintenance, but some simple things must be done periodically. It is possible to let the air conditioning dealer handle all of them. However, for those of you who like to do things yourself, here are a few practical maintenance tips (for systems with common ductwork for heating and cooling).

When summer begins, *reset dampers for air conditioning.* (Damper adjustment is required only if there are separate ducts for the cool air.)

See that air inlets and outlets, both indoors and out, are free from obstruction and clean of accumulated dust.

Clean and replace filters. Wash the electronic air cleaner.

Lubricate where called for. This is generally limited to fan motors and bearings.

Turn on the power for at least one day—24 hours—before you start the compressor. Run the fan only, with the cooling thermostat set high. In the compressors of many makes of air conditioners, power is required to pre-warm and improve the lubricating qualities of the compressor oil. Even when this is not a necessity, a 24-hour warm-up can do no possible harm. Remember to keep the fan on continuous air circulation operation all season for even temperature control throughout the house. This means keep the fan switch in the *ON* position, not *AUTO.*

If there is an auxiliary drain pan under the unit, as is the case in many attic installations, be sure this pan is cleaned and that the condensate drain is open. Flush with a pitcher of water to check run-off because insects sometimes block drains. If your unit has a condensate pump, be sure it is clean and working.

When there is piping going outside, check the condition of the insulation, concrete foundations and exposed metal surfaces for rust. Make sure that concrete foundations have not been broken or tilted by frost action.

You should also look at air intake and discharge vents. Make sure that both are open and free of leaves and other garden debris. Is there a lock on the outside electric box to prevent the prying hands of children?

Pick a day when outside temperatures are in the mid-60's for a test run. After a 24-hour warm-up, run the equipment for five or ten minutes by dropping the thermostat to below room temperature. Listen well for any unusual noises, either indoors or out. If any unusual noises persist, call in your dealer.

Be sure to have the unit serviced every year. The compressor has a five-year warranty. If not serviced, many will fail shortly after that. It's worth the service call to have the system periodically checked.

To reduce operating costs, the following things are advisable.

Prevent the escape of cold air by making sure register fireplace flues and heating ducts are closed.

Get a special timer or a thermostat with this device. The air conditioner can be turned off in the morning and the timer set to turn it back on late in the afternoon. This is a good investment for the working family. The living area will be cool when the first person returns home. The unit will not be operating all day when no one is there to enjoy it, running up the utility bill in the process.

Find a comfortable thermostat setting, say 78° F, and then don't change it unnecessarily. Remember a change of one or two degrees in your thermostat can affect your operating costs considerably.

Keep heat out of the area to be cooled by weather-sealing the window installation. Use blinds, shades, or awnings on windows in direct sunlight. Keep doors closed. Cut down on heat-producing activities during the hot hours of the day as much as possible, scheduling cooking for the early morning and late afternoon hours. The same is true for humidity-producing activities such as bathing and mopping.

Be certain all ducts are insulated, especially in hot spaces like attics.

INSPECTION

If you are buying a resale home, have the unit checked out by a home inspector or air conditioning service man. Determine the age of the unit and what service the owner gave it. My experience is that 90% of the owners do no servicing unless the unit stops cooling. This means that electric compressors will fail after five to eight years. The service man can estimate future life of the unit. The other parts of the system will last the life of the furnace.

If you plan to install a new air conditioning system using a present forced warm air system, then replace the furnace if it is over 15 years old.

Heat pumps are checked in a manner similar to that of air conditioners. The heat pump compressor has a five- to eight-year life if not maintained.

SUMMARY

Air conditioning can be considered an investment rather than an expenditure if care is taken in its purchase, installation, and maintenance. Have the unit serviced every few years. A well-working system can add to the comfort of your home and health of your family. Have a cool summer!

17.
Air and Water
Treatment Systems

INTRODUCTION

Breathe air we must—some 35 pounds of it a day. While you can't do much singlehandedly to clean up the gunk that fouls the atmosphere outdoors, you can have purer air indoors. The air in your home can be treated by your heating and air conditioning units plus special devices like humidifiers, dehumidifiers, and ventilation fans. Also by treatment, can you have purer, more delicious water. In many areas of the United States, drinking water has to be conditioned, as it is hard, highly acid, and foul-smelling.

This chapter discusses these special devices. Each section will discuss the operation, maintenance, and inspection.

DEHUMIDIFIERS

You can easily determine if your home can use a dehumidifier, if the house, crawl space, or basement shows any of these symptoms: black, moldy-looking blotches of mildew on insulation batts and wood structural members; wetness on insulation batts; mildew on stored luggage, books, clothing, or furniture; rust on workshop tools and metal accessories; a moldy odor; sticking drawers and doors; and condensation on cold water pipes.

Basements, crawl spaces, and attics are usually the only places where humidity goes high enough for a long enough period to cause damage. You must control the cause of the high humidity before the humidifier will work properly. How can you tell whether condensation or seepage is to blame for your basement's dampness? There are several possible clues. Seepage will tend to be confined to one part of the space. It may show up as a trickle of water through the wall or a damp section of wall. Condensation will be greatest during periods of high outdoor humidity, and seepage will be greatest after heavy rains. Seepage is controllable, and Chapter 13 discusses methods of control.

A typical dehumidifier uses freon as a refrigerant and operates like an air conditioner, a freezer, or a refrigerator. The refrigerant boils in an evaporator coil, picking up heat from the air passing over the coil and thus cooling that air. The freon is then pumped by the compressor into a condenser coil where it becomes liquid again, giving up heat to the air passing over that coil. The freon liquid moves on to the evaporator to complete the circuit. When the basement air is cooled at the evaporator, it loses some of its moisture-holding capacity and the excess moisture condenses onto the evaporator coil and drips into the unit's condensate pan. The air that flows out of the unit is dryer, with less relative humidity.

Condensate is disposed of by emptying a pan or by draining, using a hose, to a sink or sump pit. An automatic overflow control will shut off the dehumidifier when the condensate pan is full. Most units have an adjustable humidistat. This control turns the appliance off and on automatically and controls the humidity level. Units without humidistats operate continuously and waste electricity. Dehumidifiers are rated by the number of pints of water they draw from the air in 24 hours. Each manufacturer makes several models with capacities to fit various spaces.

A few precautions will give you the most efficient operation of your dehumidifier. To avoid overloading, keep outdoor air from entering the basement by keeping doors and windows closed. Do not operate the dehumidifier below 65° F, or when the relative humidity is below 50%. If the unit is run when either temperature or humidity is too low, ice will form on the evaporator coil, cutting the unit's efficiency and causing possible damage.

At the beginning of the high humidity season, set the dehumidifier for continuous operation for two or three weeks to dry out the space. After this period, adjust the humidistat dial until the unit shuts off. A desirable operating level is indicated on most dials by the word "normal." Do not run the humidifier when the space is heated as it is wasteful. A single dehumidifier should suffice if its capacity is large enough.

When cleaning, always disconnect the power cord before doing any work on the unit. Clean dust off the evaporator and condenser coils periodically. Clean fan motor and blade. Lubricate the fan motor. When you store your dehumidifier for the off season, make sure all parts are dry to prevent rust.

HUMIDIFIERS

During the heating season, if your home's humidity is low, and if your throat and lips are dry, then you're a candidate for a humidifier. This device introduces moisture into the house to raise the relative humidity. Central units to cover an entire house and self-contained smaller units for one room are available. You will find that you are able to comfortably reduce the room temperature by 2° to 5° when the humidity is kept at 35%. Operating costs for electricity and water are low and should be offset by living at a lower room temperature.

The three main kinds of humidifiers are the atomizing kind that uses a spray nozzle to inject water into the air, the vaporization type that ejects steam vapor into the air, and the surface evaporator type that uses plates or a rotating sponge surface from which the water is evaporated. Of the three, the atomizing type that sprays water is the most efficient and the least expensive to operate. Check with your physician on the safest unit, as mold can build to unsafe levels with some units. The unit should be automatically operated to keep a uniform relative humidity. As the outside temperature changes, adjust the relative humidity required as shown in the humidifier instructions. An automatic humidistat will vary with outside temperature changes.

You should consider a humidifier that will cover the entire house regardless of the type of heating system you have. The size depends on the cubic footage of your house, the lowest temperature experienced outdoors, and the tightness of your home construction. The unit can be located in the outlet of the hot air furnace. It can also be located in a closet, hallway, or living room. Water vapor will automatically spread itself throughout the house.

Some homeowners may have humidifiers and still suffer from dry air. This is usually because the unit is too small for the house, or because it clogs up quickly with the impurities found in most city and well water. Proper humidity control requires large quantities of water—literally hundreds of gallons of water—added to the indoor air to provide comfort. Water in many parts of the United States is extremely hard, carrying large amounts of minerals, which means the humidifier must be periodically cleaned if it is to operate properly.

In the absorption type, water is metered by a float to a series of absorbent plates. Air from the furnace is blown over these plates, picking up moisture. This type clogs up easily with salts and minerals. You should inspect the plates or pads monthly and either clean or replace them. Check the float and the water inlet to be sure they are clean and working. Check the overflow outlet to be sure it is clean—in case of an overflow. Otherwise, you will have water dripping into the top of the furnace, causing rust and possible failure by rusting as well as cracking of the heat exchanger. This is a common problem.

The spray unit requires very little maintenance. Just keep the spray orifice free of salt. This can be done with a soft scraper or thin wire. Then check the humidity control to see if the water valve opens when the furnace temperature rises—usually above 100°F.

If your humidifier is different from the ones I've described, then here are some general maintenance suggestions. Before you work on an electrical unit, disconnect water and electric lines that go to the humidifier. Empty and clean the water reservoir. Check the water intake valve that supplies the reservoir (very often this is a needle valve operated by a hollow plastic float). Use a thin wire to clean out the hole in the valve that usually clogs up. Some humidifiers have a revolving wheel that picks up the water from the reservoir. The wheel may be covered with a mesh or thin layer of plastic foam. Lime deposits on the mesh or foam prevent the humidifier from working efficiently. If you cannot remove the lime or mineral deposits, then it is best to replace the mesh or plastic foam. Replacements are available from your dealer. Remove all accumulations of lime or minerals from the interior of the humidifier. The electric motor should be lubricated at least once a year with two or three drops of light machine oil. Check your manufacturer's instructions for details. Caulk all cracks and separations in the humidifier housing where it joins the furnace duct work. With all parts cleaned, simply put everything back together in the reverse order. In some hard water areas, be sure to make minor maintenance checks as frequently as once a month. When your inspection reveals a lot of mineral deposits, then give it a complete cleaning and check.

AIR FILTERS

You can't clean up the dirt and pollution that fouls the outdoor air, but you can have purer air indoors by using an electronic air cleaner.

These units can remove up to 90% or more of the floating microscopic particles that stain your walls and furnishings and bring on allergic sneezes.

An electronic cleaner can be installed in any house served by a ducted heating system. The unit is installed in the return air duct or at a point just before the duct enters the furnace or air conditioner. Return air is drawn through the cleaner before it is heated or cooled and recirculated. The cleaner operates on regular 120-volt current. No special wiring is required and the cost is about the same as burning a 75-watt bulb.

No air cleaner or filter can rid your home of all dust and allergens. The best a cleaner can do is to reduce the particle count to a minimum. My experience indicates that homeowners who use these units find the benefits more than outweigh the installation and operating costs.

VENTILATION

The areas where ventilation is often required are the attic, basement, and crawl space. The need for ventilation is apparent when the air is damp. Moisture condenses as the air cools down or where the moist air contacts a cold surface. The inlet and outlet vents should be located properly for good circulation of air through the enclosed space. These vents not only keep the space dry in winter, but keep hot air moving from the space during the summer and help to cool the house.

The rule of thumb for adequate attic ventilation is one square foot of ventilator for each 150 feet of floor space. This can be accomplished by installing louvers in gables and soffit vents. It is a good idea to install an attic ventilating fan with its own thermostat to remove hot air in the summer months. The attic temperature will drop from 150° F to near outside temperature. This can be a big saving in air conditioning load.

Kitchens and bathrooms can produce moisture, heat, and objectionable odors. In a tight, all electric house this can produce very high humidity and mold conditions. Space ventilation can relieve this condition. A room requires at least three air changes to freshen the air.

Observe the size and location of crawl space vents. There should be at least four vents located near building corners for optimum cross ventilation. For further information on ventilation, consult Chapters 25 and 26.

WATER CONDITIONING

Water conditioning today is a big industry because water can cause problems to the homeowner and manufacturing plant. Water is usually less than ideal and often it leaves scale in pipes or it is hard. As such, it doesn't clean as effectively as it could. It may stain fixtures with rust. It can contain sulfur and be foul-smelling. It may be cloudy or brown and have a bad taste. Some water is highly corrosive and may be unsafe to drink. It may even cause mottled teeth. Have your water checked if the area is known for poor quality water.

Water conditioning simply means processing water to improve its quality for an intended use. The process removes or neutralizes the problem-causing materials in water such as minerals, gases, organic substances, acids, and disease-producing organisms.

Hardness is caused by dissolved calcium and magnesium in the water. These two minerals are easily removed from water by water conditioning equipment. It is simple to detect hard water since soap will not lather in it. Instead, it forms a curd that leaves a sticky deposit on surfaces, hair, or clothing. To treat, the water conditioning company hooks up a portable appliance to your water line, and periodically replaces the unit with a freshly-recharged one. No electrical connection or drain is necessary. Special portable water conditioning units also remove or counteract other water impurities, such as cloudiness. Some multi-purpose service water softeners remove chlorine and other taste- and odor-producing substances, as well as sediment and hardness.

If your water is hard, it may be economical to buy or rent a permanently-installed water conditioning appliance. Today's units are completely automatic and provide an unlimited supply of softened water. Automatic water softeners can be recharged on a pre-set schedule that is governed by a timer.

Iron is another water problem in the United States. It ruins the flavor of coffee and tea and stains plumbing fixtures and laundry. Sulfur will cause water to smell like rotten eggs. Acid water rusts or corrodes metal plumbing systems. When copper pipes corrode, you'll find blue-green stains in your sink or bathtub. When iron pipes rust, the stains are brownish. Acid water shortens the life of water-using appliances, plumbing systems, and plumbing fixtures. A simple feeding system, attached to your water supply, removes iron and sulfur and counteracts acidity. It can also provide safe drinking water. The feeder system injects measured quantities of water treatment substances into your water supply.

Simple water filters are available to make cloudy or silt-laden water clear. They have a renewable cellulose element. Similar filters with activated carbon elements are available to remove chlorine and other taste- and odor-producing substances from water. These filters are installed under the sink and are attached to the cold water line.

In buying a water conditioner, you should be aware that no single type of water conditioning equipment will cure all water problems. A consultation with a water conditioning specialist is usually best. Your water should be sampled and analyzed to determine the proper type and size of water conditioning equipment needed. Some tests can be made at the house. Others may be sent to an analytical laboratory for analysis. In buying equipment, it is better to have a unit that is oversized, rather than one that is undersized. Correcting water problems should be the primary consideration for selection of the equipment. A higher priced unit may cost less to operate and give greater satisfaction.

SUMMARY

The air and water treatment devices discussed require periodic treatment, maintenance, and inspection for safe operation. Get on a regular preventive maintenance schedule as discussed in Chapter 32. Equipment to perform at peak operation must be kept in top condition. Air treatment devices can cause mold growth if not properly cleaned and this, in turn, can cause upper respiratory problems in man. Water treatment adds salt to the water, so check with your doctor on the use of this equipment.

As a rule, you won't need a dehumidifier if you have air conditioning. But you may want to consider one if you notice symptoms of excess moisture such as musty, moldy odors, mildew, peeling interior paint, sweating of cold pipes and basement walls, rusty metal objects, or warping or swelling of wood. A humidifier performs exactly the opposite function of a dehumidifier. Signs that you may need one are uncomfortable, dry body conditions, static electricity, cracks in house and furniture, and drooping plants. Shop around before you buy.

18.
Plumbing

INTRODUCTION

The plumbing system remains a mystery to most homeowners because large sections of the system are concealed in the walls and floors and the remaining portions are simply taken for granted. As a result, little concern is given to the maintenance and operation of the system.

This chapter will attempt to give a general understanding of what the system is composed of, how it operates, and problem areas.

TECHNICAL INFORMATION

Plumbing Systems. The home water supply comes from either the municipality, private water systems, or individual well sources. Many different types of wells and pumping systems are used. Many well or private sources require water treatment systems that can handle anything from heavy mineral deposits to bacteria in the water. Water is moved through the home by pressure provided by either the well pumping system or gravity from high reservoirs or tall water towers kept filled by pumps. This pressure averages to about 40 pounds per square inch.

There are two plumbing systems in your house. They can suffer from leaking, pipes clogged with rust and salt deposits, and age.

Water Supply System. The water supply system provides water for kitchen, bathroom, laundry, and other household uses, with the supply kept under constant pressure to ensure full-force flow from faucets and valves. Each fixture should have a separate shut-off valve on the line to the fixture so repairs can be made. Every home should have a main shut-off valve, usually located near the water meter, where the supply enters the house. Everyone in the house should know where these valves are located and how to use them. If a plumbing emergency occurs, a quickly turned shut-off valve may prevent flooding and the resulting damage. These valves should be opened and closed periodically.

The Drainage System. The next part of the plumbing system drains waste water from all home fixtures and vents gas to the atmosphere. The wastes are collected through house drains and pipes into a large main sewer pipe and are then carried off by gravity into the public sewer system or to a private disposal system on the property. There is a water trap in the drain for each fixture. This U-shaped bend in the drain pipe is constantly filled with water, thereby blocking sewer gases from escaping into the house.

The main vertical pipes that receive discharges from sinks and other fixtures are known as waste lines. All of these pipes run to the roof of the home and are called vent stacks. This pipe is left open at the top and in some homes there is an outside fresh air vent near the basement. The purpose of the vent is to admit air so that a vacuum is not created and to allow sewer gases to leave the system. Drainage pipes are sometimes termed DWV pipes (drain, waste, and vent). Since the drainage pipes are the largest and most difficult to install, the entire plumbing system is normally designed around them.

Water Supply Pipes. Many materials are used for plumbing piping. Local codes determine which piping materials may be used. The quality of water in an area along with wholesale supplies generally dictate the availability of particular materials in a community. Pipes generally available for potable water supply and distribution lines include galvanized iron or steel, copper, brass, and plastics. Each has several types and grades.

Galvanized steel. Galvanized steel has been extensively used for home and out-of-doors distribution lines and in individual water wells. It resists mechanical damage, thus making it the best pipe for installing under roadways or to faucets subject to abuse. Galvanized steel pipe should last 20 to 30 years buried in most soils and much longer if no inside corrosion occurs. It will easily withstand the pressures found in most homeowner water systems.

Copper. The initial cost of copper pipe is high, but several advantages make it a much used potable water pipe. Few tools are needed in making repairs or additions to copper plumbing. Soft temper tubing bends easily, eliminating the need for many fittings. Its ease in being pulled through wall openings makes it an excellent material for use by the do-it-yourself homeowner. Hard temper copper pipe is difficult to bend and requires fittings. This pipe should be used in exposed locations because it makes a much neater installation. Solder type copper fittings provide an easy and secure means of making plumbing connections. Don't connect copper piping directly to steel, as electrolysis may cause corrosion and eventually leakage at the joint. Nonconducting adapters should be used for these connections.

Plastics. Plastics are the newcomers in plumbing. They are easy to install and newer materials are being developed. Because of its smooth interior and resistance to corrosion, plastic pipe has less friction than other commonly used materials. Recent developments in some plastics have made them usable in hot as well as cold lines and drainage and stack vent lines. All plastic pipe should be clearly marked with the pressure rating, manufacturer's name or trademark, and NSF (National Sanitation Foundation) insignia. Most municipal codes now allow plastic pipe. Check with your supplier for the correct application techniques and local code requirements.

Polyethelene pipe is used extensively for lawn sprinkler systems, in water wells, and in supply lines to homes and outbuildings. It is not recommended for use where high temperatures occur. Extended exposure to direct sunlight will cause deterioration. It withstands some freezing but should be buried below the frost line or drained before freezing occurs when used for lawn sprinkling.

Drainage and Vent System Pipes. Drain, waste, and vent (DWV) pipe must carry solids and chemically active materials, and provide for the free flow of water. Because DWV pipe is not under pressure, it must be larger than water lines. There is a large choice of materials for DWV piping not installed in the ground. You may use cast iron, galvanized iron or steel, wrought iron or steel, copper, lead, and plastic pipe.

Drain pipe underground must be cast iron, hard temper copper, or plastic DWV piping, depending on the code requirements. Lines going to sewers or other waste disposal areas and not in the same trench with water lines may be cast iron, concrete vitrified clay tile, bituminized fiber, plastic asbestos, cement, or copper. In case of burial in the same trench with later lines, only cast iron, hard temper copper, or plastic (PVC or ABS) are acceptable.

No matter what types of pipe are selected, make sure the size is adequate. Remember that local plumbing codes specify the minimum size as well as the type that may be installed for particular uses. This is important in northern climates where vent pipes can freeze closed if the size is too small in diameter.

There are several do-it-yourself books and magazines on the market that provide information on selecting and installing plumbing. Life expectancy of pipes before the joints start to leak vary. The average galvanized steel pipe should last 20 to 30 years; yellow brass—20 to 25 years; red brass—50 to 60 years; copper—50 to 60 years; and wrought iron—25 to 40 years. The life of plastic pipe has not been determined, but it should outlast copper if properly supported. Clay and cement pipes have an indefinite life span.

PROBLEMS

Most people have been faced with old piping, poor water pressure, leaky faucets and joints, clogged drains, running toilet bowls, and leaking connections at fixtures. Due to the high cost of hiring a plumber, the homeowner should learn how to take care of as many problems as he can.

The Water Supply System.
Leaks. The water supply system of 15 to 20 years old should present only minor problems, such as a dripping faucet or a leaking supply valve to a toilet. Either condition may be easily corrected. Typical problems of older water supply systems are leaks due to faulty joints and low pressure. Many "plumbing" leaks are caulking or grouting leaks in and around the tub and shower areas. So keep your bathrooms tightly caulked to maintain their water-tightness. Check with your local plumbing inspector for specific leak problems.

Sediment. Periodically drain the water heater for sediment which collects at the bottom. Sediment can be removed by opening the drain valve near the bottom of the heater and drawing out a bucket of water. The water temperature control is located on the heater and may be adjusted for a range of 110° to 130° F. Temperature should not be set above 140° F to save energy and increase the life of the heater.

Freezing. If weather temperatures approach freezing in your locality, turn off exterior non-frostproof water connections, such as hose bibs, to prevent freezing and cracking of pipes. Allow the outside hose bib to remain open and draining after the inside valve is closed. Protect from freezing all pipes in ceilings above unheated garages, water supply fixtures on outside walls, and exposed sewer pipes.

Hard or corrosive water. If hard water is present, a water softener will help minimize mineral deposit build-up inside the water pipe and sewer pipe. Check with local authorities, as some sections of the country have highly corrosive water.

Sweating, corrosion, and clogging. Cold water pipes should be insulated to prevent sweating, which will cause premature corrosion. This is especially true for well water. Cast iron pipes can be painted with an anti-rust paint to retard rusting. The main drawbacks to galvanized and brass piping are inside mineral deposits from hard water and corrosion due to acid, alkaline, or hard water, which reduce the flow. Acid water will cause iron staining on bathroom fixtures. Copper is very resistant to corrosion except when carrying water containing free CO_2 (carbon dioxide). Acid water or water containing free CO_2 will remove enough copper to cause blue-green stain on fixtures. Some bad tasting water may occur.

Lead plumbing. In 95% of the cases, the presence of a leg tub in a bathroom indicates lead waste plumbing over to the main cast iron stack. Lead plumbing cannot be repaired if it springs a leak; it must be replaced. Many local codes require that lead plumbing be changed if a bath is remodeled. This is not a major expense, but it prevents partial remodeling other than simple replacement of a lavatory or toilet.

Water hammer. This is the knocking often heard in pipes when a valve is closed. It is a serious threat to rigid plastic pipe. Water hammer arrestors installed at critical points in the line eliminate the problem.

Pressure. Low water pressure may be due to clogged pipes, poor well or municipal pressure, or a stuck pressure-reducing valve. Have a plumber correct this.

Drainage Problems. Drainage systems work on gravity alone; therefore, proper pitch is important to the system. Improper pitch may leave water in the pipe, thus restricting the flow and shortening the pipe life.

Blockage. Most drainage problems are caused by blockage due to negligence of the owner, by too many bends or elbows in the system, or by poor venting. Poor drainage can occur due to a vacuum caused by improper venting inside the pipe. If the homeowner did the plumbing alterations, check to be sure a vent appears at the roof line—some people terminate them in the attic, causing an odor. Blocked drains often are caused by foreign objects in the system. Homeowners sometimes can release clogged material and restore a free flow of water by using the suction cup device known as a "plumber's helper," or a wire snake.

Lack of use. If a drain is not used for several months, water in the traps may be lost through evaporation and sewer odors will enter the house. When there is a possibility of this, pour water into the house drain.

Pipes. All vent pipes should terminate above the roof line. Drainage and water pipes should be hung properly so house settlement will not cause any stress on the pipes. All fixtures should be vented with the right size pipe.

Leaks. Drainage pipes can leak due to faulty joints or corrosion cracks caused by house settlement and rust, especially when the pipe runs through damp areas or floors. Plastic pipe can leak if not properly hung.

MAINTENANCE

Maintenance of plumbing is a minor undertaking, except when equipment and the pipes are seriously misused or clogged. The only other time plumbing maintenance can be a serious problem is when you live in a region with hard or corrosive water. Such water can clog or corrode pipes in a few years unless the water is specially treated. Some plumbing maintenance can be done by any homeowner who can handle a few simple wrenches and other plumber's tools.

Leaks. A leaky faucet is repaired by putting in a new washer. Remember to turn off the water feeding into the faucet before you loosen it. If the faucet is old, you may have to have it replaced by a plumber.

Blockage. If a lavatory or sink gets clogged, try cleaning the trap under the sink. The toilet may be unstuck with a rubber plunger or one of the widely available solvents. If the job is beyond these simple devices, a plumber should be called to clean out the trap and the drain line of the fixture.

Caulking. Watch out for the tightness of the joint between your bathtub and shower stall and the wall. Should the caulking in these joints dry out and become loose, it can result in a slow leak which, over the months, ends up causing damage to the wall framing and dripping through to the ceiling below. Recaulk this joint whenever the material has dried. Do the same thing to kitchen sinks built into countertops.

Pipes. If the water runs rusty brown, especially from the hot water taps, then replace the corroded pipes with copper or plastic water lines. The cost is surprisingly low for the assurance that there will be no rust and no leaks thereafter.

INSPECTION

Much grief can be avoided if an examination of the plumbing system is made before buying a home and during homeownership. A good inspection would include many items.

To inspect plumbing systems, look for wet spots or stains on ceilings, floors, and walls. This could indicate a present or a past problem. Remember that some stains or spots can be caused by roof or gutter leaks. Check pipes for wet spots, discoloration, rust, and mineral deposits. Notice if some older pipes were already replaced. If so, you can expect further replacement of the remaining piping as other leaks occur.

Ask the homeowner if the house is on city water and sewers. If not, ask to be shown the septic system and well system and their location.

As you go through the house, try all fixtures, and observe for leaks. Most of the plumbing system is hidden and you must look for latent defects.

Check with your potential neighbors and town officials for water and sewage problems. Don't wait until you move in to find the septic's back-up.

Check to see if the house has a well or uses city water, and if it is on city sewers or some private sewer system. Details on wells can be found in Chapter 21, and septic tanks are discussed in Chapter 22.

Water pressure and flow are important. Check all faucets to see if flow is adequate. Flush toilets at the same time. Note if the hot water has the same flow as the cold. Often, hot water piping and coils are clogged with scale. If the flow is poor, try to determine the cause; i.e., municipal pressure, well regulator set too low, clogged faucet screen, small pipes, etc.

Check water shut-off valves at the service entrance or meter to be sure they will turn and close.

Observe the piping material and the size. Look for leaks at the fitting joints, and stains on the ceilings, floors, and walls. Leaks or stains can also be visible at the exterior overhangs. Check for faucet leaks.

Check for water hammer and other noises when fixtures are quickly closed. If there is an air chamber and you experience a water hammer, then the chamber is water-logged.

Have the water from private wells analyzed for purity (potability) and mineral content. See if any water treatment devices are necessary.

Operate all shower heads, water sprays, and mixing valves for proper operation.

Check all platforms, pedestals, and supports for corrosion, missing or loose connections, and defects.

There must be no cross-connection between a well and a municipal water supply.

Are all exposed pipes subject to freezing protected with insulation or heating devices? Look carefully at pipes in garages.

Note any high pitched whistle sounds made when a toilet is flushed or a valve opened slowly. A simple adjustment can correct this.

Noise in water and sewer pipes are caused by undersized water pipes, plastic drain pipes, or incorrectly positioned pipes. Insulating materials can muffle the noise.

Check all sinks, toilets, showers, and tubs for drainage. Fill each unit with water and note the drain flow. Note also any sucking sound as the fixture drains, since this might mean poor or clogged venting.

Observe all shower tile, pans, and shower drains, as these are bad leakers.

Check all ceilings under fixtures for leaks. Note any damp rot in floors and walls.

Check for a leaking toilet seal. See if the bowl is secure to the floor.

Check how long it takes for hot water to arrive to a faucet, and whether it remains continually hot or becomes tepid. The problem could be a long run of pipe and a poor hot water heater.

Observe all sewer and vent piping for leaks, rust, loose connections, clogging, splits, and material defects. Check to see if there is a roof vent pipe over all fixtures. Some municipalities require a fresh air vent at the cellar level. You can see if there is a vent screen at the exterior foundation wall.

Is there a sewer cleanout plug in the cellar or outside? If the house is below the street sewer line, then special holding tanks and pumps are needed (very expensive). Are all plugs in tight?

In some areas, because of street flooding, the sewer lines will have a special "backwater valve," or large closing valve. Do they work?

Observe the condition of all fixtures and connections for wear, rust, and chips.

Check the hot water heater (see Chapter 20 for details).

SUMMARY

If your house is over 20 years old, you can expect plumbing problems, so be careful in your inspection. Following the maze of plumbing pipes is not simple, nor is determining the quality of the system. I feel that in purchasing a home, or in an existing home, the home buyer or owner should be aware that plumbing can be improved, altered, and fixtures updated—leaving only the problem of cost. For those of you who own a home, be certain to correct minor clogged pipes and leaks immediately, before they turn into major cost problems.

19.
Bathrooms and Showers

INTRODUCTION

The bathroom is a very important place. A well-planned bath area adds greatly to the liveability of a home. Prospective home owners give high priority to conveniently located, well-equipped, and nicely decorated bathrooms. More bathroom remodeling jobs are sold each year than any other single type of home improvement. But remodeling can be expensive, and—more important—leaks, undetected, can cause structural damage.

The purpose of this chapter is to introduce you to the various bathroom fixtures, and their maintenance, operation, and inspection.

TECHNICAL INFORMATION

Toilets.   Most residential toilets consist of a bowl and attached tank that stores sufficient water to create a proper flushing action. Old city homes may have a water storage unit at the ceiling level. When the flush lever on a toilet is depressed it lifts a plug off its seat and the water flows into the flushing unit. As the water flows out of the tank, a float valve admits water back into the tank. When the tank refills, the float rises until the valve is turned off. The float can be adjusted to give a proper water level for flushing.

Toilets may be wall-hung or a pedestal type. The flushing process may be a simple washdown, a reverse trap, or a siphon-action design. Washdown toilets are the cheapest and have the least efficient cleaning action. Best of all are toilets with siphon-action, for they clean themselves thoroughly and flush quietly.

171

The quality of the materials in the flushing mechanism increases with the cost of the toilet. The best seats are made of high-impact, fade-resistant plastic and have nylon hinges.

Sinks.   There are several basic kinds of sinks: metal-rimmed, self-rimming, undercounter mounted, and those which are in one piece with the countertop. They come in a wide range of styles, sizes, colors, materials, and prices. The best bathroom sinks are made either of porcelain over cast iron or of vitreous china. Cheaper porcelain or enamel on steel sinks, which are most popular, tend to chip but give good service. For maximum convenience and adaptability, choose the largest basin built into the largest countertop.

Bathtubs.   Cast iron tubs were used years ago, but enameled steel, acrylic, or molded fiberglass are more common today. Tubs and shower units are available today as complete systems ready for installation. Many new homes use these units.

Shower Stalls.   A separate shower stall is troublesome because of a tendency to leak. Shower stalls are normally found in the master bedroom. The usual type of construction includes the floor pan of concrete or fiberglass covered with ceramic tile and the walls covered with ceramic tile. Anything but a one-piece floor pan will eventually leak, and other wall coverings rarely work. One-piece fiberglass pans are good. Lead pans covered with tile usually leak with normal house settlement.

A less expensive prefabricated steel model is also used. Here the floor pan is also a one-piece concrete pan and the walls are painted steel or galvanized iron. An attached door or a rod with a curtain is satisfactory.

The new one-piece fiberglass stall or complete tub enclosure comes in many shapes and colors, and cleans easily. The most practical and least expensive arrangement is to have the shower located over the end of the tub. A shower rod with a double curtain works quite satisfactorily.

Two other features are desirable in a shower for convenience and safety: an automatic temperature control in which the shower nozzle water is automatically kept at a constant temperature and an automatic diverter valve, which switches the water supply back to the tub spigot when the shower is turned off. It is safer but not always installed.

Walls and Floors. In the majority of homes, we find ceramic tile used for bathroom walls and often for floors, too. It is attractive, available in a variety of colors, easy to keep clean, and so rugged that if properly installed, it will last as long as the house. It should cover the entire wall and ceiling area around a shower stall or tub, but a tile wainscot about three feet high is all you need around the rest of the room.

Poor installation of tile is often found. If not put up properly, tiles will begin to loosen and fall off. Best installation is when the tile is set in a cement backing known as a "mud job." However, a well-applied mastic cement does a sound job. Tile can also be applied to a gypsum board wall. This can save money, but special care is required to prevent moisture ruining the wallboard—a common problem. There are also a variety of plastic tiles and plastic-tile boards available. These are poor substitutes for ceramic tile, but with care, they can be kept water-tight.

Many homeowners prefer a ceramic tile floor for its good looks and rugged wearing qualities or a floor of marble, terrazzo, or even flagstone. However, a resilient tile floor is an adequate covering. Rugs tend to stain.

Bathroom Fixtures.

Faucets. Good-quality faucets are made of thick brass, not zinc or aluminum die castings. Tough protective coatings of nickel and chrome are applied in the factory over the brass body. This gives a durable finish that will not require too frequent cleaning. Good faucet sets also can be identified by the manufacturer's name stamped on them. No manufacturer puts his name on his cheapest-grade faucets.

Shower valves. The combination valve consists of two compression stops cast in one body, which is fitted with a spray delivery pipe. The temperature of the water is regulated manually. The most desirable type of water supply device for a shower is the single handle mixing valve. These valves have been carefully designed to provide safe operation. The most convenient is the automatic temperature control valve that keeps the water at a pre-set temperature.

Shower nozzle. You can purchase a new water-saving nozzle that will not clog or corrode. It has a flexible joint to adjust the spray direction. It can also have a volume spray control, enabling you to adjust from a fine to a coarse spray. If you have hard water, a self-cleaning head is another good feature.

Ventilation. Every bathroom should be ventilated by a window or exhaust fan. Local building code requires this. If possible, do not locate the tub under the window. To help prevent excessive humidity in the house, the exhaust fan should be vented to the outside. New ceiling fans contain the fan, light, and heating devices in one unit.

Lighting. The well-lighted bathroom has good, glare-free general illumination and properly placed area lights over sinks and dressing counters.

Heating. Some bathrooms are not properly planned for heating. Ceramic tile can get cold from the walls, and a heating device of sufficient size is needed. Do not use portable units. Ceiling heat fans are satisfactory as an alternative heat source. Keep all hot pipes or radiators covered.

PROBLEMS

Leaks. The ceilings under bathrooms frequently show evidence of water staining from above. This trouble is usually caused by overflow or leaks in the fixture connections or pipes. A tub, sink, or toilet has usually overflowed at least once in any house, and each time it does, the water will find a way to the ceiling beneath. The best prevention against floor leaking is a well-fitted shower door or curtain and some care on the part of the person using the bathroom.

Pipes. Ceiling stains in the room beneath the bathroom can be identification of serious and expensive pipe repair. If a water-supply pipe is leaking, the ceiling plaster below will be wet and dripping.

Tubs. Tub or tub showers should have an access door on the wall in back of the spigots; look here to observe leaks. Also causing water leaks on the ceiling are the leaks that occur at the wall and the tub top. This can be prevented by adequately caulking and maintaining the joints. Another leak source is the tub overflow drain. This drain usually has a poor gasket. Consequently, when the tub is full, the water will leak onto the ceiling below.

Showers. In older houses, inspection of the ceiling under the shower will usually show telltale marks of leaking. New painting or papering in this area may be suspect as it may have been done to hide leak marks. Leaking can take place through the ceramic tile walls, at the joint between the tile wall and floor pan, and around the floor pan drain. If you live in a house with a tile shower floor, and it's past ten years old, you could be in for possible trouble. What happens is that the tile grout breaks and allows water to leak into the lead pan. The lead eventually wears out and the water will start to leak onto the ceiling below. If the leak is slow, it may cause rot in the ceiling joints before it is noticeable on the plaster below.

To repair this type of leak, the plumber must remove the tile floor, the lead pan, and the first two rows of tile. He or she should then examine the drain piping and trap—more than likely this should also be replaced—and check the tile backing and supports for rot. Because the walls tend to crack and the house settle, the plumber must install sheet lead in such a manner that any escaping water will be confined and conveyed to the terminal drain.

Ceramic tile walls are most susceptible to leaking, but this problem is less likely if the grout is maintained. Fiberglass units are waterproof, although early units developed hairline cracks because of poor installation techniques. They are easily repaired.

Walls. Waterproofed wall covering around the tub and shower are essential to the protection of adjacent walls, floors, and ceilings. Ceramic tile applied with cement is probably the most permanent of these coverings. A mastic or glue application is second best and waterproofing is highly dependent on well-maintained caulking. If water works through the joints, the mastic base may deteriorate. Plastic tile, if installed correctly, can give fair protection.

Toilet. The toilet can be a source of trouble. The mechanism in the tank may be malfunctioning or there may be a leak in the bowl itself. An inspection of the tank parts will reveal their condition. They are easily repaired. Water leaks at the bottom of the bowl may be caused by a cracked bowl or tank, a loose pipe fitting, or a loose wax seal at the floor flange. In the summer, it may be due to condensation on the tank or pipes. All problems are correctable but must be found early before wood decay occurs.

How to Find the Cause of the Leak. If the ceiling below is wet or stained, go upstairs and identify the area. It could be an overflow, a leaking shower, poor wax seal, or a leaking pipe. Try to isolate the leak to a particular fixture by viewing all access doors. As a last resort, break a hole in the ceiling and observe the leak. You or your plumber can repair the leak.

Water Pressure. Test the water pressure from a faucet. Then turn on another faucet to see if the pressure drops. Inadequate water pressure may be due to low water main pressure on your street, an undersized water supply pipe and meter to the house, or undersized or old water pipes, clogged up with scale, in the house. Correcting these can be expensive. Well pressure can be adjusted, and some houses have regulating valves on city mains that can be adjusted. If the shower fails to develop a good jet stream but the other plumbing outlets have good pressure, then all you may need is to clean the scale out of the shower head. Otherwise, a new inexpensive shower head may be installed.

Tiles. The little white lines between the tiles of your bathroom walls and floors are made of a material called "grout," and this can be another problem area. This has to be just the opposite of tub caulk—hard and rigid. Until recently, you had to buy a powdered grout which was mixed with water and then applied. Today, manufacturers make a ready-mixed grout that is easily applied wherever old grout has chipped out. Like the tub caulk, it is widely available in small tubes or cans. Good grouting will prevent leaks. Loose tiles will eventually confront the owner of even the best-tiled bathroom. Here again, a specialized material in small tubes with strong adhesive properties is recommended. You have probably noticed that it's the grout between the tiles—rather than the tiles themselves—that seems to attract the most stubborn dirt. This dirt is easily removed with a commercially prepared compound.

MAINTENANCE

The Plumbing Fixture Manufacturers Association suggests that by following a few simple rules, you can give your new plumbing fixtures and tile extra years of usefulness and beauty.

Wash your bathroom fixtures regularly with soap and warm water. Many homemakers have turned their shiny new fixtures dull within a short period by ignoring this simple advice, just as many others have cut thousands of tiny marks into china surfaces by using harsh abrasive cleansers.

When cleaning bathroom walls or the shower head, don't stand in the tub with your shoes on. Use a slide-proof bathmat to protect the tub's finish or take your shoes off.

If you overpack a medicine cabinet, containers may fall from it and break on a lavatory below, scratching the enamel finish. Chips can be repaired with a special paint. Don't sit or lean on bathroom sinks.

Bathroom fixtures should not be used as receptacles for photo-

graphic developing solutions because stains are almost certain to result.

When a faucet starts dripping, have it repaired immediately or hard-water mineral deposits may appear on the basin.

Never ignore a stain on a fixture once it appears. If soap and warm water fail to remove it, try using a simple cleaning solution. This usually does the trick, unless neglect has given the stain too much of a head start. Then rub a mild abrasive cleanser lightly against the stain with a coarse cloth. Use plenty of water.

Never use any cleanser with an acid or bleach content, even as a last resort. Acids will etch the surface of the fixture and bleaches will dull the gloss. With their use, subsequent cleaning becomes more difficult and your fixtures are subject to a deeper staining.

To clean tile floors, walls, and showers, use warm water and a detergent. Do not use soap for cleaning as this will leave an unsightly deposit. After each shower, wipe the tile surface dry to remove soap and water.

Never use a harsh abrasive cleaning compound or steel wool on any tile, for these can damage the finish. Never use a solvent on plastic tile, for this can ruin it.

If the joints between the tile become badly soiled, you can often improve matters by wiping with a household bleach. The only other solution is to scrape away the grout and replace it with a commercial grout mixture. Low quality tile may discolor in time and there is no remedy for this. If clay or ceramic tiles become covered with fine cracks, there is usually no cure. Some homeowners have successfully painted discolored tile. See your paint store manager.

Finally, *keep all valves, toilet mechanisms, pipes, and fixtures leak-free.* If you do see a problem, correct it immediately, before extensive damage is caused.

INSPECTION

If you are considering buying a previously occupied house, you should examine and evaluate the condition of the plumbing.

Try operating the bathroom devices and watching the drainage. You may feel shy about turning on the water and flushing toilets. Don't be. The house is your investment, and you will inherit problems unless you detect them prior to purchase. You have every right to inspect and question.

The following suggests features that should not be overlooked.

Are there *water stains* in the building, indicating leaks in the water-supply or drainage piping? If so, have the leaks been corrected satisfactorily?

Is the *flow of water* from the faucets good and strong, indicating absence of corrosion or scaling in the supply piping?

Do the fixtures *drain quickly* and quietly and maintain the water seals in the traps, indicating an adequately vented drainage system?

Are all *fixtures and piping firmly anchored* or supported?

Does the *toilet flush completely* and shut off completely? Does the tank refill quietly?

Do *faucets, valves, and stoppers* operate freely and close completely?

Are the *fixtures* chipped and stained? Do they need to be replaced?

Observe the condition of the *shower floor*. Does it look dirty? Is the tile cracked? Are there numerous patches with caulking compound? What is the condition of its door?

Next, put a stopper in the *floor drain* and fill the shower with four inches of water. Watch to see if it goes down, and observe the ceiling below.

Go to the *ceiling below*. Do you see any stains? Is the ceiling crazed? cracked? Even if it is painted over, observe closely around the light fixtures—is there any rust?

One requirement is a good *ventilating fan* for removing odors and excess humidity in the air. Such humidity can be harmful to the walls, paint, paper, and insulation. Check for proper operation in air-flow; does the fan force air out of the room?

Are there adequate heat, lighting and convenience *outlets*?

Do fixtures have easily accessible *shut-off faucets*? How long does it take the hot water to arrive and does it maintain a hot temperature?

What kind of *floor* is there? Is it cleanable?

Are there adequate *storage areas*, a large *medicine cabinet*, and *mirrors*?

Beware of an old house with only one bathroom. This will cause family inconvenience. A house with two or three bathrooms makes for better living and a higher resale value.

REMODELING YOUR BATHROOM

Today, a bathroom can be anything you want it to be. With a little imagination, you can make your daily life more enjoyable. The size of the family will largely determine the number of bathrooms needed. Particular individual needs and desires must also be taken into account. If you can have only one bathroom, it must serve many purposes. Therefore, it should be as large as possible.

Remodeling could include gutting the entire room, knocking out a wall, replacing a fixture, or installing a new wall surfacing. Because options in remodeling are limited by space and plumbing arrangement, planning in advance is perhaps even more important than when one is building new. Plan for ample electrical outlets properly grounded. Never use extension cords in a bathroom, nor metal pull cords on lights.

When planning additional storage, consider built-in closets or shelves. A wise rule to follow in choosing new fixtures or accessories for the bathroom is to buy only what you need. Bath shops, often associated with plumbing shops, are an excellent place to browse. They can give you a sense of the range of possibilities available and enable you to visualize how various things would fit together. Department stores also will often have bathroom accessories and aids in stock.

For help in planning and collecting ideas and information, there are numerous home magazines to consult, as well as planning literature put out by all the leading manufacturers.

If you decide on adding a half-bath or full-bath, be sure to get three quotes. But first decide exactly what you want and where it will go. New baths can be very expensive if the sewer lines are in another section of the house.

SUMMARY

The bathroom should get the most thorough inspection of any room in the house, including the kitchen. Many things can go wrong there, and if it is not designed well, the home owner will be subject to inconvenience and constant replacements for years. Remodeling is costly and the expense may not be recovered when you sell.

20.
Hot Water Heaters

INTRODUCTION

Water heaters, whether they are electric, oil, or gas fired, are the least troublesome of all appliances to operate. They suffer few mechanical failures.

TECHNICAL INFORMATION

Instantaneous Heaters. Instantaneous heaters or indirect units are often used in houses with hot water (hydronic) or steam heat boilers. They consist of a coil in the boiler or a heat exchanger on the side of the boiler. A storage tank is sometimes used, but the general principle is to pipe the hot water through the coil and directly to the faucets. The boiler must run all year if you are to have hot water.

Storage Type. This chapter deals mainly with the storage type hot water heater. Basically, this unit consists of a tank for holding water and the means to heat it. Heat can come through gas, electricity, or oil. Cold water is received at the top of the tank and conducted to the bottom of the tank by a dip tube. The introduction of the cold water at the bottom activates the thermostat and also avoids diluting the hot water remaining at the top. When a hot water tap is turned on, the hot water exits from the tank at the top and simultaneously cold water enters the tank through the dip tube at the bottom. The tank is always full and kept at a preset temperature, usually 140° F. There is a magnesium anode rod in the tank to prevent electrolite damage to the metal fittings inside the tank.

PROBLEMS AND SOLUTIONS

Instantaneous Water Heaters.

Inadequate capacity. Instantaneous water heaters are seldom designed with adequate capacity and so often run short of water. If you buy a replacement unit, be sure to get one with a minimum rating of 3.75 gallons per minute. Check to be sure the heater is an approved indirect water heater. Insist on a storage tank; otherwise, the water temperature will vary with usage. Water directly from the coil is hot (160° to 200° F) and a manual mixing valve or automatic valve should be installed in the line.

Dirty coil. The coil tends to clog up with scale, reducing efficiency and requiring cleaning. You will know it is time to clean the coils when the hot water pressure or flow is lower than the cold water pressure. Cleaning is usually done by your fuel supplier.

With increased fuel prices, it is inefficient to maintain a hot temperature in a boiler for the only purpose of heating hot water during the summer months. Consider a storage type unit for the summer.

Flow restrictor. Shower nozzles are available today that cut the flow of shower water from 5 to 1.6 gallons per minute. This can produce a real savings for a modest cost.

Storage Tank Type.

Water temperature is too hot. Adjust the control dial to bring the temperature down to 120° F. Use a thermometer to measure the temperature of the water.

"Water hammer." This banging noise can be controlled by the installation of arresting devices available from your plumber or local plumbing supply store.

Rusty water. This condition usually means that the heater is very old. However, it could mean a problem with the water supply. Drain out the tank to remove sediment and scale and make the unit operate more effectively. Be sure to drain the tank regularly from the start. If you try it on an old tank, you may not get the valve to seat properly.

Leaking relief valve. The valve may need replacement, the temperature of the hot water may be too high for the setting of the relief valve, or excess pressure may be building up in the hot water line when the heater is on. Since these problems can be dangerous, call a plumber.

Crackling or sizzling burner. This is often caused by condensation in the tank or by a minute leak in the burner compartment. It means you need a new heater.

Rumbling heater. This is usually caused by sediment collecting on the bottom of the tank. Water gets under the sediment and when heated, flashes into steam, making a sound. Usually this is not serious. Be sure to flush the tank every month until the water runs clean. Follow directions in securing the heater and also lift the safety valve.

Long wait for hot water. This condition may be the result of the faucet being too far from the heater. The answer is a circulating water system—something you may wish to discuss with a plumber.

Not enough hot water. The heater capacity may be too small for the needs of your family, the thermostat may not be working, or the piping connection may be wrong. On indirect type heaters, the mixing valve may be too wide open. Undersized storage heaters do not last as long as properly sized units.

Expected Life. Gas hot water heaters usually last from five to ten years, depending on use and care. Electric units last from ten to fifteen years, and oil fired units average seven years. Electric units may need a coil cleaning occasionally. You can tell when a gas heater is wearing by inspecting the burner compartment for leaks and excessive rust flakes.

MAINTENANCE

If properly maintained, your water heater will provide years of dependable trouble-free service. It is suggested that a regular maintenance service be followed.

Periodically have a service person inspect the thermostat, burners, relief valve, and venting system. Drain water from the unit to clear away sediment.

Visually inspect the burner while firing, and the pilot burner flame with the main burner off. The normal color of the flame is blue-orange. The tip of the flame will have a slight yellow tint. Your gas company or installer can adjust this correctly. If you notice any odor of gas, call your gas company immediately. Open windows and shut off the main gas valve.

Keep the area near the water heater free of flammable liquids and other combustible materials.

Make certain that the flow of air to the heater is adequate and that ventilation is not obstructed.

Check the flue pipe to be sure it is clean and securely attached. Sometimes the caulking at the chimney has broken loose.

In certain areas, the water contains very aggressive elements. Periodic inspection of the anode rod is necessary to determine if replacement is warranted. As the anode rod is consumed, it protects the glass lined tank.

The energy crisis demands that you keep the temperature setting as low as possible and that you conserve hot water.

BUYING A NEW HOT WATER HEATER

Tank Capacity. The tank capacity depends on whether you get a gas, oil, or electric heater. The minimum size for gas should be 40 gallons. For a large family, a high recovery heater with a special burner or increased tank capacity should be installed for an adequate supply. A full load of clothes in an automatic washer takes from 25 to 40 gallons of water, most of which may be hot water. Washing dishes by hand takes four gallons, while an automatic dishwasher takes five to six gallons. A bath consumes 15 gallons of water and the average shower takes 12 gallons. This is why you can easily run out of hot water with multiple usages.

Electric heaters have low recovery rates and are expensive to operate. The smallest unit to install is one with a 66-gallon capacity. If you have automatic clothes or dish washers and a family of four, you need an 80-gallon unit. Check with your public utility for off-peak control and special meters.

Oil fired units cost more initially than electric or gas units but have the best recovery rate. These are high quality heaters that will not only last ten or more years, but provide all the hot water you will ever need at any given time. They are usually used in those homes not serviced by natural gas.

Gas units are most common where the area is serviced by natural gas. They are clean and efficient. Units come in 30- to 75-gallon capacities with variable capacity flame units for quicker recovery. Bottled gas units should be avoided.

Quality.   Water heater quality depends on the kind of tank material and the guarantee you get. For most applications, a high quality glass lined tank with a 10 to 15 year unconditional warranty is the best. Read the warranty carefully because some are worthless. Understand the recovery features and cost.

Water heaters also come in ceramic lined, aluminum, copper, and galvanized tanks. It is important to check with your supplier on the best material, capacity, and fuel for your area. Some utilities will install and rent a unit to you with a full warranty.

Installation.   The heater must be installed in accordance with local codes, utility requirements, and the manufacturer's direction. Some municipalities require a permit. Keep the manufacturer's instructions near the unit for reference. Some pointers are given below.

A gas and oil fired water heater must be connected by a flue to a chimney. Building codes in your area may require a larger flue for a larger heater, because the volume of waste gas is more. For replacement heaters, get professional advice or follow the manufacturer's instructions carefully. If the unit is electric, a larger electric line may be mandatory, and it should be protected.

The water lines should be connected to the hot and cold pipes labeled on the top of the heater. Many are not, and efficiency is cut down this way.

The flue pipe should not run more than ten feet and be properly secured to each section. Two gas appliance flues may be connected to the same chimney, providing the code requirements are followed.

For safety, there should be a pressure and temperature relief valve at the top of the hot water heater. This will prevent excess pressure from destroying the tank. The valve should be piped to a sink drain or to within four inches of the floor (if the pipe won't freeze) to prevent flooding the area if the safety lifts. Be certain that your tank has this valve.

Look for a local pipe shut-off valve to secure the heater if there is a leak, for draining water from the tank, or for securing the unit.

When installing a new heater, have the plumber use unions for easy installation the next time.

Consider an auxiliary catch pan or a hose so that in the event of a leak, the resulting flow of water will not cause damage to the surroundings or equipment.

Do not store combustibles near the unit. Always keep a fresh air supply to the unit for combustion. Do not install a gas or oil unit in a sealed closet or furnace room.

Should you have any questions about a new unit, or if it requires an adjustment, first contact your installer. If the problem is not solved to your satisfaction, then contact the manufacturer. Remember to keep all warranty certificates.

EVALUATION

If you are buying a house, you should check the condition of the hot water heater. Try to determine the age of the unit by noting the date on the plumber's tag or the name plate. Inspect the fittings at the top of the tank for corrosion and look for rust spots at the seams of the tank. Examine the burners to see if they are clogged and if there is extensive rust flaking in the burner compartment. This usually means a short life. Check to see if the temperature of the water is high. This means the unit has worked hard and a shorter life is indicated. The average expected life is a good gauge of the remaining life in the present unit.

SOLAR WATER HEATERS

In various parts of the United States, solar water heaters have been used successfully for years. Check with your local governments for government rebates on the use of solar units.

SUMMARY

Properly maintained, your water heater will provide years of dependable trouble-free service. It is suggested that a regular maintenance service be followed. Periodically have a service person inspect the thermostat, burners, relief valve, and venting system. Periodically drain water from the unit to clear away sediment. If you need a new unit, evaluate your requirements and purchase a good quality heater.

Should you have any questions about a new unit, or if your unit requires an adjustment, contact your installer. Should the problem not be solved to your satisfaction, then contact the manufacturer. Remember to keep all warranty certificates.

21.
Private Water Wells

INTRODUCTION

The owner or prospective owner of an individual water supply has to be more knowledgeable about sanitation and well construction than the city dweller who depends on a municipality for such service. Fifty million people in the United States depend on privately owned well water. Although many well owners may boast of the superior taste and quality of their water, surveys show that approximately two-thirds of these private wells have some serious mechanical or other defect which often results in an outbreak of waterborne diseases. Fortunately, it is possible to prevent the risk of waterborne disease with proper attention to location, construction, and testing of well water and supply. This chapter will cover those preventive measures, including inspection of the well and the steps to take in contracting to drill a new well.

TECHNICAL INFORMATION

A simple, direct pumping system consists of the well, a pump controlled by a pressure switch, a pressure tank, and the distribution system.

Pump and Pressure Switch. Water is pumped out with either a jet pump placed next to a storage pressure tank in the basement or well house, or a submersible pump that actually fits down into the wall casing. Both are satisfactory. A pressure switch setting of 30 to 50 pounds per square inch is recommended for these systems. It will provide adequate pressure for lawn sprinkling, "first aid" fire protection, and modern automatic laundry equipment.

Pressure Tank.   The pressure tank is sometimes called a hydropneumatic tank. It contains a small volume of water and a larger volume of compressed air which expands and contracts, depending on the water pressure. This compressed air supplies the energy which delivers the water to household faucets and fixtures, eliminating the necessity of pump starts for every small water demand—although most suburban homes will have only the pressure storage tank.

Many rural homes require intermediate storage systems to provide good service. Intermediate storage is atmospheric storage located between the source of supply and the distribution pump, carefully planned and constructed to preserve water quality. The intermediate storage tank is in effect the source of supply of the distribution system. It is filled at a low and prolonged rate from a well which may be of low yield. The well pump may have a low capacity as compared to the delivery pump and pressure tank drawing water from the intermediate storage area.

PROBLEMS

Rate of Flow.   The rate of flow is the amount of water that can be pumped out of the well with constant use before it starts churning mud and sand and becomes dry. A well of ample capacity will not greatly increase the overall cost of a home, yet it will add more to comfortable modern living. A well should produce between five and seven gallons per minute. A well that produces less than four gallons per minute precludes watering the lawn. This figure should be your minimum supply unless you are willing to provide some special intermediate storage apparatus. Some sections of the country can only get a flow of one-half gallon per minute, while the county codes allow a two-gallon per minute minimum. If waterflow problems occur, the capacity or well recovery can be measured by a well digger and a solution recommended.

Polluted Water.   Wells that are too shallow or too close to septic or cesspools can become polluted. A well is considered unsatisfactory when the coliform and bacteria count in the water is too high. You should have a test done before you move in. Local codes state how deep (usually over 50 feet), how far away from the nearest septic tank or cesspool (minimum 25 feet), and how far away from the drain field (100 feet) a well should be. In some cases, municipal authorities will allow spring water cisterns to be used if an acceptable home chlorinating or treatment system is installed.

Malfunctioning Equipment.   The pump and holding water tank can be located in the cellar or in a cement enclosure located in the ground near the house. The pump can also be a submersible unit in the well casing with a holding tank at ground level. Possible equipment troubles may be traced to the items below.

Submersible pump. The first sign of a problem is poor recovery of pressure. Average life is ten years.

Ground level pumps. Problems are accompanied by excessive pump noises, bearing noises, and hot motors. Repair or replacement vary in costs, depending on whether the nozzle and piping in the well need to be replaced. Average life is 10 to 15 years.

Pipes and water tanks. Rusting can be a cause of malfunction. Average life is five to ten years.

Pressure switches. They have a five-year life expectancy and then they start to malfunction.

Smashed pipes. Heavy equipment or heavy frost can destroy pipes, particularly where the water tank is in a cement structure in the ground.

Water Quality.   Mineral and chemical content of water is important and should be determined by testing. A high mineral content, often called "hard" water, may soon clog home humidifier systems. Hot water heating systems are also made less efficient by minerals that form hard scales and sludges. In these cases, a water softener may be desirable.

Too "soft" a water or one with too low a mineral content will taste flat and is likely to corrode pipes and tanks. Know the quality of your water before purchasing new equipment.

MAINTENANCE TIPS

Inspection.   Your inspection of the well should include a visual examination of the pump motor and pressure storage tank. Inspect all piping, gauges, water tanks, and valves for rust and signs of leaking. A routine examination should include the following steps.

Run water simultaneously from several faucets for about 15 minutes and note the pressure fluctuations. Near the end of the test, look for mud and cloudiness in the water, an indication that the water is being drawn off faster than it is being supplied. This running of the water will also help test the effectiveness of the septic system.

Check the tank and piping to make sure it is insulated to prevent excessive condensation in the summer.

Check if there is a *pilot light* that indicates when the well pump is running. This is usually installed on a well of low yield and signals the homeowner to shut off the pump when the water level drops.

Feel the water tank for the cold section that locates the level of the water. Since well water is usually about 52° F, there will often be a sweat mark on the tank. A full tank will cause the pump to rapidly cycle since water is incompressible and can cause excessive pump wear. Many tanks have an air valve at the top, and a bicycle pump can be used to lower the level in the tank and give an air cushion. Newer tanks have a collapsible interior with an air cushion and the problem does not appear.

Records and Tests. If the well is new, pertinent information is usually available from the county sanitarian. Ask questions of the present owner and contact the local pump and well digger for service records.

You should obtain a *well log*. This includes the location of the well, the depth of the well, the capacity (in gallons per minute), the name of the well digger, and the amount of casing tube used. If the homeowner doesn't have the log, you may obtain this from the municipal files, usually those of the health officers. Particularly note the items listed below.

1. Rate of water flow.
2. Depth of the well. (Depth will vary in different areas, and while 100 feet is the average, it is not uncommon to drill 200 to 500 feet to reach pure water in some areas. Old wells of 20 to 30 feet deep are no longer satisfactory and in most cases are no longer approved. The best wells are drilled wells, which are usually encased with six-inch pipe through dirt layers and into rock.)
3. Location of the well. (Sooner or later, the well will need servicing and you should record its location in advance. The well should be

uphill from both the house and septic system and 100 feet from the leaching area; however, local codes may vary.)

Have a *Potability test done.* The county Environmental Health Officer or a local testing laboratory can test a sample of the water for possible contamination. There is a small charge.

Ask the homeowner if he or his neighbors have had any well problems. Check with neighbors and the municipal authorities on local well problems.

NEW WELLS

The home buyer will need to determine that a safe, adequate water supply can be developed at a proper distance from the sanitation field. In planning a new well, you should also be thoroughly informed as to local ordinances regarding well construction.

Local conditions vary throughout the country. Except for a few areas of creviced limestone and sink holes or areas of fractured rock under a very shallow mantle of soil, it is not difficult to have a safe well from a bacteriological standpoint. State and local health authorities can warn you of any other problems typical to the area.

In a few places, fluorides may be too high. Some areas have high concentrations of nitrates, and excessive iron and manganese or hardness are also common local problems. High chloride content or salt water intrusion are problems in certain areas. Tests for these chemicals are not too costly but are usually not requested unless the problem is known to be common to the area.

In developing a water supply, remember that avoidance of a poor source of supply is many times better than trying to provide remedial treatment.

Local Ordinances.   An application and a permit are usually required to locate and construct a well or to alter an existing one. These are usually issued by the Health Officer of the municipality. The Health Officer will require a potable water test of the new system. This procedure for the tests is explained in the local or state code and must be followed.

In most counties, no new individual water supply system may be put in use and no new dwelling or building depending upon such a system may be occupied or sold until the water supply system has been certified by the Board of Health. For such certification, the Board of Health requires (1) a written report by a professional engineer, licensed in the state, certifying that the system has been constructed in accordance with the terms of the application for the permit and applicable codes currently in effect; and (2) a report from an approved laboratory indicating that the water meets the potable water standards of the State Department of Health on a sample taken by the Sanitary Inspector of the Board of Health.

Contractor and Written Contract.   You can find and select a well drilling contractor by consulting the National Water Well Association for a member in your area. Your building contractor or local health officer may also help. Check on the well contractor's reliability and reputation.

Be certain to insist on a written contract explaining how the well will be constructed and itemizing all costs and materials. Do not accept a "per foot" charge.

The contract should include the size of the hole; the inside diameter of the casing; an estimate of the well's depth; an estimate of the casing's depth; how the well is to be sealed; how the well will be sterilized; specification that a well log will be furnished; a guarantee of materials and workmanship; the distance the well will be from sources of contamination; assurance that a flow test of four or more hours will be made in order to determine the well's sustainable yield; a guarantee that any undesirable formations will be sealed off; what depth the cement grouting will extend; what type of pump and pump capacity will be provided or recommended; whether the well will be capped on completion; whether any abandoned well hole will be sealed; whether the well will be pumped until clear; assurance that the water supply system will be tested and free from coliform and bacteria; and whether the well driller carries statutory compensation and liability insurance.

SUMMARY

If you have gone to the trouble to test your well, searched for possible paths of contamination and removed them, and designed the system for adequate flows so that there is no competition for water between fixtures and water uses which occur simultaneously, then you may very well have the best quality water for miles around!

For further information, an excellent guide for well location and construction is *Water Sources for the Farmstead and Rural Home.*

Write for FB2244, to Superintendent of Documents, Government Printing Office, Washington, D.C. 20202, and enclose 15 cents. In addition, most states have published similar bulletins. You can also obtain information from your local health department or environmental protection agency. Or write the National Water Well Association, 88 Broad Street, Columbus, Ohio 48215.

22.
Private Sewage
Disposal Systems

INTRODUCTION

Private sewage systems in the United States use one of four methods: tanks with absorption fields, seepage beds or seepage pits, Clivus Multrum systems, and oxygen (aerobic) systems. This chapter discusses in detail the septic system which is the major method used in the United States to dispose of household sewage.

When your septic system is functioning properly, it can inexpensively dispose of domestic sewage wastes with little or no ecological damage. However, like the rhyme, "When she is good, she is very, very good, but when she is bad, she is horrid," a malfunctioning septic system is ill-smelling, offensive, and expensive to repair. In the long run, the septic system is likely to be costlier and more troublesome than a public sewage hook-up. If you have no alternative to a septic system, then you should make every effort to understand the three main parts of the system; i.e., the soil, the tank, and the absorption field.

TECHNICAL INFORMATION

Sewage.   Household sewage consists of the water-carried wastes from the bathroom, the kitchen, the laundry, and other plumbing fixtures. It includes human excreta, toilet paper, dishwater, food scraps, wash water, bits of soap, grease, hair, lint, bleach, cleaning compounds, and sweepings. It may also include ground food wastes and backwash from regenerating water conditioning equipment.

Paper cartons, wrappers, newspapers, sticks and stones, and discarded clothing are rubbish, not sewage, and should be kept out of sewage disposal systems. Storm drainage from roofs, sump pumps, and areaways also should be kept out of septic tank systems and other sewage disposal facilities, as they overburden the system.

Cesspool.   The cesspool is a lined and covered excavation in the ground that receives the discharge of domestic sewage or other organic wastes from a drainage system. It is so designed as to retain organic matter and solids but permits the untreated liquids to seep through the bottom and sides. Cement blocks or stone are used without mortar in the joints. The size is usually five feet in diameter by ten feet deep.

The cesspool cannot be considered an effective method of sewage disposal since its mode of operation is dependent upon the discharge of the sewage into pervious underground strata. The increasing need for water makes even the discharge into "unusable" water strata a questionable practice when considered in the light of future needs. If pervious strata are not located, the cesspool will overflow, thus causing a surface nuisance. For the most part, municipalities have outlawed cesspools. If yours malfunctions, the town will require that a new septic system be installed.

Clivus Multrum.   This type of system is a self-contained method for the treatment of organic wastes. It wastes no water, for it uses none. It protects all bodies of water from the waste products of toilet and kitchen by retaining them in an impervious container from which there is no effluent. It preserves the nutrients in these waste materiels by converting them to a rich humus suitable for gardens. It needs no external supply of energy or chemicals to effect the decomposition, as the energy is inherent in the wastes, and the micro-organisms present in them do the work of conversion. Since it has no moving parts, it requires virtually no maintenance other than the annual removal of a few pails of humus a year. As the wastes are converted to a usable product on the site, there is no need for water or sewer hook-up.

Clivus Multrum means, literally, "inclining compost room." The Multrum consists of an impervious container set at such an angle that the organic wastes slide in a glacier-like fashion down the sloping bottom at a rate slow enough to ensure that they will be thoroughly decomposed by the time they reach the storage chamber. Tubes connect the container to the kitchen chute and toilet. A draft, which is maintained by natural convection, ensures that the process is essentially aerobic (one in which oxygen-breathing organisms do the work), and that the bathroom and kitchen are kept free of odors at all times. Some people report that the aerobic action slows down in very cold basements. For further information, write Clivus Multrum, USA, 14A Eliot Street, Cambridge, Mass. 02138.

The Aerobic System. In areas where there is no municipal system, and the soil percolation test will not permit a septic-absorption system, an aerobic system can be used.

This system provides the compartmentalization, hydraulic flows, and oxygen necessary to optimize the aerobic process. The process entraps and retains organic solids until necessary oxidation takes place, even under extreme shock or overload conditions. Living habits can change wastewater characteristics, and if a solids or sludge build-up is noticed after several years of operation, all internal parts can readily be removed for servicing and the tank can be easily pumped. In up to 95% of the cases, treatment is achieved and the effluent (treated wastewater) is semi-clear, odorless, and acceptable in many states for surface or stream discharges. It requires less tile field than septic tank effluent in soils with good percolation and helps prevent clogging of tile fields.

In many cases, the use of the Aerobic Wastewater Treatment System will permit the use of land for building that would be unsuitable for septic tank installations. The tank is cylindrical, of 1000 gallon capacity at the water line, and made of fiberglass-reinforced plastic designed and tested to withstand physical pressures and loads far in excess of actual requirements. It is impervious to chemical attack inside and out as a result of carefully controlled finishes. For further details, see your town sanitarian.

The Soil. The soil must be porous enough to absorb the effluent put into it. The capacity of your soil to absorb liquids is measured by a percolation test reading. From this reading, the square feet of absorption area per bedroom is calculated. Your local health department can advise you about the percolation test procedures required and can also give you advice on local soil surveys.

Septic Tank. The second part of the system is the septic tank, the function of which is to separate the solids contained in the sewage from the liquid. The sewage entering your septic tank contains 99.9% water and 0.1% solids. The solids cause all the trouble.

A modern septic system has a grease trap tank to take the kitchen wastes. Not all solids decompose, and after a time the tank can fill up and the solids go right through and clog the absorption system. This is why you should pump out the septic tank every two or three years.

Absorption System.   The absorption portion of the system is the most critical part of the facility. If it is constructed improperly or abused by you then it will have a short life and cause many problems. The absorption system consists of a network of perforated pipes laid in a bed of stone in a pattern approved by the local health officer. The stone bed spreads out the effluent and allows it greater contact with the earth surface, which absorbs and purifies it. In very porous soils, you can use a seepage bed or tank rather than lateral absorption fields.

There is always solid matter (both suspended and dissolved) in the effluent that hasn't been completely stabilized or digested moving out of the tank to the absorption field. Further digestion is carried on by bacteria present in the soil in the absorption field. In the absorption field, perforated pipe or tile that has been spaced apart is used to allow the effluent to trickle out. The tile or pipe is placed beneath the ground, surrounded by gravel. The gravel evenly disperses the effluent as it trickles to the soil below. Under the present pattern of use, all absorption fields are destined to fail eventually (if well-designed and constructed, average life is 20 years) because of a very thin layer of scum and other matter that slowly forms on the surface of the soil, just beneath the gravel. This layer becomes impervious to liquid, and ultimately clogs the entire system.

In the meantime, other factors can cause absorption field failure, such as poorly drained soils, soils with extremely low absorption characteristics, and so forth. This type of land can become a boggy mess, and was never meant to have a septic system. In a given area of good soil, some systems will fail and others will not, and this is due primarily to design and construction as well as the type of maintenance the system receives. A failure, for example, can be caused by a tank overloaded with scum and sludge—a tank which needs cleaning.

There are two basic types of shallow absorption fields. The conventional type has tile laid beneath the ground in individual trenches from 24 to 36 inches wide. This type is used most often. Fields on the side of hills, in rock formation soils, and near a high water table are usually doomed to failure, so check carefully. The second type, called a seepage bed, consists of one big trench, usually over ten feet wide. A seepage bed is as good as the conventional trench type, and is less costly. Both types are recommended by FHA and the U.S. Public Health Service. Seepage pits are commonly used in addition to the absorption field, in cases where the field itself is not adequate. Beneath the ground, these pits can be over 20 feet in depth. They use open-jointed structural linings to allow effluent to seep out. These pits are frequently banned by code because they are prone to polluting underground water. However, if the percolation test is good, the code will allow the pit with a septic tank.

MAINTENANCE

Below are some maintenance pointers that we have successfully recommended for septic systems.

To facilitate cleaning and maintenance, *you should have a diagram of the septic tank system*, showing the location of the house, the septic tank manholes, the piping, and the soil absorption system. If you are buying from another owner, get the map plus the results of the percolation test and the engineer's design sketch of the system. If you are dealing with a builder, be certain he or she is following acceptable septic tank design procedures. Your health department can help and will be glad to discuss this with you.

Don't cover an absorption field with extra fill, swimming pools, driveways, or other things that will prevent it from working.

Don't drive cars or heavy equipment over the tank or field, as the pipes will be broken and crushed.

Don't plant trees or shrubs at or near the field or the roots will clog the system.

Don't use colored or printed toilet paper, as the dyes prevent the paper from breaking down and the tank becomes full of sludge quicker.

Be certain to fix all leaking faucets or toilets to prevent overloading the system. Pipe all dishwater and clothes washer drains to a drywell system.

Don't waste your money on chemicals or biological septic aids or cleaners. They could cause failure of the absorption field.

Don't use the toilet as a garbage disposal.

Don't let water collect over the drainfields and don't discharge footing drain sumps or leader drains to the system.

Educate the family and your company on water conservation; it will postpone system failure (and reduce water bills).

Inspect the sludge and scum level in the tank every few years and have it pumped out if necessary. Neglect of the septic tank is the most frequent cause of damage to soil absorption systems. When the tank is not cleaned, solids build up until they are carried into the underground soil absorption system, where they block the flow of the liquid into the soil. When this happens, the system must be rebuilt—a costly undertaking. The precautions of periodic inspection and cleaning of the tank prevent this needless expense and work.

If you do install a new drain field, connect a bypass valve to the old system. Drying out of the old system in a number of months may return it to serviceability. Switching after long rest periods will prolong the lives of both systems.

INSPECTING THE SYSTEM

Since the system is not visible, you must evaluate it by asking questions and noting the telltale signs of possible failure.

Questions.   If you are purchasing a home with a septic system, you should ask the following questions.

Ask the town sanitarian or engineer if there are any violations against the present property and if there are any private sewage system problems in the immediate area. Get a copy of the engineer's design report that is sometimes available in the town office. Ask for a map locating the tank and leaching area. Service companies charge an extra fee to locate the tank for pumping.

Ask the home owner when the system was installed. Has it been altered, improved, or enlarged? What are the reasons?

Ask for the service record of tank pumping. A pumping record of every three to four years is considered a good preventive maintenance schedule. By design, all systems are eventually doomed to failure, but with regular tank cleaning, a system will last 20 to 30 years.

Is there recovery room on your lot? There may be no room to place a new system and the soil will become saturated. In some areas, the field is too small to do the job. Discuss possible problems with neighbors.

Find out when municipal sewers will be installed. Where is the near-

est well? Does the town perform a dye test to see if the system is polluting streams and lakes?

Testing the System.   The best way to evaluate the septic tank is to
open it and measure the sludge level, but often this is not practical. To
check the functioning of a system, flush all toilets three to five times,
and run the water continuously into a tub for 15 to 30 minutes. Ask the
homeowner if there has been any trouble with the system.

A problem in a septic system makes itself known in one of several
ways. Home drains will back up and sewage won't flow into the system,
indicating that the septic tank is filled or the pipes are crushed, or that
the drainfield has been flooded by heavy rains (if the latter, the condition will eventually abate). Low-lying drain vents boil over with sewage, a sign that the septic tank is filled (drains have a gurgling sound
and fixtures drain very slowly). If the ground above the drainfield sud-
denly erupts with effluent (breakout), check with the town on the water
table and breakout problems in the area; ask to have a dye test per-
formed to be sure the breakout is sewage. If the grass takes on a dark
hue and starts to grow more vigorously above the drainfield than elsewhere, you have a problem (black mold may also be observed).
Another sign of trouble is a sewage odor on the property, especially in
the summer. Finally, when there is snow on the ground, a bare spot
may help you locate the tank or leaching area problems.

Correcting Problems.   If the septic tank or sewage line is blocked, it
can be an inexpensive job ($100 to $200) to pump and clear the tank.
But if the absorption fields are contaminated, it may mean installing a
new field and that cost starts at $2,000. So it pays to carefully check the
system and then to maintain it.

SUMMARY

The disposal of sewage from residences on an individual basis in rural
areas or sparsely settled suburban localities is usually solved satisfactorily by the use of a septic tank followed by a drainage field, or—in
localities with tight soil or high water tables—by the use of submerged
or sand filters. The use of individual systems rarely proves effective
over a long period of time in thickly populated areas because of overloading the soil. Remember that septic systems are intended only as a
stop-gap measure of waste disposal. If your wait for sewers is to be a

long one, then you should do all in your power to have as good a system as you can get and to maintain it properly.

For more detailed information concerning special conditions in your area, consult your local or state health department. Public Health Service Publication No. 526, *Manual of Septic Tank Practice*, may also be helpful in providing additional information, including cleaning procedures for septic tank systems designed in accordance with this manual. It can be secured from the Superintendent of Documents, U.S. Government Printing Office, Washington, D.C. 20402.

23.
Fireplaces
and Chimneys

INTRODUCTION

Gathering at the fireside for comfort and fellowship is a custom as ancient as the use of fire. Fireplaces, long appreciated for their aesthetic value, are being looked to as a source of supplemental heat, for use on chilly fall mornings when the central heating system is turned off, or during emergencies. Most fireplaces are inefficient, tend to smoke, and are rarely used except for entertaining company.

This chapter will increase your understanding of the proper construction of chimneys and fireplaces—information which is essential for continued safety and efficiency of operation. This knowledge should add to your enjoyment of your fireplace for many years to come.

TECHNICAL INFORMATION

The two fundamental parts of a fireplace are the chimney, which vents products of combustion, and the firebox, in which the fire is built and by which heat is reflected into the room. It is a good idea to be familiar with the several specific terms used in connection with the fireplace.

The Chimney.   *The flue* that is inside a masonry exterior carries combustion gases out of the house. A flue liner should be used. Brick flues in older homes should be inspected periodically for leaks.

The smoke chamber is the area that connects the damper with the flue and directs the flow of gases into the chimney.

The smoke shelf is an essential part of every fireplace. It is the horizontal surface just behind the damper that helps prevent downdrafts from reaching the fire by turning any downdraft back up the chimney.

The damper is used to close the flue when the fireplace is not in use. Every fireplace should have one that seals the entire throat. With a well-designed, properly installed damper you can regulate the draft, close the flue to prevent loss of heat from the room when there is no fire in the fireplace, and adjust the throat opening according to the type of fire so you can reduce loss of heat. Glass doors on the front of the fireplace perform a similar function.

The Fireplace.   *The fire chamber* is the area where the fire burns. It should be lined with fire brick or a prefabricated steel fireplace.

Fire brick is a special heat-resistant brick set with fire clay. Be sure to keep these mortar joints well-set.

The hearth is where the fire is built. It protects the floor from sparks and embers and is supported by a concrete or brick arch. Check to be sure the contractor removed all wood forms, as they are a fire hazard.

The ash dump and cleanout door are installed in the basement or on the exterior to simplify ash removal. Be careful to secure this door to prevent fires in a basement.

Construction.

The Chimney. All fireplaces and fuel-burning equipment such as stoves and furnaces require some type of chimney. The chimney must be designed and built so that it produces sufficient draft to supply an adequate quantity of fresh air to the fire and to expel smoke and gases emitted by the fire or equipment. A chimney located entirely inside a building has a better draft than an exterior chimney, because the masonry retains heat longer when protected from cold outside air.

The chimney is usually the heaviest part of a building and it must rest on a solid foundation to prevent differential settlement in the building. Concrete footings are recommended. They must be designed to distribute the load over an area wide enough to avoid exceeding the safe load-bearing capacity of the soil.

A chimney should extend at least three feet above flat roofs and at least two feet above a roof ridge or raised part of a roof within ten feet of the chimney. This is critical to give good draft and properly vent other fuel burning units. Proper construction of the flue is important. Its size (area), height, shape, tightness, and smoothness determine the effectiveness of the chimney in producing adequate draft and in expelling smoke and gases.

Lined flues are definitely recommended for brick chimneys. When the flue is not lined, mortar and bricks directly exposed to the action of flue gases disintegrate. This disintegration, plus that caused by temperature changes, can open cracks in the masonry which will reduce the draft and increase the fire hazard. However, flue linings may be omitted if the chimney walls are made of reinforced concrete at least six inches thick or brick at least eight inches thick.

A minimum thickness of eight inches is recommended for the outside wall of a chimney exposed to the weather. Brick chimneys that extend through the roof may sway enough in heavy winds to open up mortar joints at the roof line. Openings to the flue at that point are dangerous, because sparks from the flue may start fires in the woodwork or roofing. A good practice is to make the upper walls eight inches thick by starting to offset the bricks at least six inches below the underside of roof joists or rafters. Keep T.V. antennas off the chimney.

Chimneys may contain more than one flue. Building codes generally require a separate flue for each fireplace, furnace, or boiler. If a chimney contains three or more lined flues, each group of two flues must be separated from the other single flue or group of two flues by brick divisions or wythes at least three and three-quarter inches thick.

No wood should be in contact with the chimney. Leave a two-inch space between the chimney walls and all wooden beams or joists unless the walls are of solid masonry eight inches thick, in which case the framing can be within one-half inch of the chimney masonry.

The Fireplace. All fireplaces are constructed in much the same way, regardless of design. But check for proper proportion to get a good draft.

The fireplace's position in the room should be coordinated with the location of the chimney so as not to spoil the exterior appearance of the house. A fireplace should harmonize in detail and proportion with the room in which it is, but safety and utility should not be sacrificed for appearance.

Metal fireplaces. Modified fireplaces are manufactured fireplace units. They are made of heavy metal and designed to be set in place and concealed by the usual brickwork or other construction. Because the correctly designed and proportioned firebox provides a ready-made form for the masonry, there is less chance of faulty construction and more chance of a smokeless fireplace.

Properly installed, well-designed units heat more efficiently than ordinary fireplaces. They circulate heat into the corners of rooms and can deliver heated air through ducts to upper and adjoining rooms. However, the metal lining of a modified fireplace may eventually rust out, and the advantage of circulating heated air through registers may then be reduced or lost.

Prefabricated fireplaces. Prefabricated fireplace and chimney units, which contain all parts needed for a complete fireplace-to-chimney installation, are on the market. The basic part of the prefabricated fireplace is a specially insulated metal firebox shell. Since it is light in weight, it can be set directly on the floor without the heavy footing required for masonry fireplaces. Prefabricated metal fireplaces and chimneys should be labeled as approved by the Underwriters' Laboratories (UL) and installed as specified by the instructions. Prefabricated fireplaces cost less than masonry fireplaces but they may be less durable. Metal fireplaces are available in black or colored finishes, and in varying sizes and shapes.

Wood stoves. Getting the most heat out of a conventional fireplace is difficult. Living room fireplaces today often create a net heat loss, using more fossil fuel—heated room air for draft—than they throw wood heat into the room. With the recent boom in wood heat interest, it seems that everyone with a welding outfit is coming out with some sort of patented fireplace grate, but few are worth much, and no conventional fireplace will hold a fire overnight.

To really heat, a fireplace should be a high, massive ceramic heat storer holding a great bed of coals and ashes. The "Rumford," as detailed in several references, is the best design. More efficient still are wood stoves. Several good designs are out that hook up to a conventional fireplace, using the existing flue and damper system.

Most efficient of all are free-standing stoves that expose all sides to room air. Located as near the center of your house as possible, they act as passive hot air circulators. Warmth radiates out from all sides. The warm air rises, moves through the living spaces, and returns cooler air along the floor. Many other new stoves are coming out now, too, but selection of type and model takes some careful thought.

For really serious home heat, you want a heavy cast iron, ceramic, or welded steel and firebrick stove that is air-tight. When doors are closed, there should not be a crack between the air inlet and the top of the flue. That way, with damper and draft, you can control precisely the amount of oxygen getting to your wood, and thus control the amount of heat produced. Air-tights are great creosote-producers, but some brands have been a bit oversold in ads, so be sure to read up on stoves before you buy. Then get competent advice or service in installing and operating it. Use the same care in selecting and using your wood-burning appliance as you do in buying any expensive appliance.

PROBLEMS AND SOLUTIONS

The Chimney.

Chimney fire. When soft wood or cannel coal is burned in a fireplace for a long period, soot will accumulate inside the flue. Occasionally, under prolonged heat, the soot may ignite and an intensely hot "chimney fire" will result until the carbon is burned away. The roar of the fire and the flames which belch out of the top of the chimney will cause alarm, but are usually not harmful to chimneys in good condition. However, nearby roofs should be inspected for live sparks and the attic inspected for any overheating *immediately*. Large amounts of salt thrown on the fire in the grate or fireplace will extinguish a chimney fire.

A fire in a fireplace can be checked in its intensity, or extinguished by first quenching the fire on the hearth and then holding a wet rug or blanket over the opening to shut off the air.

Sparks. Some fuels, such as sawdust, burning paper, and other trash, emit sparks when burned. To limit the possibility of setting the house on fire, a metal spark arrester should be installed on the chimney top. Arresters may be required when chimneys are on or near combustible roofs, woodland, lumber, or other combustible materials. They are not recommended when burning soft coal, because they may become plugged with soot. Spark arresters do not entirely eliminate the discharge of sparks, but if properly built and installed, they greatly reduce the hazard. They should be made of rust-resistant material and should have screen openings not larger than five-eighths of an inch nor smaller than five-sixteenths of an inch.

Creosote deposits. Creosote may form in chimneys, especially when wood is burned and in cold weather. When it ignites, it makes a hot fire which may crack the masonry and char adjacent timbers. It is very hard to remove. The only safe method is to chip it from the masonry with a blade, and you must be careful not to knock out mortar joints or damage the flue lining.

Downdrafts. A chimney, especially on an outside wall, may be so cold prior to the start of a fire that a downdraft exists. Therefore, before starting a fire, crumpled newspapers placed at the fireplace damper level should be ignited to warm the chimney and induce an updraft. Rain hoods are used to keep rain out of chimneys and to prevent downdraft due to nearby buildings, trees, or other objects. Common types are the arched brick hood and the flat-stone or cast concrete cap. If the hood covers more than one flue, it should be divided by wythes so that each flue has a separate section. The area of the hood opening for each flue must be larger than the area of the flue.

The Fireplace.

Wood ignition. Dry wood has an ignition temperature as low as 250° F. At no point should the wood structure of the house come in contact with the hot surfaces of the chimney or fireplace. Prefabricated fireplaces are available which can be installed with zero clearance. Suitable screens in front of fireplaces minimize the danger of brands and sparks.

Hot surfaces. Hoods and canopies, as well as screens and glass fronts, can become hot from the fire. Children should be specifically warned of this hazard.

Flash fire. Do not burn old Christmas trees, holly wreaths, cardboard boxes, excelsior, or other highly flammable materials which can make a flash fire far beyond the capacity of the fireplace. Charcoal lighter fluids, kerosene, or gasoline should never be used in the fireplace.

Smoking fireplace. Fireplaces may operate well most of the time, but smoke on occasion. This may occur when the wind is from a particular direction or is gusty. A fireplace that smokes should be examined to make certain that the essential requirements of construction have been fulfilled. If it is clear that the chimney is not stopped up with fallen brick, and the mortar joints are not loose, several simple corrective measures should be tried before drastic solutions considered. It takes a lot of air to make a good draft in a chimney. In tightly built homes, it may be necessary to open a window an inch or so to supply air for the fireplace. You can also use an outside air duct to the hearth. A chimney, especially on an outside wall, may be so cold prior to the start of a fire that a downdraft exists. The fire should be started with a small amount of dry tinder at the back of the hearth until the chimney is well-heated. The amount of combustible material in the fireplace should not be too great at any time.

The flue area should not be less than one-twelfth of the area of the fireplace opening. To determine whether the fireplace opening is in correct proportion to the flue area, hold a piece of sheet metal across the top of the fireplace opening and then gradually lower it, making the opening smaller until smoke ceases to enter the room. Mark the lower edge of the sides of the fireplace. The opening may then be reduced by building a metal shield or hood across the top so that its lower edge is at the marks made during the test. Another way to reduce the opening is to raise the hearth by laying one or two courses of brick over the old hearth. The sides may be made narrower where further reductions are necessary.

Another cause for smokiness is lack of ventilation for the interior. New caulking and weatherstripping techniques now can make a house so tight that there are few air inlets to provide air for drafts such as fires need; the result is that the unlighted fireplace becomes an inlet for outdoor air necessary to fuel burning equipment needing oxygen. Then, when the fireplace is lighted, the draft down the chimney is likely to drive smoke into the room. Opening a window an inch or two may let in enough oxygen so the fire will burn satisfactorily.

Occasionally a fireplace smokes all the time because of too small a flue. Some remedies for this include decreasing the fireplace opening by raising the back hearth; installing a canopy hood; raising the chimney height to 20 feet to increase the draft; installing a draft inducer to deflect downdrafts; and trimming the tall trees.

When no other remedy works, consider a fan that forces air up the chimney.

USE OF FIREPLACES

Fuels. Fuels and their present and predicted availability are of importance as you make a choice of supplemental heating. Plan to use the fuel which is now most readily available and which will probably be available for a long period of time. Wood, coal, and natural gas can be burned in fireplaces, Franklin stoves, and circulator heaters. These fuels, liquified petroleum gas, and fuel oil can be burned on circulator heaters. Pound for pound, dry, heavy hardwoods have about half the heating value of coal and a third the heating value of oil.

Kindling the Fire. You can become an expert fireplace manager, and here's how.

Lay a fire carefully. For kindling, use a few small branches with the bark cut into curls along the sides. Lay medium-sized pieces of wood above the kindling and a few larger pieces of wood on top of the fire. Lay the fire toward the center and back of the fireplace, leaving space for air to circulate around and between the wood.

Place a tightly rolled and tied piece of paper in among the kindling and light it. In cold weather, you may want to light one end of a rolled paper and hold it, with extreme care, just below the open damper in the top of the firebox. Hold it there a few seconds to warm the flue so that it will draw well. Then tuck the lighted paper in among the kindling at the base of the fire. Close the fire screen quickly. Fan the blaze gently, if necessary, until the wood burns readily.

A fireplace fire requires about five times as much air as is needed for liberal ventilation, in order to keep burning. You may need to open a window slightly to bring in enough fresh air to keep the fire going, if your house is insulated and completely weatherstripped. To keep smoke from entering the room, turn off kitchen and bathroom exhaust fans and close registers of forced air heating systems which are near the fireplace.

After the fire is started, adjust the damper to control the draft, so that there is enough to keep the fire burning but the amount of heat escaping up the chimney is kept at a minimum. Fireplaces are only about 15% efficient. Use only enough fuel to keep the fire as hot as you need. The heated firebox will reflect heat and glowing coals add comfort.

INSPECTION AND MAINTENANCE

The Chimney. Along with their beauty, pleasure, and comfort, fireplaces may have hazards and shortcomings. However, proper inspection and maintenance can eliminate many unnecessary problems and repairs.

Chimneys should be checked every fall for defects. A routine inspection should include the following items.

If there is an outside chimney, check to be sure it is snug against the side of the house. Cracks developing between the chimney and house could indicate serious structural trouble, or they could be caused by pressure from a TV antenna. Sometimes the only remedy available is to anchor the chimney to the house with large "U" bolts and then caulk the separation.

The chimney exterior should be examined to determine the soundness of the mortar joints. If mortar crumbles, leaving openings in the joints, host gases can creep into the house and cause possible suffocation or fire.

Build a very small fire in the fireplace and cover the top of the chimney. Use chalk to mark mortar joints where smoke seeps from the chimney. Point up the mortar joints and replace broken, eroded, or porous stones and bricks.

Check the top of the chimney to be sure the cement cap is sound. If there are water stains in the fireplace hearth, then consider installing a flue cap of slate. Check inside the chimney for broken flue linings and examine flashings for evidence of rust, corrosion, or open joints. Without a lining in good condition, the fireplace may not be safe, and the cost of a new lining is prohibitive. A good chimney cap screen is also essential to keep out leaves, squirrels, and birds.

Check inside the hearth and smoke chamber for loose brick and mortar.

Inspect the mortar around the firebricks and grout them, if necessary.

Go into the cellar under the hearth and check that the brick or cement arch that supports the hearth of the fireplace is in place and secure.

Check flues to make sure they are in good condition at all times.

Check for any water problem in ash cleanout.

Cleaning.   A wood burning fireplace requires little maintenance and no repair. The main job is to occasionally clean the flue. *Cleaning* of a chimney is needed every three or four years, particularly if you have oil heat. If you use gas as a fuel, it is a wise precaution to have the gas company check the cleanliness and drawing powers of the flue. Once a chimney becomes clogged with soot, there is a dangerous possibility of a back flow of flue gases into the home. Certain chemical compounds may be used in the removal of soot deposits from the chimney. Metallic chlorides, which are vaporized by a hot fire and then deposited on the surface of the soot to lower its ignition temperature, are one possible method of treatment. Common rock salt is not the most effective remover, but it is widely used because it is cheap, readily available, and easy to handle. Use two or three cupfuls per application.

If there is not too great an offset in the chimney, you can dislodge soot and loose material by pulling a weighted sack of straw up and down in the flue. Remember to seal the front of a fireplace when cleaning the flue to keep soot out of the room. Be sure to also clean out the ash pit. Never use the ash pit to get rid of hot coals as these may cause a fire when they hit the cellar through an inadvertently open flue door.

If the inspection shows defects that cannot be readily repaired or reached for repair, you should tear the masonry down and rebuild properly. Do not use the old bricks that have been impregnated with soot and creosote in the new work, because they will stain plaster whenever dampness occurs. Soot and creosote stains are almost impossible to remove.

The Fireplace.   Some things you can check yourself. Look for evidence of recent use. An exceptionally clean fireplace might mean that it can't be used. Check for loose bricks or a cracked iron lining in the firebox. Make sure the damper operates properly.

SUMMARY

When you are buying a resale home, it is a good decision to have the fireplace examined and inspected. If you want a fireplace in your new home, than have your architect offer his experience and skill as to proportion, size, location, and design of the fireplace so that it is in harmony with the room and fulfills its requirements. If you are having problems with smoking or poor heat, try some of the suggestions in this chapter.

Lastly, keep the flue clean to avoid fires, and grout all loose mortar.

REFERENCE: *Fireplaces and Chimneys,* Farmers Bulletin #1889, U.S. Department of Agriculture, 1971, Catalog A 1.9:1889/7.

24.
Termites and Other Wood-Destroying Insects

INTRODUCTION

Wood-destroying insects and fungi cause damage to a house, and early detection of pests and decay may help homeowners avoid expensive repairs. This chapter discusses control, inspection, and treatment of pests.

If you are buying a resale house, the mortgage company may require a termite inspection and treatment before they issue a mortgage. Be certain there is a contractual understanding between you and the seller as to who will pay for the termite inspection and who will correct any damage. Custom differs in many states. If your new home is financed through an FHA-insured mortgage and is located in a termite-prone area, HUD requires protective measures against termite infestation.

The initial damage from termites is usually minor and rarely affects structural integrity. However, if termites go undetected, they can cause extenside damage. Therefore, your home should be inspected yearly for signs of termites or other wood pests. Remember that although chemical treatment can be effective for ten years, you must not stop periodically inspecting.

TECHNICAL INFORMATION

Termite Identification. Winged ants are sometimes mistaken for swarming termites. The true termite has a pear-shaped body, while the ant has a narrow, wasp-like waist. Termites have paddle-shaped wings of equal length, while ants have front wings that are longer than their hind wings.

Reproductive termites have yellow-brown to black bodies and two pairs of long, white, opaque wings of equal size. They swarm from their colony in groups, most frequently after a rain on the first warm day of spring. They may, however, take flight during the summer or fall in warmer parts of the country. In heated buildings, flights may occur even in winter. Attracted by strong light, the swarming termites gather about windows and doors when they emerge within buildings.

When the swarm alights, the termites shed their wings. They are poor fliers and cover only short distances. A pile of discarded wings indicates a well-established colony nearby.

Termite Varieties and Typical Damage.

Damp wood termites. These pests occur in southern Florida, the Southwestern states, and along the Pacific Coast. Preferring damp wood, they rarely damage houses but may be found in house construction where wet lumber is used.

Drywood termites. This variety is found in a narrow strip along the Atlantic Coast from Cape Henry, Virginia to the Florida Keys, westward along the coast of the Gulf of Mexico to the Pacific Coast and into northern California. There also is a local infestation in Tacoma, Washington. Drywood termites are a serious problem in parts of the tropics, including Puerto Rico and Hawaii.

Distinguished by a reddish head, blackish body, and four wings of the same size, reproductive drywood termites may swarm several times a year. Their presence indicates a nearby colony.

Damage is indicated by clean cavities cut across the grain in solid dry wood. The cavities may contain slightly compressed pellets of partially digested wood resembling coarse sand and sawdust. Telltale piles of pellets accumulate under the push-out holes through which the termites clear their galleries or work areas.

Subterranean termites. These are the most destructuve of all wood-destroying insects in the United States. They heavily infest California, the Mississippi and Ohio River valleys, and the southern United States in an area roughly encompassing South Carolina, Georgia, Alabama, Mississippi, Louisiana, Florida, and eastern Texas. Other parts of the United States experience moderate to slight infestation. Hawaii and Puerto Rico are heavily infested, while Alaska has no termite activity.

Damage may not be noticeable on wood surfaces because termites avoid exposure to air by constructing galleries within the material they attack. Tunnels may be seen along the grain of the wood and specks of excrement may appear on the walls of galleries when the exterior surface of a timber is stripped away. Often, the wood is completely honeycombed, leaving little more than a thin shell.

When the subterranean termites cannot gain direct access to wood from the soil, they build tubes of earth and partly digested wood, crossing such obstacles as concrete or brick foundation walls and even the "termite shields" provided by some builders.

INSPECTING FOR TERMITES

It is a good idea to call in a professional to check out your home for termite infestation. However, you can order Department of Agriculture publications from your County Agriculture Agent and, with some study, do the inspection yourself. The required inspection tools include a flashlight, a step ladder, a long screw driver, a sharp, pointed probing tool or knife, and a small hammer.

Symptoms.　There are three common signs that indicate a termite infestation. One is the presence of swarms of winged termites. Another is the discovery of one or more shelter mud tubes going up the wall or under wooden sills or wool carpets. The third sign is wood that collapses easily when probed with an ice pick, pocket knife, or screw driver, or when tapped with a hammer.

Where and How to Look.　Start to inspect those areas where termites gain easy access, such as grade level entrances, garages, exterior stairs, and places where siding touches the ground. Examine exterior foundation walls and crawl spaces for termite tubes, while using a hammer to sound walls, sills, and frames for damage. A dead sound indicates decay; a hollow sound indicates possible termite damage. With a sharp instrument like a screw driver or knife, probe exposed wood posts, landings, stairways, entrance door frames and thresholds, garage sills and studs, and any areas where wood touches the ground.

In the basement, you should check the sump pit, the intersection of floor slab with chimney and foundation, areas where pipes penetrate the foundation, and stair carriages where joints contact foundation wall or floor slab.

If your house is built on a slab or with part of the basement finished, termites may enter behind furred walls undetected. You should look for piles of wood dust sifted down beside baseboards or for bulging or loose wall board finish. Examine areas under heating elements for wood dust or partly digested wood. Slab houses are especially vulnerable to termite attack. Check bathroom partitions and flooring around toilets where water leaks and condensation may cause decay and attract termites.

Carefully inspect for sloping floors, doors that won't close, windows out of plumb, and roof lines that are not level. Then pay particular attention to girders and other structural members, which, if damaged, will cause settling. Check floor joints and sills or beams on the foundation where flashing is missing. Even the attic should be checked in older homes and in southern climates, where flying drywood termites abound.

If you are inspecting with an eye to purchasing, look for signs of recent termite treatment as small covered holes about the size of dimes. You will find them in the walks or patios about 18 to 24 inches apart, inside the basement concrete floor next to a wall (and in the wall if it is hollow), and in the wood sills. These holes are drilled for the chemical poison injection. Some firms do not drill the sill but instead pressure-apply the treatment.

SOLUTIONS

The rate at which damage proceeds is extremely variable, but it is usually comparatively slow. This means that no one should feel compelled to rush into a job of termite control before taking sufficient time to study the matter thoroughly. Buildings not supplied with heat during the winter months are very rarely subject to serious termite attack. Termite colonies also vary considerably in colony strength, which directly influences the rate and extent of damage.

Structural Modification.   As a first step in the control of an established infestation, the building should be carefully examined to locate all construction factors making the building susceptible to attack. Each factor should be studied to determine whether it might be structurally modified to reduce susceptibility to termites. An example of such structural modification might be the providing of ventilation in enclosed cellar or crawl space areas or other areas not provided with full cellar excavation. Be sure to remove any lumber from such places. Window wells around casement windows which serve to lower the soil level around cellar window frames, also reduce termite susceptibility and aid in control.

Insecticides.   The second step in control is the installation of chemical soil insecticides as barriers to the passage of termites to and from the soil adjacent to the building. Since termites cannot successfully attack a building unless they can pass from the soil to the wood and back again, sound termite control depends upon eliminating that freedom of passage. If this is done, the termites in the soil are prevented from attacking the wood of the building, while those trapped in the building will die from lack of moisture.

Almost all firms guarantee soil treatments for one year. Extensive testing by government experts and others, however, indicates that recommended chemicals currently in use actually are effective for ten years or longer.

OTHER COMMON PESTS AND THEIR TREATMENT

Carpenter Ants.   Next to termites, the most common menace to the wood members of your house is the hardy species of North American ants called carpenter ants. Carpenter ants, usually black, vary in size from one-quarter inch to three-quarters of an inch. They are equipped with especially strong pinchers which serve them well when chiseling through wood. Unlike termites, which devour wood, carpenter ants thrive on a relatively sweet diet. Their tunneling and chiseling is not carried out for food, but rather as a way of establishing a nest from which they can seek sweets. The number of ants in a colony will vary from a few, in a newly established nest, to many thousands in an older one.

All types of buildings are fair game for carpenter ants but their favorite targets are houses without basements or with partial basements, low foundation structures, and porches. The presence of an occasional ant is not cause for concern, but if you often see numbers of ants, you should look for damage. A telltale sign is the discovery of piles of discarded wood fragments. Carpenter ants hibernate in wood, sometimes infesting stacked fire logs. Avoid bringing infested logs indoors until you are ready to burn them; otherwise the revived ants will scatter throughout the house. Chlordane is the usual control method. Check for other recommended chemicals.

Powder-Post Beetles.   These pests infest hardwood flooring, leaving an accumulation of fine dust and powder around a hole in the wood. A spray insecticide will control them in most cases, although serious damage may necessitate fumigation by a pest-control company. With a little sanding, cutting, filling with plastic wood, and repainting, the damaged structures can be made to look almost as if they were new.

Carpenter Bees.   These insects are more an annoyance than a real threat to the structure of a house. They drill through wood to form tunnels in which they store food and lay eggs.

Flat-Headed Borers.   These insects complete a life cycle in one or two years but may live 30 or 40 years before emerging from infested wood. Larvae of three or four years old are found in the woodwork of buildings standing for only one or two years, indicating that stored lumber is a source of infestation.

   The borer leaves an elliptical, tunneled imperfection in wood. Tunneling is done by larvae of all kinds and by adults of some species of borer. This pest does not re-infest seasoned lumber; therefore, treatment is usually unnecessary when infestation is found in existing construction.

MAINTENANCE TIPS

The best way to control termites is to build a house so they can't get in. The following are some factors to consider.

Termite Shields.   Metal sheets, properly joined and shaped and placed between the top of the foundation and the sills, have been a means of termite protection. When correctly designed and installed, these shields will give as complete protection as can be had, provided other construction features of the building do not allow the termites to enter. The basic principle of the shield is to force the termites to come to the surface of the masonry where their mud tubes can be seen. Unfortunately, the shields are usually poorly applied.

Door Frames.   Doors leading to cellars from outside stairways and garage door frames in houses built with attached garages are frequent sources of trouble. Do not extend frames into or through concrete, and use factory-treated wood in all construction touching the floor.

Wood Construction in Basement or Cellar. The use of wood in finishing basement areas usually creates conditions highly favorable to termites. Wooden floors are particularly subject to attack, and noncellulose tile or other such flooring material should be used. In constructing sidewalls, all furring strips, door frames, partition studs, and similar members should be made from factory-treated lumber. No wood member of any kind should extend through the basement or cellar floor.

Slab Construction Homes. Modern slab construction homes having wood partition walls are subject to termite attack as a result of termite penetration through cracks in the slab, plumbing, and other utility holes in the slab, or through expansion joints. If the house is built on a slab, the slab should be either of the monolithic or suspended type, and the top should be at least eight inches above grade. The siding should not come within six inches of the ground.

Wooden Porches and Steps. The bottom step should rest on a concrete base projecting at least six inches above the soil. Porch support should rest on similar bases. Lattice work under a porch should not come in contact with the soil.

Cellar or Basement Windows. To prevent infestation, use metal frames or factory-treated wooden cellar window frames.

Presence of Wood in the Soil and Near the House. All stumps, branches, and other wood debris should be removed from the site before construction is started. This helps to destroy colonies already established at the building site.

Wood Buried in the Fill Around the Foundation Walls. Avoid burying scrap lumber and form boards, inside as well as out. Never leave scrap lumber under building or porches.

Excessive Soil Moisture. The outside soil level should be kept at least six inches below all woodwork, and adequate provision should be made to remove rain water. Drainage tile properly installed around the outside of foundation footings is also an advantage. Leaky, defective plumbing is sometimes a contributing factor in termite infestation.

Easily Penetrated Foundations. Walls constructed of stone, hollow concrete block, hollow tile, or brick often develop cracks through which the termite can pass.

Insufficient Clearance Between Floor Joists and Soil Under Unexcavated Part.   A minimum space of 18 inches should be observed at all points. Never allow wood to remain in such places. Plenty of cross ventilation should be provided in crawl spaces.

Earth-Filled or Masonry Porches and Steps.   A major cause of termite attack on residences is this type of construction. As usually employed, soil or masonry is placed in contact with the wood of the house (door saddles, sills, joist, sheathing, etc.), providing ideal conditions for termite entry.

SUMMARY

Homeowners and buyers should be alert to the inspection and control of wood pests. Your local County Agricultural Agent has numerous bulletins on wood pests, and he is available for consultation.

Local infestation control companies offer yearly inspections and guarantees against infestation. Whether you "do it youself" or hire a company, be certain to be alert to wood pests.

25.
Wood Rot, Mold,
and Fungus

INTRODUCTION

In properly designed houses that are well-built and well-maintained, decay causes little damage and most damage can be avoided. Prevention is cheap; cure is sometimes costly. Wood decay is caused by minute plants called fungi, visible when many of them occur together. Some fungi merely discolor the wood, but decay fungi destroy the fibers. Decay must take place under moist conditions and in wet wood, but it may be found dry in the final stages. Dry rot is a misnomer. Mold is a growth of minute fungi that will form on vegetable or animal matter and is associated with decay. Odor usually accompanies mold and decay.

The purpose of this chapter is to help you recognize the signs of wood decay and aid you in preventing their reoccurrence.

TECHNICAL INFORMATION

Molds and Fungus.   Mildew is a growth produced on the surface of different materials by molds. Molds are simple plants belonging to the group known as fungi. Molds that cause mildew grow on anything that will provide food, such as cotton, linen, silk, wool, leather, and paper. Many man-made fibers are resistant to mildew. Mildew flourishes in cellars, crawl spaces, clothing closets, and other spaces that are damp and warm and have poor air circulation. Under these conditions, mold can grow on the inside and outside of your home. Mildew is most often on the north side of a house where the sun seldom shines. It occurs on roofs, siding, and foundation. Molds are also likely to grow in a newly-built house because of moisture in the building materials.

As the molds grow, they cause damage. They discolor fabrics and affect them so severely that the fabrics rot and fall apart. Mildew is not easy to recognize and is often mistaken for dirt. The color may be green, red, purple, gray, or white. The homeowner who paints over mildew will soon have his new paint job ruined. One way to determine if a mildew problem exists is to simply wash the affected area with an ordinary household bleach. If the blotches on the house begin to lighten in color in about two minutes, the condition is mildew. Dirt will not be affected by the bleach. Musty odors are a sure sign of mildew growth before any mold is visible. By removing the moist conditions causing the odor, you may prevent further damaging mold growth.

Wood Rot.   Wood decay is caused by airborne spores, which produce minute plant-like growths called fungi, consisting of many microscopic threads. Fungi work in damp wood to cause decay. White decay fungi are usually caused by improper ventilation, inadequate flashing, vapor barriers, or surface sealant. Brown decay causes wood fibers to shrink, crack, and crumble. Fungi spread from moist soil or wood into dry wood by conducting water to wood through vinelike structures. Occasionally, they cause great damage to buildings, but fortunately most fungi cannot conduct moisture in this way.

Serious decay damage can be caused by one or more errors in construction or maintenance: undrained soil and insufficient ventilation under crawl spaces; wood such as grade stakes, concrete forms, or stumps buried in the soil under houses; wooden structural members in direct contact with the soil; the use of unseasoned and infected lumber; the use of sheathing paper that is not a good moisture barrier; no flashing at windows, doors, and roof edges; inadequate paint maintenance; no rain gutters and leaders; poorly ventilated attics; and leaks in roofs, piping, kitchen appliances, and bathrooms.

Decay is evident behind painted surfaces when a light tap on the suspected area with the handle of a screwdriver or knife produces a dead sound. Usually the painted surface will be severely checked at the decayed area. Odor and stains are also an indication of decay.

CONTROLLING DECAY AND MOLD

Dry rot can turn beams and joists into masses of powder that won't support your home. Try to control causes of dampness. Otherwise, mold spores, usually present in the air, will settle on articles and have ideal conditions for growth. Properly installed air conditioning systems remove moisture from the air by taking up warm air, cooling it, and circulating the cool air back into the room. In non-air conditioned homes and in those having no air conditioning in the basement, mechanical dehumidifiers are useful. A humidistat can be attached to the unit to control the humidity in a room. Drain the condensate into a sump or a sink. When using air conditioners or dehumidifiers, keep windows and doors closed. If necessary, you can get rid of the dampness by heating the house for a short time. Then open doors and windows to let the moisture-laden air out. An exhaust fan may be used to force it out.

Proper ventilation is the renewing and circulation of air. These air movements are of great importance in removing excess moisture. When the air outside is dry, ventilation allows the dry air to enter, take up excess moisture, and be carried outside. When natural breezes are not sufficient, electric fans can be used. They should be of the proper type and size to do a specific job. Chemicals that absorb moisture, such as silica gel, activated alumina, or calcium chloride, may be used to absorb moisture from the air. They are not too effective in a large space.

To get rid of mildew, mix together three ounces of trisodium phosphate (TSP); one ounce of a powder detergent; one quart of household bleach; and three quarts of warm water. This will provide you with a gallon of a solution that will remove mildew. Scrub the affected area thoroughly with a bristle brush, and follow the scrubbing with a rinsing of clear water. It may be necessary to repeat this a few times.

To eliminate musty odors on cement floors, bathroom floors, and tiled walls, scrub with a dilute chlorine bleach solution: one cup of liquid chlorine bleach to a gallon of water. Rinse with clear water and wipe dry. Keep windows open until walls and floors are thoroughly dry. On other washable surfaces such as wood and asphalt tiles, scrub with a solution of trisodium phosphate (four to six tablespoons to a gallon of water) and then rinse and dry thoroughly.

If the house has a wood porch or steps, replacement of decayed boards or bases of pillars should be made with treated or decay-resistant wood. Protect the lower part of the structure from coming in contact with moisture. Use kiln-dried wood and build in a way that will keep wood dry most of the time. Fungi will grow in wood only when it contains more than 20% moisture—so keep moisture away.

In crawl spaces, keep all vents open for natural cross air circulation.

Place a vapor-resistant cover over the ground or cement slab. This will stop moisture vapor from rising. Then insulate the ceiling joists in the crawl space with the vapor barrier toward the ground. Grade away from the foundation so rain water will not collect there. In some very wet areas, a sump pump may be needed to keep the space dry.

Seal all roof, vent, chimney, window, and door flashings periodically. Minor house settlement will cause these flashings to leak unless they are sealed. Decay in trim framing, rafters, windows, or door frames often means that flashings are leaking or that more flashing is needed. If cracks open up so that water runs into them, use a caulking gun to fill the voids.

Good foundation drainage will prevent water penetration. Moist building sites should be well-drained. The soil surface should slope away from the house at a 15° angle for three feet and downspouts should discharge into drains, masonry gutters, or splash blocks that lead the water away from the house. Dense shrubbery or vines planted too close to the house can interfere with drainage and air movement and thus promote fungus growth.

If you are going to use wood in exposed joists and bases of uprights and columns, then be sure they are treated with water-repellent preservatives. Set all columns on concrete or steel pads set above the ground level. Be sure water will not lay on the wood but will drain away properly.

INSPECTION AND MAINTENANCE

Chapter 33 includes a preventive maintenance checklist. As part of this periodic inspection, you should be checking for mold, decay, and fungus. Chapter 26 discusses condensation and moisture problems that bear directly on rot and molds.

In mid-winter, examine attics for condensation, moisture, or frost accumulation and decay, especially at the eave level at the north side of the house. If paint failures are especially troublesome on the north wall or dark stains develop from moisture seeping out from under the siding, it may indicate moisture condensation in the walls. Attic condensation difficulties can be corrected easily by increased ventilation and proper roof drainage.

Do not build with infected lumber that is wet. Lumber becomes dangerous if it is stored so that it cannot dry. During construction, store lumber off the ground, protect it from rain, and allow air to circulate between the boards. Use only seasoned and sound lumber. Compared with green lumber, it has better nail-holding capacity, it shrinks and warps less, and it is safer from decay. The west coast uses a great deal of green lumber.

Chemical treatment against decay is especially likely to repay its cost for porches, outside steps, and railings made of wood of low natural durability. Allow no wood to be in contact with the soil unless the wood is thoroughly impregnated with a suitable preservative. Protect wood posts resting on concrete floors from floor moisture by placing them on raised concrete bases or by using treated or naturally durable wood.

Window sash may discolor or decay, especially in the colder climates where water condenses on the inside of the glass in winter and runs down into the wood and surrounding plaster. Storm sash is effective in decreasing such condensation. Keep the humidity level low and adjust it as the temperature changes.

Paint is not a preservative. However, it helps prevent decay by protecting wood from intermittent wetting, especially if applied to ends and edges as well as to exposed faces, and if it is maintained so as to allow the fewest possible cracks at joints. When applied to wood that is not seasoned, it may favor decay by hindering further drying. Design the construction, wherever possible, to shed rain water. Overhanging roofs and proper flashings help to protect woodwork. Some decay is to be expected in porch steps, floors, railings, or pillars exposed to rain. This, however, can be much delayed by good maintenance.

Keep closets, dresser drawers, basements, and any place where mildew is likely to grow as clean as possible. Soil on articles can supply sufficient food for mildew to start growing when moisture and temperatures are right. Greasy films, such as those that form on kitchen walls, also contain many nutrients for mildew organisms. Don't give the mold growth a chance to weaken or rot the material: remove mildew spots as soon as they are discovered. Sun and air fabrics thoroughly. If any mildew spots remain, wash at once with soap or detergent and water. Rinse well and dry in the sun. If any stain remains, use bleach, but first test colored fabrics for colorfastness to the bleach.

Dampness in a basement is often caused by condensation of warm, moist air on cooler surfaces. Excessive moisture may indicate that outside drainage is not adequate. Replace cracked or defective mortar, clean the walls, and apply a waterproof paint.

In damp summer weather, keep papers and books as dry as possible to help control mold growth. To protect leather against mildew, treat with low-pressure aerosol formulations that carry specific directions. Never let clothing or other fabric articles lie around damp or wet. Dry soiled clothes before putting them into the hamper. If clothing or household textiles are not treated with a mildew-resistant finish, be sure to wash or dry-clean them before sorting, as soiled articles are more likely to mildew than clean ones.

Indoor wood surfaces covered with enamel or oil-resin paint rarely mildew unless conditions are very favorable to mold growth. Softer paints on outdoor surfaces mildew more readily. Molds feed on the oil and minerals in the paint and cause a dirty-looking discoloration. They may penetrate the paint film deeply, even to the underlying wood. Buy paint that has a mildew additive. If your paint dealer doesn't have a mildew-resistant paint of the color you desire, you can add a mildew-cide to any kind of paint. It will make a non-mildew-resistant paint mildew-proof.

SUMMARY

No house will stand neglect for long. A building frequently requires correction or compensation for the shortcomings in the original construction and for normal aging, settlement, and neglect. Inspection and continued care are needed. Excessive moisture, poor construction, and inadequate ventilation produce wood rot, mold, and fungus. Preventive maintenance will correct and prevent these conditions.

26.
Condensation and
Moisture Problems

INTRODUCTION

Did you know that water is the cause of more premature failure and deterioration in your home than any other single factor? The penetration of water into your home, as vapor, liquid, or ice, can cause paint failure, discoloration, decay, foundation failure, termites, and many other serious problems.

Many older homes are in need of improvement because excessive moisture and condensation have caused decay and unsightly deterioration. A knowledge of ventilation requirements has made it easy and inexpensive to reduce moisture problems in most homes. The purpose of this chapter is to help you understand the cause of moisture problems and to suggest steps to be taken to eliminate excessive moisture conditions in your home.

TECHNICAL INFORMATION AND POTENTIAL PROBLEMS

Condensation.   Over 95% of the buildings I've inspected have had a moisture and condensation problem. Water can come from the exterior as rain or snow, from below the house as either liquid or vapor, or from within the house as vapor produced by family activities. It is important that the house be checked thoroughly for all symptoms of moisture damage, that the causes be corrected, and the damage be repaired. In some cases, water leaks are the cause of this trouble, but generally, problems are due to condensation of excessive moisture in the air. Condensation can be described as the change in moisture from a vapor to a liquid. Water vapor within the house, when unrestricted, can move through the walls and ceilings during the heating season to a cold surface where it condenses, collecting generally in the form of ice or frost. Later it will cause rot, mold, and decay.

The effects of condensation may be seen as damp spots on ceilings and inside surfaces of exterior walls; water and ice on inside surfaces of windows; moisture and stains on basement side walls and floors; severe rusting of metal parts in the basement; water filled blisters on outside paint surfaces; white salt crystals, called efflorescence, on the inside of basement walls; black mold at the base of walls; and marbles of ice on attic floors or rafters.

Solutions.   Reducing high relative humidities within the house to permissible levels is often necessary to minimize condensation problems. Discontinue the use of room-size humidifiers or reduce the output of automatic humidifiers until conditions are improved. Use exhaust fans and dehumidifiers to eliminate high relative humidities within the house. Where possible, decrease the activities that produce excessive moisture.

Water vapor moving through the walls and ceilings can create major maintenance problems and make frequent repainting necessary. Properly installed wall and ceiling vapor barriers and the proper use of insulation and ventilation can avoid most of these difficulties. The way to get rid of moisture once it is in the house is to ventilate. Do this a few minutes in the morning and at night, especially on those dry days during the winter season. There are several ways of properly ventilating—by ridge ventilators, louvers, pipe stacks, fans, or a combination of several methods. The kind of ventilation your home requires depends on the specific situation you face. If bathrooms and kitchens are poorly ventilated, you can use wall ventilators or a pipe stack, or you can put a fan in a hood, ceiling, or wall. One air change per minute is recommended. Be especially careful in a tight, all-electric heated house.

If you have a flat roof or shed roof house and it has an attic, then it too should be ventilated. Small under-eave ventilators will help remove hot air, especially if accompanied by a fan. The air circulation will keep the attic cool as well and prevent temperatures rising to over 160°. These temperatures can buckle a built-up roof and radiate heat into the rooms below far into the night. It is practically impossible to prevent accumulation of moisture by ventilation of a flat roof.

Therefore, these roofs must have an efficient vapor barrier under the roof insulation.

If your basement is damp, it must be ventilated. Use a ventilator that can be installed in the foundation wall. These are especially needed in crawl spaces, where a minimum amount of ventilation is necessary. Provide at least four foundation vents (8 x 16 inch units) which can be closed during the heating season. Window fans can be used in a basement window. If the situation is serious, than a dehumidifier can be used. Most cellars need a dehumidifier.

If insulation is placed on the attic floor of gable or hip roofs, and efficient vapor barriers are properly installed, attic ventilation is not necessary except to remove summer heat. Ventilating minimizes the condensation problem, but the best solution is to prevent the vapor from reaching the attic. When an attic is to be ventilated, there should be a vent in either end of the gable roof or at the high point of a hip roof; cornice vents at the eave are necessary to promote circulation; ventilated air must be distributed over the full area of the attic, including all areas behind and above second floor rooms; and the total area of openings should be at least one-quarter square inch per square foot of attic floor area or 250 square inches per 1000 square feet, with the area distributed between the ventilators at the gable, hip, or ridge.

Attic fans, while not needed for the winter, are almost essential for warm climates or where a house does not enjoy cool prevailing winds. An attic exhaust fan placed in one gable end of the house will effectively reduce the overhead heat load. The most widely used size is 24 inches in diameter, with sizes up to 48 inches for larger houses. Plan to mechanically ventilate one to two attic air changes per minute, or at least six cubic feet per hour per square foot of attic floor area. This represents 6000 cubic feet of air per hour. Your fan dealer can help you select the correct size.

Proper insulation can make a home more comfortable in extremes of temperature and will lower heating and air conditioning costs by reducing heat loss and gain. Insulation keeps surface temperatures of walls, floors, and ceilings at an even level. A loose filling or plaster resin blown into the walls or attic under pressure, a batt or blanket, or a reflective material can be used. The "R" value will vary with the chosen material's thickness, form, and shape, and with the method of installation. Most new houses have from two to three and one-half inches of insulation in the walls and six or more inches in the ceilings. Unfortunately, the more efficient the insulation is in retarding heat transfer, the colder the outer surfaces become, and unless moisture is restricted from entering the wall or ceiling, the greater the potential for moisture condensation. Applying insulation may produce water vapor condensation in house walls unless a vapor barrier is installed on the side of the wall that is warm under winter conditions. This is very important to prevent rot and mold build-up.

Vapor barriers help prevent water vapor condensation in walls and attics and protect the insulation and structure. Asphalt-coated paper, aluminum foil, and polyethylene film are good vapor barriers. Inspect your house and check with the builder or previous occupant to determine the amount of insulation and vapor barrier installed. It is expensive to insulate an existing house if the original job has been inadequately done. Be sure to ask the installer how he intends to put in a vapor barrier.

The cause of condensation and frost on the windows is that the house air is too warm and moist. When this air strikes a colder surface it gives up some of the moisture by condensing just as dew forms on grass in the summer. Since the walls are insulated and warm, the only cold surface is your window, which is chilled by the outside air. Surface condensation can be minimized by the use of storm windows or by replacing single glass with insulated glass. When storms do not prevent condensation on the window surface, the relative humidity in the room must be reduced.

Other Moisture Problems.   Variations in climate, soil, and drainage conditions in your locality govern the degree of moisture and dampness that threatens your home. The source of unwanted water can be downspout run-off, window wells, slope drainage, low-lying areas or wet spots, roofs without gutters, or flooding.

To rid yourself of unwanted water, first find a location to dispose of the water. This could be a low spot at least 20 feet away from where the water collects. If local ordinances permit, you may run piping to the curb or to the storm sewers. Check your local laws. You may already have a low spot, ditch, or gully in a remote section of your property to which you can run a pipe (be sure this doesn't cause problems for your neighbor). If none of these solutions are possible, then you can always dig a leaching trench right on your own property. The leaching trench is sized by the amount of water it is to disperse. The trench consists of a gravel bed into which a perforated pipe is installed. The pipe evenly distributes the water to the trench, where it is absorbed by the soil. Your local lumber yard can help you design the proper size trench. Next, collect the unwanted water at its source. For downspouts, pipe the water away from the foundation to the disposal spot. For window wells and wet spots, install a drain box and connect this by underground pipe to the disposal area. If your house is located on a slope and your trouble comes from that direction, you should dig a swale or trench and put a pipe and gravel into it. Then run the pipe to your disposal area. If the run-off is too great in a storm, you may have to build a diverter wall to direct and funnel the water to a drain.

If you are building a new house, you can stop drainage problems before they begin. Grade the land so the house is high and all ground water will run away from the foundation. Pipe all downspouts to a disposal area. Don't let any water collect at the foundation wall. Another cause of wet basements is ground water close to or higher than the basement floor. Sometimes the only solution is foundation footing drains and a sump pump. This is always good insurance. In extremely wet areas, or if you are on the side of a hill, it is good practice to install a four-inch pipe in sand and gravel under the cellar floor and connect it to a disposal area. To prevent heaving and settling of a driveway or walk and to prevent retention of puddles, install four-inch diameter pipe under or at each side of the walk to drain water away. If you plan to live on the side of a hill you must expect heavy water flows in severe rain storms. This may mean you can't have a cellar. Still, you must provide means to prevent heavy run-off from reaching the house. The preventive measures are a drainage trench on a slope, walls to direct the water to large underground drains, and the grading of the land to direct the water to a disposal area. Determine if there are local soil or water conditions that may create problems. Add fill dirt where improper grading prevents runoff. Trees or shrubs planted too close to the foundation may cause dampness in the basement.

MAINTENANCE AND INSPECTION METHODS

Regular inspection and maintenance can help you avoid costly repairs resulting from undetected condensation and moisture problems. The following list will aid you in your regular program.

Look for broken, loose, blistered, missing, or damaged roof shingles. They should be replaced. All open joints should be caulked.

Check the roof eaves for evidence of leaks. Are the soffits rotted? Is the paint blistering?

Gutters must be kept clean. Standing water can back up and force its way under the roof. Check for splits or cracks in the gutter. In some cases, these can be patched with fiberglass and roofing cement.

See if the downspouts are properly connected to the gutters. Be sure that when the water hits the ground, it is directed away. It is a good idea to pipe the water to the street or to a low spot far from the foundation.

Be certain that all flashing around the chimneys, vent pipes, and roof valleys, and at the juncture of roofs and walls, have not corroded or rusted. If damaged, apply roofing cement to all joints and replace the rusted section.

Skylights are a source of leaks on flat roofs. Look for loose putty, cracked glass, and paint blisters.

Inspect the chimney. Look for broken flue lining and make certain that all the bricks are pointed. Examine flashings for evidence of rust, corrosion, or open joints. Look into the hearth for evidence of leaks and loose mortar. Seal the cement cap. Check to be sure all attic and crawl space ventilators are open.

Check the exterior walls. Brick walls should be kept well-pointed. The flashings, as well as the window drip caps, should be checked. In some cases, it is necessary to apply a waterproofing coating. Stucco siding should be checked for cracks, and repairs should be made. Stucco walls need repainting or waterproofing every ten years. Since masonry is a brittle material, any cracks or loose crumbling mortar joints should be repaired immediately to prevent the freezing of water in cracks.

Cedar shakes will need a coating of stain and preservative every five years. If not, the shingle will dry out and buckle, allowing moisture to penetrate. All painted surfaces should be checked thoroughly for paint failure like peeling, crazing, and caulking, as well as for signs of normal wear. Spot painting should be done as required.

Basement walls should be examined from the inside for signs of dampness, water stains, white salts, mildew, and cracks. There are materials to repair basement walls from the inside; however, any serious water penetration must be repaired from the outside, at its cause. This should be done by a reputable company. Check your crawl spaces to determine whether drainage is good. The crawl space should have a moisture barrier, adequate ventilation, and insulation.

Inspect all doors, windows, and related trim for paint failure. Look for cracked or loose caulking around frames and trim. Check weather-stripping of doors and windows for damage and fit.

Condensation is also a bathroom problem. Is there an exhaust fan? Is the wall covering coming loose? Kitchens and utility rooms cause a tremendous amount of moisture. Is there adequate ventilation?

In the attic, do you see stains on the insulation surface? Are the roofing nails rusted? Are there signs of leaks at the chimney and roof vents?

Check the landscaping at the foundation. Does it slope away at a 15° angle for at least fix feet? The ground around the house should be graded so there are no low pockets or places where water can collect against the foundation. Settlement of the soil frequently occurs around a building, due to settling and improper back-filling. Water that is allowed to stand against the foundation walls can seep into the basement, crawl space, and underslab air ducts. Proper grading of the soil will correct this.

Check all ventilation fans and filters for proper operation.

SUMMARY

Condensation and moisture problems vary in their type and intensity in various sections of the United States. Be certain to question the homeowner, neighbors, and municipal inspectors as to the type and extent of the problem. This applies also to the soil and tree root conditions that may cause foundation instability. The home inspector or engineer can advise you, too.

27.
Kitchen and Appliances

INTRODUCTION

A kitchen may be used for many activities, but it is essentially a workroom for food preparation. The primary concerns are convenience and ease in the basic kitchen processes. Safe kitchens are well-lighted, well-ventilated, and planned for efficiency. It is costly to correct errors and eliminate hazards after the kitchen has been completed and the equipment installed. Planning for efficiency and use in the early stages of construction will prevent expensive and major structural changes in the future. This chapter discusses remodeling and the purchase, maintenance, and use of appliances.

REMODELING KITCHENS

The average kitchen has a useful life of 15 to 20 years. When you are ready to remodel, do some shopping to determine the style, use, and equipment you want. Is the room to have a dual purpose, serving as a family room and eating area as well as a food preparation room? Do you want the clothes washer in the kitchen?

When you are ready to start, measure your room accurately and draw its plan on graph paper. You will need two sketches: one showing your present kitchen, and the other showing how it will be after structural changes and after cabinets and appliances are installed. Your plan should also include the locations of heating and air conditioning ducts, lighting fixtures, electric outlets, and switches. The placement of doors, windows, and adjacent rooms gives either a straight line, L-shaped, parallel wall, broken U, or U-shaped arrangement.

Sketch in all closets and storage areas. Detailed notes will be of help to the architect or builder who will prepare the working drawings for the electrician, plumber, and carpenter.

For efficiency, think of your kitchen as having four work centers providing room to prepare, cook, serve, and clean up, each with its own equipment, counter, and storage space. The heart of the kitchen is the work triangle, which is formed by lines connecting the sink, range, and refrigerator. The sum of the sides of the work triangle should not exceed 21 feet. As the major activity area in the kitchen, this triangle should be out of the path of most traffic through the room to adjacent areas. The size of the dining area is determined by the number of persons to be served, the type of furniture, and clearances for passage and serving.

In addition to adequate fluorescent or incandescent ceiling fixtures, area lighting is desirable at the sink and other work centers as well as at the dining area. Fixtures beneath wall cabinets reduce annoying shadows on work surfaces. One duplex convenience outlet for every four feet of counter is recommended, with a minimum of one outlet for each counter where portable appliances are likely to be used. Special purpose outlets are located in places where appliances are permanently installed, and these should be on separate circuits.

APPLIANCES

As a homeowner, you will purchase thousands of dollars of equipment. If buying is properly planned, you can save 20% of the cost by using the information prepared by consumer testing groups. Read carefully to make certain that appliances are compared on a basis important to you. The appliance should carry an Underwriters' Laboratories seal signifying that the product design meets safety requirements.

Using credit effectively or not at all can cut your costs up to 18%. Time your purchases of appliances and equipment to take advantage of special promotions. Appliances are frequently marked down at least twice a year. Some of the biggest bargains are offered by sellers who plan to make their profit on installment contracts. Buying for cash from these credit sellers will save you money.

Check the appliance warranty. Almost all warranties cover parts and labor for a specified period of time, and some also cover defective parts (but not service costs) for an additional period. Warranties do not generally provide for replacement of the entire appliance. Find out who is responsible for service and who will handle any claims under a guarantee or warranty. Terms and conditions vary widely. Be sure to read and ask questions about the guarantee so you will know its terms and your rights and obligations.

Service contracts or agreements are forms of insurance. Their purpose is to assure you that you will get service on your mechanical and electrical equipment after the warranty runs out. Some contracts will pay for inspection only. Others will pay for an inspection and the labor to make repairs. Others will cover labor, parts, and inspection. As a general rule, it does not pay for you to order a service contract. The majority of firms issuing contracts expect to make a profit. This means that their appliance service records tell them that their customers as a group will require less service than they paid for.

Ranges (*Expected Life of 15 to 20 Years*).   Many of the same features are found on electric and gas ranges. These include take-apart units, burners and surface tops that can be lifted for easy cleaning; removable oven doors and oven liners that can be washed at the sink; and self-cleaning ovens that use high temperatures to remove oven soils, or are lined with a material which encourages the breakdown of oven soils at baking temperatures and programmed cooking. It is wise to choose a range with controls located at the front or side and without storage areas above the burners. This reduces the risk of burns from spattering grease, boiling water, or steam, and lessens the danger of garments catching fire when you reach over hot burners. Eliminate clutter around the range, particularly flammables that can ignite if they come into contact with heating elements. Keep a small fire extinguisher on hand, charged and ready to use. Keep a box of baking soda handy as it makes a good flame extinguisher.

Good maintenance, including periodic cleaning, assures more economical and efficient operation of your range. Adjust burners to a blue flame, clean burner parts and recalibrate, and adjust or replace thermostats as needed. Your gas or electric range manual has complete maintenance instructions.

Ventilation Fans (*Expected Life of 15 to 20 Years*).   A range hood dispels odors, grease, heat, and contaminants. A safely designed range hood should have rounded corners. It should be installed at such a height that the lower edge does not restrict the view of utensils on the rear heating elements. For best ventilation, have a short, direct duct route with few turns. Exhaust systems within the hood should direct their flow to the outside and not into an attic or unused space. The motor blower assembly should be easy to remove for cleaning off grease and for oiling the motor bearings. Filters should also be maintained to insure efficient operation. Don't leave exhaust fans on longer than necessary as it wastes energy.

Microwave Ovens (*Expected Life of 15 to 20 Years*). This is a new, popular method of cooking. Microwave energy enters the food directly and molecular agitation inside the food produces heat. Cooking times are much shorter than usual but browning will not take place, except for something as large as a roast that requires longer to cook. Recent units have browning cycles. The oven has special locks and seals designed to keep microwave energy in and protect the user. Some heart pacemakers are affected by microwave energy, so a pacemaker wearer should consult his physician before purchasing a microwave oven. Energy costs are lower than those of conventional stoves.

Refrigerators (*Expected life of 10 to 15 Years*). About 30% of the refrigerators sold are side-by-side refrigerator-freezers that come in sizes from 30 to 60 inches wide. These models offer storage at a convenient height, and the narrow doors do not require as much space to open. Some have a third door for ice cubes and some include icemakers, which eliminate the tray-filling job. Compact refrigerators are available and may be useful for the family room or for a vacation home.

Frost-free refrigerators are also available. Temperatures in these units are even throughout the unit, and foods cool to safe storage temperatures faster. However, the cost of operating a frost-free refrigerator may be almost double that of automatic defrost refrigerators with manual defrost freezers. No matter what type of refrigerator you have, proper exterior ventilation and temperature settings greatly affect its operating costs. Set the temperature at 36° to 42° F for the refrigerator and 0° to 10° F for the freezer. If your refrigerator and freezer has number settings, consult your owner's operating booklet, or call the dealer who handles the make of the unit you have. Cool hot foods at least 30 minutes at room temperature before placing in the refrigerator. If you don't, the refrigerator will have to work hard to maintain its temperature. Dust or dirt should not be allowed to accumulate on the coils or the operation will be impaired, and sufficiently cold temperatures cannot be maintained. Other parts that are most likely to require servicing include the temperature regulator, the fan that cools the condenser, the timers and switches used in self-defrosting, and the fans used to circulate air within a frost-free refrigerator or freezer. In addition, gaskets on refrigerators and freezers deteriorate over time and should be replaced.

Food Waste Disposals (*Average Life of 10 to 15 Years*).   Most disposers will grind small bones, fruit rinds, and seeds, but metals, glass, and china should be avoided. To make the best use of a disposer, all wastes should be ground immediately. Foods decay rapidly and the acid that develops can corrode metal disposer parts and cause odors. Cold water is a must to solidify fats so they won't congeal in drain pipes and clog them. In a continuous feed disposer, wastes can be fed continuously during the disposing process, whereas a batch feed type will operate only with the cover on. Anti-jamming and reset devices are features that protect the motor from overheating and allow you to get the disposer back into operation when stalled.

Never put your hand or a wrench into the disposal to free it without securing the switch. Injuries occur when attempting to extract or touch an item placed in the disposal unit while it is operating. Use tongs, rather than your hand, to retrieve objects that have fallen in, and use a broom handle or similar tool to loosen a jam. Some cities will not allow disposals because of fear of overloading the sewage system.

Waste Compactors.   Waste compactors reduce the volume of trash leaving the home and thus simplify waste disposal. Bottles, cans, cartons, and waste paper can be compacted. The compactor should be operated after each addition to the disposal. Odors may develop with the decaying process and disinfectant sprays delay, but do not stop, food decomposition. Key locks are available on all models. In some, they prevent operation of the compactors. On others, they prevent opening the door as well. Special trash bags may be required and can be relatively expensive. Sometimes any standard sized heavy-duty plastic bag can be used.

Dishwashers (*Expected Life of 8 to 12 Years*).   The family's role in getting clean dishes is important. Water must be soft and hot (130° to 140° F) and the right amount of a proper detergent must be used. In choosing a machine, the homeowner has a number of cycle choices. Regular and Rinse and Hold are used most often, although Soak, Utensil, Short, Gentle, and Fine China cycles are also offered. A large single load can be washed as effectively and more economically than several smaller loads. The dishwasher instruction book will say what can and cannot be washed and will provide charts for proper loading of racks.

Before placing the dishes in the dishwasher, regularly check the filter screen located over the drain in the bottom of the dishwasher and remove accumulated particles. Always place sharp items in the basket with their points down. If you find a utensil has slipped through the bottom of the tub, do not attempt to remove it immediately since touching the heating element could produce a bad burn.

Clothes Dryers (*Expected Life of 10 to 15 Years*) **and Clothes Washers** (*Expected Life of 5 to 8 Years*). These appliances may be part of the modern kitchen but most likely are found in the utility room. Unfortunately, automatic washers probably have a higher frequency of repair than any other major appliance. This is because of the complexity of the appliance and the high humidity to which the functioning parts are exposed. Parts most likely to require service include the timer that controls cycling of the washer, the pump for circulating water and emptying the washer, the transmission, and the motor. Get a washer with as few gadgets as possible and check on the unit's past service record.

It is recommended that clothes dryers be vented to the exterior. This will prevent accumulation of lint and moisture and will also give it an adequate air supply to operate at peak efficiency. The vent pipe should have few turns in it and be kept free of lint buildup. Otherwise, you may get a back-pressure that will affect dryer performance.

MAINTENANCE AND INSPECTION

Maintain home equipment regularly to prevent breakdown. Lubricate the ventilating fan, the vacuum cleaner, the washing machine, and the dishwasher as noted in their operating manuals, and keep traps, vents, and dirt-collection devices cleaned out. Any appliance that must overcome clogged valves or dry bearings will break down sooner than a clean, well-maintained machine. Follow directions on cleaning, loading, and using your appliances.

If an appliance problem occurs, check the instruction manual. It will tell you what to do and may even save a service call. If you've misplaced your manual here's a quick checklist of common problems. If the appliance operates on electricity, make certain it is plugged in. If it runs on gas, check to see that the pilot is lit. Check for blown fuses or tripped circuit breakers, which can result from overloads on the electrical system. Are the doors securely closed? (Most washers and dryers have electrical interlocks which prevent operation if doors are not fully closed.) Examine the controls to see if they are set properly (a refrigerator won't work if the temperature control dial has been inadvertently turned to OFF). If a dishwasher or automatic washer will not fill with water, see if the main water supply is at the regular pressure. Check your U.S. Agriculture County Cooperative Extension Service for a book on servicing home equipment. Many of the faults that interrupt equipment service can be fixed quickly at little or no cost.

If your appliance or equipment came equipped with a service manual and diagrams of parts and functions, study it to see if you can buy a part and install it yourself. Write to the manufacturer for information on servicing the equipment and obtaining parts. If service is needed, an authorized service person should be contacted. The brand, model number, and a detailed description of the problem should be relayed to the person taking the message. The consumer must realize that service call costs cover not only the technician's time in the home, but time traveling between jobs, costs of training the service technician, fringe benefits for the technician, tools, truck, a building with utilities, parts inventory investment, office personnel, and taxes. This can amount to over $40 per hour.

The service company expects an adult to be at home at the time of the service call, or other arrangements to be made if the consumer cannot be at home.

If you are buying a resale home, run all the appliances through a complete cycle. Get all instruction booklets and warranties. Note the exterior condition for signs of wear. Most appliances are warranted only for the first year of operation and these are quite limited. Recheck all units again prior to closing.

SUMMARY

Any appliance that must overcome obstacles like partially clogged valves or noisy bearings will break down sooner than will a clean, well-maintained machine. Therefore, maintain your home equipment to prevent breakdown and follow directions on cleaning, lubricating, loading, and using your appliances. If you are planning a new kitchen, do your homework and lay out the floor plan to reach all your objectives. Kitchen remodeling is one of the top home improvement projects. As such, there is plenty of free advice available to help you get your remodeling dollars' worth.

PART III.
MAINTAINING
YOUR HOME

28.
Home Improvement Economics

INTRODUCTION

Many people invest great time and expense into remodeling their homes firmly convinced that the increased sales value of their home will reap them handsome profits for their efforts. If you too are part of this "improve to move" syndrome, you had better read this chapter carefully.

This chapter examines the advantages and disadvantages of home improvements. At the end of the chapter are listed some average home improvement costs. Chapter 28 discusses how to avoid falling victim to the racket boys or to poor workmanship when buying services.

ADVANTAGES AND DISADVANTAGES OF IMPROVING TO SELL.

Disadvantages.   Many leading home experts feel that for the family wishing to improve its housing, the most economical course of action is to move. So unless you are remodeling solely to satisfy yourself or to improve the comfort of your home, the facts against improving far outweigh those in favor of it. Even the most profitable (best return) improvement you could make will return only about 50 to 75% of the original investment. In other words, for every dollar you invest into renovating those kitchen cabinets, perhaps 50 cents will be returned. Unfortunately, most improvements reap much lower returns than that.

A partial explanation for the low cost return on improvements is the fact that it costs more than twice as much to improve an older house than to build the same convenience into a new home. The eventual buyer of your house will rarely pay a premium for a home improvement; to him, a room is a room. If you add a porch for $5,000 that would have cost the original builder $2,000, all a buyer is willing to pay (or the market will bear) is $2,000.

Another explanation is that increasing numbers of modern home buyers are searching for no frills houses. Their reasons vary; some prefer to remodel according to their own personal tastes, while others are much more attracted to a lower sales price than to a newly remodeled bathroom.

Advantages.   Of course, there are exceptions to every rule. Due to skyrocketing prices of land and construction some people are more inclined to improve rather than move. Not only is it less expensive and troublesome than moving but major improvements often lessen the burden of painting and other minor fix-up chores that so many homeowners are plagued with. However, for any improvement to be profitable it must meet the following demands.

Good workmanship.   Nothing is less attractive to the prospective buyer than poor workmanship. If you don't have the know-how and are reluctant to hire someone who does, don't remodel.

Appropriateness.   Improvements must tie in with the architectural style of the neighborhood. An English Tudor home in a block of brownstone apartment buildings is not going to be a hot item on the sales market. The improvement should also be in proportion to the value of your home. A $15,000 kitchen in a $30,000 home is a luxury few home buyers will appreciate.

If improving your home would make its sales price higher than those in the neighborhood, it would be wise to abandon your thoughts of improving. Most people prefer a $50,000 home to be in a $60,000 neighborhood rather than a neighborhood in which most houses are valued at $40,000. On the other hand, if others in your neighborhood are improving their homes as well as raising the overall neighborhood sales value, then remodeling may be a reasonable and profitable undertaking. So too, if your home is presently below the sales value of your neighbors' homes, renovations that would raise your home's value to the same level as theirs would more than likely be a wise investment.

Necessity.   Although a new roof or improved driveway may not boost the sales value of your home, the lack of such improvements could definitely reduce the house's value. Such improvements also add greatly to your own comfort and convenience while you occupy the house.

Visibility. The way a house looks is perhaps one of the biggest boosts to its sale. A freshly painted house, both inside and out, is certainly more likely to attract customers than a poorly maintained home, even though the first may be of lower quality. The installation of new carpeting will have a greater return than boosting the electric capacity of your home. Although the latter is a far better renovation in the long run, the carpeting is clearly the more visible and immediately appealing improvement. Similar "unseen and better left undone" improvments include the replacing of galvanized pipes with copper and exterior improvements such as the application of siding or cedar shingles, or the installation of storm windows. It is worthwhile, however, to give your home an interior face lift by patching cracks, fixing loose hinges, covering watermarks, and uncluttering closets and storage spaces.

WORTHWHILE IMPROVEMENTS

Worthwhile improvements with an eye to eventual resale usually have to do with improving living space in the home. Once again, I must restate that a worthwhile improvement (profitable) usually indicates a return of 50 to 75% of the original investment. If those returns are satisfactory to you and if you can adjust your personal home preferences to those in demand on the sales market, you may even be able to increase your comfort and house value without a high cost penalty. Those improvements presently in demand on the resale market are related to the four living areas of your home; i.e., the bedroom, the kitchen, the bathroom, and the family room. These four are the candidates most likely to return the greatest percentage of your original investment.

Kitchen. Usually, improvements costing up to 10% of the overall value of the house are profitable. The total cost of kitchens varies from $5,000 to $10,000 complete with appliances.

Bathroom. If you own a $50,000 home with three or more bedrooms, it just isn't complete, according to modern standards, without two full baths and one main floor powder room. The cost of a full bath is about $4,500 to $5,500, while a powder room runs about $1,500 to $2,000.

New family room.   Any room which adds to the living space will give a good return.

Bedroom.   Usually a third or fourth bedroom is a worthwhile improvement. However, if you must travel through one bedroom to reach another, this renovation would be unsatisfactory and better left undone.

In addition to the "big four" of home improvements, there are several other renovations which may prove profitable.

Central air conditioning.   This should be at least a three-ton central unit priced at approximately $1,500 to $2,000. Single room units do not generally affect house value. Installation of a central air conditioning system is only profitable, however, if you can utilize existing air ducts such as those used in central heating.

Fireplace.   A free-standing fireplace is usually a nice plus in home renovations. However, a built-in chimney and fireplace are usually not recommended as the cost is too high in proportion to the return.

Two-car garage.   If the climate is warm, a carport is an even better choice.

Energy conservation measures.   Conservation measures are an all-around plus. The lack of insulation may actually cause the house value to drop. Furthermore, the practice of energy conservation measures adds considerably to your own comfort as well as lowering your heating bills.

QUESTIONABLE IMPROVEMENTS

Although many of these improvements may not add to the sales value of your house, or return a high percentage of the original investment, they could very possibly be a deciding factor in the quick sale of your home.

Outdoor living area.   Most outdoor improvements are chancy. These particular improvements may bring back 25% of the investment. Other outdoor improvements, such as barbecue pits and backyard sheds, may return nothing.

Landscaping.   Many people avoid homes with extensive landscaping due to the increased burden of maintenance.

Basement rec room.   The great rec room craze of yesteryear is over. Now the rec room is regarded by the home buyer as merely an added expense. In addition, children seem to avoid these "play" areas.

Swimming pool.   Although in some fashionable areas a pool may add considerably to house value, in most cases it is a negative investment. A $5,000 pool *may* add $1,000 to the sales value. Common complaints lodged against pools are that they are hazardous, particularly if small children are in the family, too expensive and troublesome to maintain, space consuming, and not particularly useful if the home is occupied by adults.

Gaudy or unorthodox decor. Very personalized decor may appear as an expensive waste to others. Gaudy carpets and drapes or decorations in wild colors often detract from the overall sales value of the house.

Converted garage. A converted garage usually loses out, even when turned into a family room. Many towns require that there be a garage available.

SUMMARY

If after reading this chapter you are still uncertain whether to move or improve, perhaps you should make a simple, written comparison of the finances involved. On one side of a sheet of paper, figure the difference in the possible selling price of your home and the price of a new home that will satisfy your needs. Estimate the expenses of making the switch: moving costs, closing costs, taxes, new furnishings, the higher costs of interest and mortgages, and possible fixing-up costs. On the other side, calculate the approximate costs for the home improvements and carrying costs. Remember to add in the additional maintenance and operating costs that improvements may bring. Now compare the two totals to see which is the lowest. Don't forget the intangible return of the excitement of being in a new home versus the comfort and security of your old neighborhood and the pleasure you may derive from transforming your tired old house into a more enjoyable, modern living space.

Repair and Remodeling Cost Estimates. As part of your plans to buy a home or improve your existing home, you will need some guidelines to compare costs. The best way to do this is to provide the same repair or remodeling specifications to three contractors and compare their price quotations. Be sure each contractor is bidding on the same specifications or your low bid may turn out in the end to be the more expensive. Also consult mail order catalogs for equipment prices.

The cost estimates that follow are "ball park" figures to be used as a guideline. They are 1978 installed prices and include labor, material, overhead, and profit. A range is given because costs vary widely over various sections of the country. Many contractors estimate by "what the traffic will bear," so a comparison is necessary. Plan ahead. Don't be caught in a rush and be forced to accept the first bid.

Since you may be referring to this book over a number of years, use the multiplier ratio that follows to arrive at a current price. The multiplier represents an inflation rate of 5%, 7%, and 10% per year. Just multiply the remodeling or repair estimate by the ratio for the current year. If you don't know the average inflation rate, then use 7%.

Inflation Rate

Year	5%	7%	10%
1978	1.00	1.00	1.00
1979	1.05	1.07	1.10
1980	1.10	1.15	1.21
1981	1.16	1.23	1.33
1982	1.22	1.31	1.46
1983	1.28	1.40	1.61

*Additions**

Extension—one floor—all crafts complete	$35–$45/SF
Extension—second story	$30–$35/SF
Attic expansion	$15–$20/SF
Garage—two car detached complete	$12–$15/SF
Garage—two car overhead door	$300–$350
Garage—two car automatic door opener	$240–$300
Carport—two car	$3,000–$3,500
Garden tool house	$750–$3,000
Porch—enclosed	$6–$10/SF
Removing or widening a load bearing wall	$25–$30/LF

Air Conditioning

Installing a three-ton unit into existing heating ducts	$2,000–$2,500
Installing a three-ton unit with new ducts	$2,500–$3,500
Annual service	$25–$50
Replacing compressor	$400–$800

*Notations used are SF = square feet and LF = linear feet.

Alarm System
Individual battery smoke alarms	$40–$80
Burglar alarm system—seven-room house	$1,500–$3,000

Basement Room $9–$12/SF

Crawl Space (24 x 50 feet)
Vapor barrier on floor	$50–$100
Perimeter insulation	$300–$350

Basement Waterproofing—French Drains $500–$2,500 ($25/LF)

Bathrooms
Adding a new bath in existing house	$2,500–$4,000
Remodeling existing bath	$1,500–$2,500
Adding ceramic tile shower	$600–$1,000
Replacing existing shower floor and lead pan	$400–$600
Grouting a tile bathroom	$50–$100
Sauna—complete	$1,500–$2,000
Adding a powder room	$1,000–$2,000

Closets—Building a New Unit	$250–$400
Dehumidifier	$100–$200

Driveway
Building a new driveway	$1.50–$1.70/SF
Resurfacing existing driveway	$.50–$.75/SF

Drainage
Raising grade at foundation	$200–$400
Piping downspouts to street	$2–$4/LF

Electrical
Rewiring house and removing old knob and tube wiring	$1,500–$3,000
Upgrading service to 150 amps	$300–$450
Convenience outlets or switches	$30–$40 each
Large electric appliance wiring	$100–$150 each
Wiring an exterior post light	$100–$150

Exterior
Painting—one coat	$.25–$.35/SF
Trim painting	$.15–$.25/LF
Patio—concrete	$2.00–$2.50/SF
Redwood deck	$7.00–$7.50/SF
Siding—aluminum	$1.50–$1.75/SF
Storm windows (each)	$40–$100

Storm doors (each)	$80–$150
Fireplace	
Masonry and brick	$2,000–$2,500
Free-standing metal	$400–up
Flashing	
Sealing house flashing to prevent leaks	$75–$125
Foundation Underpinning	$1,000–up
Gutters and Leaders, Aluminum	$2–$3/LF
Heating	
Replacing 125,000 BTU boiler	$1,500–$2,000
Replacing 125,000 BTU furnace	$600–$1,000
Replacing a radiator	$300–$400
Radiant heat coil leak repair	$150–up
Cleaning chimney	$75–$150
Replacing zone valve	$50–$75
Replacing a circulating pump	$150–$200
Insulation	
Walls	$1.00–$1.20/SF
Ceiling	$.40–$.80/SF
Interior Work	
Doors	$100–$150
Entrance door	$250–$400
Sliding doors—patio	$500–$900
Floor coverings—asphalt tile	$.70–$1.00/SF
Painting a 12 x 12 foot room	$100–$150
Disappearing attic stairway	$150–$300
Sanding and refinishing wood floor	$.50–$.75/SF
Kitchen: Remodeling With Appliances	$3,000–$10,000
Landscaping	
Lawn care by season	$.05–$.10/SF
Tree removal	$100–up
Plumbing	
New sewer line—house to street	$8–$12/LF
Replacing rusted water pipes in cellar	$300–$350
Replacing rusted water pipes in walls	$400–$600
Hot water heater	$250–$400
Septic Tank	
Cleaning and pumping	$75–$125
Installing a new tank	$800–$1,000
Installing a new absorption field	$2,000–up

Swimming Pool—In Ground	$3,500–up
Roofing	
Asphalt—applied over old shingle	$75–$100/100 SF
Ripping off old shingles	$30–$50/100 SF
Wood	$2.00–$2.50/100 SF
Flat roofing	$100–$150/100 SF
Termite Control—Seven-Room House	$350–$500
Termite Inspection and Warranty	$10–$35
Wells	
Replacing basement pump	$150–$200
Replacing submersible pump	$400–$700
Drilling a new well	$10–$20/foot
Replacing tanks and controls	$300–$400

29.
Buying Services for the Home

INTRODUCTION

Once a learned colleague of mine told me that a person's chances of having a nervous breakdown are highest during the period of remodeling his or her house. And it's true that starting a home remodeling job can be a nerve-wracking experience. Many homeowners find alterations and repairs to be complicated, troublesome, and extremely frustrating. But don't despair! By clearly acquainting you with the various aspects involved in buying services, this chapter will prove that remodeling is not the mammoth task many think. You'll discover that the pleasure derived from the increased comfort and beauty of your newly modeled home is well worth any hassles you might possibly encounter.

WHEN TO GET THE JOB DONE

As with most businesses, there are on and off seasons in the home remodeling industry. During the peak construction seasons (spring and fall), workers are swamped and prices soar. Of course, some emergency repairs can't wait until the appropriate time, but if at all possible it would be to your advantage to hire workers for indoor improvements in winter and for any other kind of improvements during the summer vacation months. During these seasons, the best skills are usually available at the lowest prices.

Some jobs, however, are regulated by season and in these cases the homeowner has little choice. For instance, spring is the best time to install new heating systems or to undergo landscaping projects, while the ideal time for installation of central air conditioning, patios, and swimming pools is in the fall. Not surprisingly, the weather also affects the home improvements schedule, as in the case of a new roof, which should be installed during a dry spell.

WHO TO GET FOR THE JOB

Once you've made the decision to remodel, you will be faced with the task of doing it yourself or choosing a competent worker to carry it out.

Do-It-Yourself. If you do the job yourself you can save approximately one half the expenses incurred by hiring a professional, but such an undertaking requires great expertise and time. Another thing to remember is that the amateur often lacks the expensive tools and discounts on materials that are available to professionals.

If you are still determined to remodel your own home despite these difficulties, then be certain you are thoroughly informed as to the construction demands and difficulties of the particular job. Perhaps instruction books available in the public library or courses in construction sometimes offered by local organizations could be of help. If you only need a little advice on your project, the dealer from whom you bought your supplies may be able to furnish answers to your questions. Further information may also be available from the manufacturers of the various materials you will be using.

Be certain to acquaint yourself with local ordinances that might affect your project. Although you may be quite good in carpentry, it is a good idea to leave structural, plumbing, and electrical work to the experts—not only because of the dangers involved, but because local ordinances affecting these phases of construction are even more intricate than those concerning routine construction projects and the job must pass inspection.

Hiring an Architect. The question of hiring an architect usually arises when discussing major home improvements. For extensive remodeling, it is usually advisable to obtain the services of an architect. In fact, on large-scale projects, an architect is sometimes required by law. His fee of 10 to 20% of the job (with a minimum fee guaranteed) is usually well worth the costly planning and construction mistakes he will help you avoid. A good professional design can make your dreams of a beautiful new addition to the house become as lovely in reality as they are on paper. The architect can also help you select and monitor a contractor. Architects don't advertise so it is advisable to contact the American Institute of Architects for information on services available in your area.

Hiring a General Contractor.   A homeowner's uneasiness about remodeling is compounded by stories of people being cheated out of their life savings because they dealt with unreliable contractors. Don't let these stories frighten you away from the vast majority of contractors who are reliable and expert in their field. If you are informed and cautious when hiring a general contractor you will more than likely discover that the advantages of hiring him far outweigh the difficulties. Not only will he save you a great deal of time and energy, but a good contractor will relieve you of the burden of responsibility of the project and control the numerous tradesmen necessary to complete the task. You'll also find his knowledge of legal codes and restrictions invaluable.

To be assured of hiring an honest, dependable contractor, check his background thoroughly. The National Home Improvement Council publishes a list of contractors that may aid you in the hiring process. Be sure the contractor you are interested in meets the following qualifications.

He Should be Established. He should have a place of business, not just a phone number or Post Office box. Check to see if he's been located in the neighborhood for a while rather than "just setting up shop."

He Should be Reliable. Check the bank for a full credit reference. Ask about him at local lumberyards, hardware stores, and wholesale suppliers. Find out if any complaints have been registered against him with the Better Business Bureau, Chamber of Commerce of the State Consumer Protection Agency. The Federal Housing Agency prints a precautionary list of contractors to avoid, so it might be a good idea to look this publication over as well. Most important of all, check with his former customers to learn if they are satisfied with his work. Don't feel uncomfortable obtaining this information as any reliable contractor will fully understand your concern. If the contractor is reluctant to supply any of the above information it might indicate a problem.

He Should be Fair. After you've completed the above inquiry and have secured the names of at least three reliable contractors, you should ask each one for an estimate to complete the project. Not only is an estimate a good way to obtain the best bargain, but it is a wise precaution in case the job is totally beyond your means at the moment.

Make certain the estimates are all based on the same written specifications. The information you give to the contractors should include a list of specifications and a sketch of the project. When taking estimates it is good to keep in mind that the lowest price is not always the best bargain. If two contractors estimate the cost at $1,000 and a third asks $300, it is more than likely an indication that many corners will be cut on the $300 bid. Remember that poor quality materials and inferior craftsmanship will cost you much more in the long term. So check each estimate carefully against the job's specifications.

CONTRACT NEGOTIATION

To avoid embarrassing and expensive misunderstandings, it is a wise precaution to insist upon a written contract. The contract should include the following information.

Details of the work to be done, including sketches.

Name, address, and phone number of the contractor, including his home number.

The *materials* that will be used, including brand names, color, quantity, and quality. It is the job of the homeowner to supply the necessary funds for materials.

Estimated start and finish dates. Most contractors start the project 10 to 15 days after signing the contract. The average remodeling job should take about 30 days to complete.

The *total cost* of the job. This should include information concerning method of payments, permit fees, and finance charges.

Specify that the final payment (usually 10 to 20%) is not paid until satisfactory completion of the project.

Insurance covering damage and liability and workmen's compensation.

Penalty clauses, if any.

Clean-up requirements.

Name, home address, and phone number of the salesman.

Don't let anyone pressure you into signing the contract until you have read it thoroughly and understand all areas covered. For a major job, it may be advisable to have a lawyer look over the contract. Your peace of mind will be well worth the lawyer's fee. After signing, be sure to get a copy of the contract right away. Never wait until the day after the contract's been completed.

FINANCING

The party's over and the bills have started to drift in. If you aren't lucky enough to have a rich relative ready to foot the bill, then you had better start looking for a bank that will—at least temporarily! It is better to make your own financial arrangements rather than working through the contractor. Shop around for loans with good terms and a low interest rate and be sure it can be paid back in a reasonable time period.

Bank Procedures.   While you check out the banks' offerings, they will be running a check on you. Banks prefer clients who are established in their neighborhood and have a good credit rating. Inquiries will also be made as to the homeowner's mortgage conditions. The bank wants a client to be thoroughly familiar with all of the job's projected costs and to be prepared with details and a schematic of the proposed work. A bank appraiser will be sent to your home to inspect the property and the quality of the neighborhood.

Available Loans.   One of the lowest interest rates can be found on a Life Insurance Policy Loan. Straight personal loans from the bank also have low interest. The personal loan is not an installment loan and security may be requested. If you put up your home as security, be certain the lender supplies you with notice of your right of cancellation under the federal truth in lending law. Under this provision, you may cancel without obligation. Two copies of the notice will be sent to you. If you should decide to cancel, sign one and send it back in letter or telegram form.

FHA Home Improvement Loans are available through banks and savings banks. Perhaps the best known is the Title I, which is available only for home improvements, and has a term of seven years. For improvements on a single family home, you can receive as much as $5,000; if you live in a home with two or more families, you can receive up to $2,500 per unit.

For a major remodeling job you can also refinance your home by obtaining a new mortgage. Although the interest is lower on a mortgage loan than on others, it will probably be higher than your original interest rate. Be sure the new loan is large enough to pay off the old mortgage as well as the remodeling costs. Credit Union Loans are also available to the home remodeler.

The highest interest loans available are the Conventional Home Improvement Installment Loan and a Finance Company Loan. Particularly try to avoid the latter as the interest rates are sometimes above 20%.

HOW TO AVOID GETTING CHEATED

The clever and successful swindler is all too aware of the human desire to get something for nothing. Therefore, be suspicious of any advertisements which boast of extremely low rates or which make exaggerated claims. Suspect the salesman who confides that your home has been chosen as a model for the rest of the neighborhood. Special factory deals should be checked thoroughly and, above all, never let anyone pressure you into signing anything. On large dollar items, check with a lawyer.

If you feel you have been cheated by a salesman or contractor, or you have obtained a faulty product, examine the facts carefully before acting. In a dispute with a contractor, consider three questions: Did I live up to the contract? Did I follow care and use instructions carefully? Have I given it a fair trial period? If your answers to these questions are "yes," you may have a legitimate complaint.

If notifying the contractor or businessman gets no results, then start letter writing. The letter should outline your complaint, tell what you've done already to get redress, and make a request for help. Keep a copy of the letter. Write first to the contractor, then to the Better Business Bureau, and finally to the Director of the Bureau of Consumer Protection in the state capital. If you get no satisfaction, contact a lawyer.

SUMMARY

When it comes right down to it, buying services is the responsibility of no one but the homeowner. Any complaints or problems which may arise are usually the direct result of poor planning. However, as a thoroughly informed consumer, I doubt that you will have any trouble in making the right decisions when buying services for your home. I hope you will be completely satisfied and proud of the result of your home remodeling job.

30.
Energy-Saving Methods

INTRODUCTION

The cost of energy will continue to rise and take a bigger bite out of your budget than ever before. This chapter will give you ideas for saving energy and returning a net savings on your home improvement investment. Be sure to get current energy-saving information from your public utility or municipality.

The first step is to take a closer look at your home by performing an *energy audit*. This means examining weatherstripping, caulking, storm windows, insulation, crawl spaces, attics, floors, and the heating and cooling systems. Professional help is available to do this audit or you can write for the excellent booklet mentioned at the end of this chapter. Once the audit is complete, the second step is to develop an action program to complete the job.

In each section of the house, there are things you can do for a small investment and those that will require a larger expenditure. These are grouped together. You job is to inspect your house and note the steps to take to reduce your bills. A check-off box is placed before each idea for your notation.

CAULK AND WEATHERSTRIP ALL DOORS
AND WINDOWS

During the winter months, considerable heat loss is caused by warm air leakage and cold air infiltration throughout the house. The reverse is true of cooled air during the summer months. Weatherstripping and caulking should be checked prior to the heating and cooling seasons.

Caulking and weatherstripping are inexpensive ways to save energy and are easily applied. Caulking compounds are available in tubes for use with a caulking gun. Weatherstripping comes as solid or flexible felt, rubber, or vinyl.

( ) Are all cracks around the windows and doors filled with caulking?

( ) Are there any open cracks between the foundation sill and the siding?

( ) Are the wood or brick siding end joints caulked?

( ) Are the doors and windows weatherstripped on all sides?

( ) Does the garage door have rubber gaskets on all sides?

( ) Are all openings to the attic or crawl space sealed and insulated?

( ) Are clapboards and shingles securely nailed, with few cracks showing?

( ) Are there drafts around the windows and doors on a windy day? (Check with a candle.)

( ) Do all doors close tightly?

STORM WINDOWS AND DOORS

Properly installed storm windows and doors can increase the efficiency of your heating and cooling system by reducing the heat loss in winter and the heat gain in the summer. The least expensive approach is to use plastic sheet storms or single pane glass or plastic. Combination storms and screens are more expensive and can still be installed by the homeowner, though many use a contractor. Local do-it-yourself stores have continuing sales on these items and they will help you with the measuring and provide installation instructions. Plastic windows cost $1, single pane units start at $10, and the combination units are $30 and up, installed. Severe northern climates require windows with three panes of glass.

( ) Are all windows covered with storms during winter (and in summer, too, if the house is air conditioned)?

( ) Do all doors have storm doors?

( ) Are there insulating shades or screens?

( ) Are the storm doors and windows tightly sealed?

WALL AND CEILING INSULATION

Adequate insulation in walls, ceilings, and crawl spaces will contribute greatly to reducing heating and cooling costs. It will also be more comfortable for those in the house. Installation of insulation can be done by the homeowner in accessible spaces; contractors can be hired to insulate the walls. Proper insulation is an investment that can pay immediate dividends to the homeowner. Check with your building supply store, do-it-yourself store, or an insulation contractor for the cost of the insulation and installation and the expected returns in lower heating bills. Note that "R" values denote insulation density. The higher the "R" value, the less the heat loss.

( )   Is there at least six inches (R-19) of insulation between the ceiling joists or roof rafters in your unfinished attic? In cold climates, go to 10 to 12 inches (R-34).

( )   Does the unfinished floored attic have less than four inches of insulation? If so, you can either put enough under the floor to equal six inches or you can insulate between the rafters and at the end wall. The floor is the best approach.

( )   Are the walls adequately insulated? They should have three and one-half inches of insulation. This can usually be observed by removing an electric convenience outlet plate. If this is not possible, then put your hand on an inside wall and the other on an outside wall. If the difference feels extreme, consider more insulation. Houses built prior to 1940 probably have no wall insulation.

( )   Are there drafts coming out of the electric outlets and switch plates, indicating no insulation and poor caulking and weatherstripping?

( )   Is your finished attic insulated a full six inches?

( )   Is the crawl space ceiling insulated with at least four inches (six inches is desirable)?

( )   Is there a vapor barrier on the crawl space dirt surface or a plastic sheet on a concrete crawl space floor to reduce condensation?

( )   Is the floor over the garage insulated a full four inches?

( )   Are the foundation walls of a heated basement that are exposed to the elements insulated? Is there insulation between the top of the foundation wall and rough flooring above?

( )   Are the walls of the crawl space insulated?

( )   Are all overhangs insulated?

( )   Are all air conditioning and heating ducts insulated in crawl spaces, attics, and garages?

( )   Check the roof after a light snow. Melted snow areas show where insulation may be lacking.

ATTIC AIR LEAKAGE AND VENTILATION

It is important to close and seal tightly all sources of air leakage from occupied areas of the house into the attic or crawl spaces. Tape up and insulate all attic doors. Maintain adequate outside ventilation to prevent condensation of moisture in or on the insulation or other basic structural elements. This can be accomplished by adequate natural or forced ventilation. The louvers in the attic and crawl spaces are designed for natural circulation. Unfortunately, these openings are usually too small to do the job. In severe climates, it may be necessary to throttle these vents in the winter to conserve heat. Thermostatically controlled attic fans are a good idea for summer use.

( ) Are there adequate vents in the attic, gable, roof or soffits, and crawl space?

( ) Are there signs of condensation in the attic or crawl space? Look for rust on nails or ice on the inside of the roof. To correct, insulate, use a vapor barrier, and ventilate the area.

( ) Do all kitchen and bathroom vents discharge only to the outside and not into the attic?

( ) Are all openings from the living area into the attic sealed and insulated?

MAINTAIN AN EFFICIENT HEATING SYSTEM

A properly functioning heating system can significantly reduce overall fuel costs. Periodic checks of the entire heating system by heating professionals will assure proper air/fuel mixture and system efficiency. Heat exchanger surfaces should be cleaned periodically. Any filters should be cleaned or replaced regularly. The chimney flue and dampers should be cleaned and adjusted as needed.

( ) Is the oil burner system cleaned and adjusted annually?

( ) Are the gas burners and pilots checked for proper burning? If the flame is yellow, have the burner adjusted. Your public utility usually provides this service.

( ) Do you have a fresh air intake to the furnace or boiler? Today's tight homes need a controlled introduction of fresh air to replace air discharged by exhaust fans and flues. If not, untreated cold replacement air will try to steal in around doors and windows. The fresh air intake brings air into the air-treating unit.

( )   Do you turn the thermostat down at least 6° from your usual setting during the sleeping hours? Do you do this during the day when you are out? There are automatic devices that will do this for you for a moderate cost.

( )   Do you lubricate all blower and motor bearings?

( )   Do you clean or replace all filters at least every month? Do you monitor the electronic air cleaner?

( )   Do you keep the winter temperature set below 68° F?

( )   Is the summer temperature kept above 76° F?

( )   If your heating unit is over 25 years old, have you had a heating contractor survey the savings you could expect from a more efficient new unit? This could result in considerable savings if you have a conversion unit from coal.

( )   Have you had the fan blades on your furnace blower cleaned of dirt build-up to increase the volume of air moved?

( )   Do you operate the furnace blower constantly? It is the only way to enjoy a full-time comfort system because if the blower stops, the treating of air stops. Gentle, constant air circulation (CAC) keeps air from stagnating and keeps temperatures even, especially in split levels, bi-levels, and large, spread out homes.

( )   Check into installing a heat pipe. This is a small pipe that is installed in the stream of hot flue gases running from your furnace to your chimney. The pipe picks up heat from the flue gases and, in turn, heats forced warm air.

( )   Check into a motorized flue damper. When the furnace is running, the damper is open, and the instant the furnace shuts off the damper closes. This saves warm air from going up the chimney.

( )   Check to be sure the valves on all radiators are packed properly, especially in a vacuum system for steam heat.

( )   Get a quote from your oil supplier on the savings possible through the installation of the new high efficiency oil burners.

( )   Check with your heating contractor on the availability of electronic spark ignition for your gas appliances that eliminate the need for a pilot light.

( )   Do you have any rooms that are abnormally warm or cold? If you do, have the system balanced.

( )   Do you annually bleed air from baseboard and radiators to keep all units uniformly hot?

( )   Do you turn off the heat in unused rooms?

( ) Is the fireplace damper capable of closing securely?

( ) Do you periodically dust duct grills and ducts to improve forced air circulation?

( ) On hot water systems, is the temperature and pressure at or near 170° F and 12 psi? If not, have it adjusted. The pressure will vary from 12 to 20 psi.

( ) Do you drain the water out of the system periodically and add a rust inhibitor?

( ) Are radiators, convectors, and baseboard units kept clean and free of air in the lines? Covers, curtains, or obstructions in front of the units will reduce their efficiency.

( ) Are all leaks in the system repaired promptly?

( ) Is there a proper pitch in all your steam lines so the condensate can drain easily and reduce noise?

( ) Are all thermostats level? Have they been cleaned and adjusted recently?

( ) For your oil burner, has a draft test been done on the chimney flue? Has a CO_2 test been done this year? Has the stack gas temperature been checked? Your service contract can cover this.

( ) Do you drain a bucket of water out of your steam water level control periodically to remove sediment? Do you maintain a proper water level? If your boiler needs water more than once a month, the system has a leak.

AIR TREATMENT DEVICES

Cleanliness and proper control features will insure efficient use of humidifiers, dehumidifiers, electronic air cleaners, fresh air intakes, and filter systems.

( ) Is the humidifier cleaned each season of salt build-up? Does the control system turn on the unit? Is the water float valve operating? Do you know when and how to adjust the humidity control to prevent excessive humidity as the outdoor temperature changes? Frost or condensation on windows or walls means the humidity control is set too high.

( ) Do you clean the dehumidifier each season? Can you drain the unit into a sink or floor drain?

( ) Do you periodically clean the mechanical or electronic air cleaner systems?

( ) Is the fresh air intake system damper working properly?

AIR CONDITIONING SYSTEMS

To derive maximum efficiency from a central air conditioning system or from room units, several factors should be considered. Choose the correct size unit (not oversized or undersized) with an energy ratio of seven or higher and operate at a constant reasonable temperature setting. For best results, keep the house conditioned during the entire season. Opening the windows allows untreated, humid air to enter. Annual maintenance is necessary to avoid overworking the compressor and other parts of the system.

( )   Do you have an annual service that checks all temperatures and pressures and adds freon if necessary? Were all filters cleaned? Is the compressor operating properly? Were all parts lubricated?

( )   Do you keep the temperature at least 6° higher during sleeping hours or if you are out?

( )   Do you adjust the dampers for summer operation? Do you keep the blower on continuous air circulation for even temperatures and non-stagnant air?

( )   Have you ever had the system balanced for even temperatures in each room? Additional registers may also help.

( )   Do you periodically flush the evaporator drain line to prevent condensate back-up and stains of surfaces by the water?

( )   Is the compressor-condenser located in the shade and on a level platform base?

( )   If you use your air conditioner all season, do you keep the storm windows closed as well as the drapes?

HOT WATER HEATERS

The cost of heating hot water can average $3 to $5 per person per month. Savings are possible by lowering the temperature to below 140° F if you have a dishwasher and below 120° F if you do not. Settings over 140° F are costly and can shorten the life of water heaters, especially those that are glass-lined.

( )   Have a serviceperson check the damper, clean the burner surfaces, and check the electrode on electric units. Be sure the flue is the right size for a new larger heater.

( )   Do you drain out a pail of water every few months to keep the bottom free of scale?

( ) For instantaneous heaters on your boiler, do you have the unit descaled when the flow of hot water drops below that coming out of the cold water tap?

( ) Do you keep the water below 140° or 120° F?

( ) Is your heater insulated? There are kits available.

OTHER ENERGY-SAVING IDEAS

( ) Keep electric light levels adequate but not excessive. Keep lights turned off when a room is not in use.

( ) Have you planted trees as windbreaker screens and for shade?

( ) Have you considered the use of a vestibule or a mud room entrance in winter to conserve heat?

( ) Check into inexpensive devices for reducing the amount of water flushed in a toilet.

( ) Do you operate dishwashers and ovens in the late evening when power loads are less and the outdoors are cooler in summer? Stop the dishwasher before the electric drying cycle and let the load air-dry overnight.

( ) Insulate all pipes and ductworks in crawl spaces and non-living areas. Insulate cold water pipes to reduce the chances of freezing in winter, especially in the garage, crawl space, and attic.

( ) Consider heating hot water by using the heat dissipated by the air conditioning condenser in the summer, or the flue gases in the winter.

( ) Does your family wear warm clothing to enable them to be comfortable at reduced air temperatures?

( ) When dehumidifiers are used in basements and crawl spaces, be sure to keep basement doors and windows closed to protect the treated air.

( ) Grade the earth away from the foundation so water will be diverted away from the house and will not penetrate basement walls.

( ) Periodic servicing and adjustments of appliances and air treatment equipment will result in better operation and replacements will be deferred.

( ) Light color roofs reflect the sun radiations more than dark colored roofs. Flat deck roofs can be sprayed or painted with a reflective paint or covered with white stone chips. In cold climates, dark colored roofs will absorb more heat.

( ) Are all your windows shaded in some manner to reduce the solar heat gain—particularly the south and west walls? Are windows covered by insulating drapes in winter?

( ) Do you lower the temperature in your bedroom at night instead of opening the windows?

( ) Gas clothes dryers must be vented outside. Venting electric clothes dryers into the house in cold climates conserves heat, but you must be sure the filter works and is kept clean.

SUMMARY

Some of the ideas listed in this chapter will cost you some money to install but many of them are absolutely free. They will all save you money, give a good return on your investment, and keep you comfortable year after year. Think about how much energy you can save with this "action program." Past experience has shown that the average energy improvement pays off in three to five years.

Call your local insulation and energy saving contractor to perform the "energy audit" and action program for you. You can do it yourself. Write for *In the Bank or Up the Chimney* (April 1975) -23-000-00297-3, $1.70, from the Superintendent of Documents, U.S. Government Printing Office, Washington, D.C. 20402.

31.
Household Emergencies and How to Cope With Them

INTRODUCTION

This chapter deals with household emergencies and how to prepare yourself, your family, and your home to meet them.

Careful planning may save your life as well as your time and money in the event of an emergency. I speak from personal experience, for a few years ago my house was struck by lightning. Fortunately, my family followed the rules I will be sharing with you, and as a result, we were calm and rational throughout the entire experience.

At the start of the electric storm, I instructed my family to keep away from the windows and electric appliances as well as to disconnect all stereos, televisions and major appliances. I also instructed them not to turn the water on or touch any faucets or sinks. When the storm increased in severity I had all the children leave the top floor and get into the center of the house. After a tremendous crash of thunder which shook the entire house, my daughter came running in to say that the picture window was smashed. Although later this was found to be untrue, a number of lights in the house did blow out. It was then that I realized our house had been struck by lightning.

My first step was to call the fire department to tell them I believed that the house had been hit by lightning. Second, I started to get all the children into the front room—but to my joy, I found they were all already there! Because we practice fire drills every six months, the children were prepared, and as a result, they reacted calmly and sensibly.

The firemen arrived in four minutes—almost at the same instant my daughter smelled smoke. The firemen rushed upstairs while I sent the family to a neighbor according to a pre-arranged plan. Although there was little if any smoke, the odor seemed over-powering. It took ten minutes to locate the cause of the odor. The smoke detectors, which sounded at the first trace of smoke, pinpointed the area of damage. The cause of the odor was a burned-out attic fan timer switch and all of its wiring. The force of the lightning bolt had blown off a small portion of the roof, jumped to the fan, and blew the switch before going to ground. Many of our neighbors had wiring and appliance damage when an electric pole was hit, but since our incoming electric line was protected with a lightning surge arrestor we had no such damage.

Are you prepared for such an emergency? Do you know the steps to take to protect your home? Remember that in many emergency situations, tradesmen will be swamped with calls and may not be readily available for your house. This chapter will help you meet those emergencies.

PRECAUTIONARY MEASURES

The following precautionary measures should be made in preparation for possible emergencies. They deal with the main sources of energy and how to stop their flow. I would recommend that you locate these emergency valves and switches today and clearly mark them. Also show each member of the family the valves and switches and inform them of their functions. Then post a sketch locating all valves and switches.

Main Water Valve.   The main water valve that shuts off all water coming into the home is located near the water meter or near the basement floor where the pipe enters the house. Clearly label the valve with a magic marker. If you have a bad water leak this is the valve to close. Be sure the valves can be turned; if not, free them up and back-off one-quarter of a turn. Then the valve will operate easily.

Main Electric Service Box.   Service boxes will have either fuses or circuit breakers. Depending upon the age of the house, there will be either a main disconnect switch, individual switches, or breakers to shut off power. Once again, be sure to label all circuits so you can locate them easily in an emergency. Circuits fail either because of a break or short in the line due to the use of too many appliances on a single circuit, or because of an overloaded appliance. Your job will be to determine what caused the circuit to fail and to take that appliance off the line. Next, reset the circuit breaker or replace the fuse. Lighting and convenience outlet circuits are usually designed for 15 amps—not for 30 amps. Do not increase the size of the fuse to accommodate the appliance, since such overfusing may cause fires.

Gas Meter.   Near the gas meter is a main cut-off valve that does not have a handle but has a square end on the valve stem. To shut off the valve, it is necessary to have a wrench, so keep one hanging nearby. You can use a monkey wrench or make a wrench from a piece of steel (3/8 x 2 inches). Cut a slot in the end of the steel piece to fit the end of the valve stem.

If you smell gas, check the pilot lights of the various gas appliances in the house. Stove burners may have been turned on but left unlit. If you cannot locate the source of escaping gas immediately and suspect a gas leak, turn off the valve at the appliance and call the gas company. You should never attempt to fix a gas leak yourself. While you are waiting, don't light matches or flames and be sure to open all windows.

When the emergency is over and the gas is turned back on make sure that all pilot lights in the house are immediately relit, after insuring that the gas to the pilot light has been off long enough for air currents to carry away any remaining gas in the room.

If pilot lights malfunction, the gas company may provide a free adjustment so that they burn correctly. Otherwise, a qualified repairman will do this for a fee. Pilot lights of furnaces and water heaters should be left burning throughout the year to prevent condensation and rusting.

Oil as Heating Fuel.   If you should have any difficulties with the oil fired boiler, secure the electric emergency switch, which is usually painted red and located at the top of the cellar stairs or near a basement window. Then call a serviceperson. Be certain to periodically check the bottom of the oil tank for leaks. These tanks tend to leak after 20 years. They can be repaired by coating the outside of the tank with a fiberglass cover.

ELECTRICAL SHUT DOWN

Each year, many sections of the country are hit with severe rain, wind, snow, or ice storms that knock out electric service for a day or a week.

To help the power company, shut off all light switches and be certain that all major appliances are in the OFF position. Many homeowners are not prepared for this stoppage and do very little to prevent damage to their heating, water, and refrigeration systems. Your knowledgeable action can save you money.

Heating Systems.   If your area has an electric stoppage, the power company should be able to tell how long the electricity will be out. If the weather is cold, your home should stay above freezing for about 12 hours. If the stoppage goes beyond that, then some action on your part will be necessary to prevent damage due to freezing. Temporarily, you can close off the room that has a fireplace. This will give you comfort in one room.

If your home is heated by *gas*, consult the furnace instruction manual on how to operate the system without power to the fan. Forced warm air systems can be operated without the blower fan since the heat will rise by gravity. Be certain to follow instructions and remain at the furnace, as it is possible to burn the heating surface.

If your house is heated by gas fired circulated *hot water*, then manually open the zone valves. The heated hot water will rise by gravity to the baseboard or radiator system.

If your furnace or boiler is heated by *oil*, an electricity stoppage will prevent the heating system from operating. Therefore, you must prevent the system from freezing. If you have forced warm air heat, no protection is necessary.

Your *steam heat* system requires no electricity to generate steam. However, you will have to remain with the boiler as the gas must be fired manually. If oil is the fuel, the boiler must be secured.

If you have hot water or steam heat, you must bleed the system of all water. This is done by securing the inlet water valve from the street or well. Put a hose at the lowest point in the system and bleed the water outside. Be certain that all zone valves are manually wide open. Open a radiator vent valve at the highest part of the system. The water should flow out.

Water System.   If the outside temperature is below freezing, you have to bleed the entire hot and cold domestic water system. Shut off the inlet valve at the meter. Then open a valve at the lowest point and the highest point and bleed the system. There will still be water in the sink, tub, and toilet traps. If this freezes, the fixture and trap will rupture.

Put anti-freeze into each trap you can't drain. Also bleed and drain the hot water heater.

Refrigeration.   You can take several steps to keep the home freezer food from spoiling. Keep the freezer door closed. Food will usually stay frozen in a fully loaded cabinet two days, and in a half-loaded cabinet more than a day. If the stoppage is longer, move the food to a freezer locker plant or add dry ice, if you can get it. (To prevent burns, wear gloves when you handle dry ice.) As a last resort, you can get friends to store the food. In most cases, it is not a good idea to refreeze food that has thawed.

Return of Power.   When the power is finally restored, the first step is to get the house heated. Turn on the water, and add water to all systems. Bleed out the air. Then follow instructions and fire the boiler.

NATURAL DISASTERS

Earthquakes, floods, hurricanes, tornados, and winter storms are some of the natural disasters that can and do strike the United States.
   The major suggestion is to be prepared. The United States Weather Service usually gives ample warning of these disasters, and radio stations will give you instructions on what to do. But always have a family escape plan and hold drills so the whole family knows what course of action to take. In the event of a bad storm, it may be a wise precaution to purchase rolls of plastic sheeting. This plastic can come in handy if the roof should start to leak. Also, during storms, it is possible for water to get into the basement. Unfortunately, once water starts to come in it is tough to stop until the rain stops. Trouble areas are clogged or worn gutters, leaders, drain systems, clogged window wells, and the soil at the foundation if it is not properly graded away. If your area loses electricity often and you need a sump pump to keep the basement or crawl space dry, then some alternate power source is needed; i.e., a portable generator or batteries.

SUMMARY

Be prepared. That's the motto for every homeowner. I've dealt with families who have experienced most of the disasters discussed. Those who were prepared had the least damage.

32.
Home Security—
Fire, Noise,
and Burglary

INTRODUCTION

The American home can be a dangerous place. In 1977, there were approximately 28,000 accidental deaths and 4 million severe injuries. Burglaries are on the rise and death or injury due to fire is common. Home safety hazards are so numerous that the education of the homeowner is essential. This chapter will introduce you to the hazards that may exist in your home and the corrective methods to use to overcome them.

FIRE

This year one home in your general neighborhood will be involved in fire. It could by *yours*. Each day hundreds of people, mostly the young and aged, die in these fires. Fire deaths occur when the simple rules of fire safety are violated.

Home Inspection for Fire Safety. A home fire safety checklist is available free from the National Fire Protection Association, 570 Atlantic Avenue, Boston, Mass. 02210. Your local fire department may make fire safety checks of homes. Some fire prevention ideas are given below.

Discard partially filled cans of little used combustible products. Store necessary cans and bottles in a cool, ventilated location out of the reach of youngsters.

Place portable fire extinguishers at strategic locations in the home (kitchen, hallway, basement) and instruct the family on proper use. Check the charge on each unit semi-annually.

Ground outdoor TV antennas securely to prevent them from conducting lightning into your home.

Call the local utility company at the first major sign of trouble; i.e., gas fumes, downed electrical lines, smoke odors.

Stop sparks from flying out of your fireplace by installing a permanent built-in screen (large mesh) that fits snugly over the exterior flue opening.

Have the heating system checked periodically.

Make sure the electric service to your house is at least 100 ampere, and that the wiring is safe. Don't overload your electrical circuits. Replace all worn or frayed electric cords. Have enough electrical circuits to take care of appliances without overloading the wiring.

Never smoke in bed. Be sure all matches and smoking materials are extinguished.

Exercise great care with portable heaters.

Keep stoves clean and free of grease.

Keep storage areas and yards free of debris. Dispose of trash regularly.

Never leave young children unattended.

Get rid of accumulations of old clothing, mattresses, curtains, drapes, lampshades, furniture, paper, magazines, and rags.

Hang up oily mops and keep oily rags in closed metal containers.

Keep home tools, machinery, motors, and appliances serviced and clean.

Cover the roof with a fire-retardant material.

Keep the grounds around your house free of dead grass, weeds, trash, and dried brush.

Keep matches in a safe place, out of the reach of children. Have plenty of ashtrays.

Fire Detectors and Extinguishers. Deadly smoke gases cause three-fourths of all fire deaths in dwellings. These slow fires usually occur when the family is sleeping. A reliable fire detecting system is a good investment. There are two basic types of fire detection systems—heat sensing and smoke detecting, powered by a battery or electricity. Heat sensors will activate when a certain temperature is reached. Smoke detectors will work even if you can't smell the smoke, and their acute sensitivity makes them more dependable than the heat sensing units in detecting smoldering or remote fires. Install smoke detectors in the basement and on each floor. Proper maintenance is also necessary to be sure the system remains in working order. It should be checked about once a year by a professional such as the installer.

There are four types of fire extinguishers, commonly designated as A, B, C, and D. Type A is for ordinary combustibles, such as wood. Type B is designed for use on flammable liquids, such as grease or paint. Type C can be used on electrical equipment, and type D is for use on metal fires. If you don't know what type of fire detection system or extinguisher would be best for you, you can obtain general advice from the fire prevention unit of your local fire department.

Lightning Protection.   Lightning protection can prevent or greatly reduce this danger of life and property. It should be considered in those areas subject to severe lightning storms. In most states, lightning protection reduces the cost of fire insurance. Lightning-protection systems should be designed to provide a direct path for the bolt to follow to ground, and to prevent damage or injury as the bolt travels the path.

If your home is not protected during a storm then stay away from metal fireplaces, stoves, water faucets, appliances, telephones, and metal windows. Stay inside the house during an electrical storm. If caught outdoors, lie down in a low protected spot. Stay away from high trees, hilltops, wire fences, and poles. Remain in an auto or truck during an electrical storm.

Escape Plan. Remember—fire protection is a family affair. Discuss the subject of fire and its prevention with all members of the family. Develop a sound fire prevention program for your home, along with an escape action plan in case of fire. Discuss this with the local fire department and obtain their literature.

Sit down with all members of your family and draw up a floor plan of your home. Figure out at least two exits from each room, especially from bedrooms. If there are porch roofs outside upstairs windows, utilize them. Make sure all windows open easily. A rope or chain ladder may be indispensable for safe escape from upper stories.

Schedule periodic family drills. Know where the fire alarm box is located. Agree on a meeting place, like the front yard, where all must assemble after evacuation so that you will know the house is vacant.

If Fire Strikes . . .   When the alarms start ringing, do not attempt to put out the fire unless you can see it is confined and you have an extinguisher handy. Do not waste time. Get out of the house as rapidly as possible. Do not stop to call the fire department; your phone may already be inoperative and you may lose your chance to escape. Pull the fire alarm quickly, or get a neighbor to call. After you escape, don't risk your life to go back into the house. The fire department is much better trained and equipped to make rescues.

When reporting a fire by fire alarm box you should know the location of the nearest alarm box to your home. The location should be memorized by everyone in the house. Know how to send an alarm: open the door to expose the hook, pull the hook all the way down once, and let go. Remain at the alarm box until fire-fighters arrive. You must give them the exact location of the fire. If you phone, give the operator your name and address and the location and type of the fire.

NOISE

A quiet place is not easy to find, even in the country. Apartment living means people above and below and perhaps alongside. Your own home, no matter how quiet, has noise pollution from all sides. Few houses are constructed with the idea of keeping out anything more than wind and weather. You can, however, take the edge off the noise that's around you. Care should be exercised in selecting mechanical equipment. Some manufacturers now include noise ratings in their specifications; many more will in the future. If noise ratings are not available to compare, it is to the home builder's advantage to shop, listen, and beware.

Careful design of home heating systems and plumbing systems will help reduce noise from inside sources. Heating and air conditioning blower noise can be reduced by keeping blower speeds and air velocity to a minimum. Sheet metal heating ducts are often a transmission medium for vibration or airborne noise. Commercially available acoustical lining may be applied to these ducts to absorb the sound. Back-to-back heating grilles in adjoining rooms should be avoided. Where outlet grilles pass through the wall, rubber padding should be used to isolate them from the structure.

Plumbing noises can be reduced by using slightly larger pipe sizes. Air compression standpipes installed above frequently used faucets or valves will reduce hammering. Pressure reducing valves will keep the pressure below 50 psi. Where water and heat pipes go through a structural member or wall, the opening should be padded with rubber and sealed to prevent airborne noises through the opening. Piping and ducting should be supported by rubber or felt padded hangers.

The following are some further ideas for a quieter home.

Use noise-absorbing materials on floors, especially in areas where there is a lot of traffic. Put rubber or plastic threads on uncarpeted stairs.

Hang heavy drapes over the windows closest to outside noise sources.

Install sound-absorbing ceiling tile in the kitchen.

Use a foam pad under blenders and mixers.

Use insulation and vibration mounts when installing dishwashers.

Install washing machines and dryers in the same room with heating and cooling equipment. Then insulate the walls and ceilings and use an outside source of air.

Remember that a hand-powered or electric lawnmower does the job with considerably less noise.

Place window and central air conditioner units not facing your neighbor's bedrooms.

Compare the noise outputs of different makes of an appliance before making your selection.

BURGLARY

There are many things which you as a homeowner or renter can do to discourage a thief from entering your house or apartment. It is important to remember that most burglars are quite cautious. Unless your home contains items of unusual value, the typical burglar will bypass it when he sees that you have taken steps to deter forced entry. I have found that 98% of all homes inspected have poor security. One of the most common ways a burglar enters a home is through unlocked or poorly locked doors.

Sliding glass patio doors are particularly vulnerable break-in points. The doors can often be removed by lifting them from the grooves they slide in. Spacers or protuding screw heads can be installed in the grooves over the door to prevent this type of removal. Most patio doors have weak latches that can easily be broken by prying the door away from the frame. Placing a piece of pipe in the bottom grooves can prevent the door from being opened if the latch is broken. There are special sliding door locks that are both strong enough and of such a design as to prevent removal of the door.

Jalousie doors (doors with glass slats that angle out) also pose problems. It is possible to turn the crank or knob that opens the glass section from outside the door. You can prevent this by removing the knob or lever when it is not in use.

When considering the installation of a new door, keep in mind the following. Install a front door peep-hole and chain guard so that you can be sure of the identity of the caller before you open the door. More expensive indoor/outdoor intercoms and monitors provide maximum protection. Be careful not to install mail slots within reach of the inside door knob or lock. It's easy for burglars to open doors through such openings.

If your primary lock is the key-in-the-knob type, it is easily attacked and should be replaced with a stronger lock, or you can install an additional lock. Exterior doors should be equipped with either a dead bolt or a self-locking dead latch. The term "dead" bolt refers to the fact that the bolt cannot be moved except by turning a knob or key. The latch or bolt should protrude at least one inch out of the lock when the bolt or latch is in a locked position. Extra protection for exterior doors can be obtained by using a chain guard which locks with a key. Be careful when buying locks. All too often what appears to be a good brass lock is nothing more than brass-plated soft metal that breaks very easily and offers little protection against forced entry.

When considering the installation of locks, keep in mind that the exterior lock cylinders of the house you are moving into should be changed, since you cannot be sure who had access to the keys in the past. Lock garage doors; unlocked doors invite the theft of expensive tools and equipment and may provide easy access to your home. Check your basement security; unlocked casement windows and basement doors can provide a perfect entry, so provide locks for your windows and doors and lock the basement door leading into the house. All windows to which a burglar can gain access should have key locks, which are easy to install and not expensive. Too many locking devices can create a fire hazard by interfering with your emergency escape. This is a major concern when a double cylinder lock is used. Be sure the key is accessible to the entire family as a safety precaution.

Burglar alarm systems range from inexpensive battery-operated units that protect a single door or window to sophisticated systems which cover the entire house and alert the police or a private protection service. For maximum protection, all doors and windows should be part of the alarm system. Sophisticated electronic systems are now available to signal the arrival of unwanted guests. Crossing the field of surveillance trips an alarm. Many police departments install these for residents who will be away for more than a few days. Check with your police department.

The majority of burglars are unwilling to enter a home when someone is in it, so any steps you take to create the illusion that the house is occupied will help to prevent forced entry. Adjust the window shades or blinds the way you would if you were at home. A house with all the shades drawn down to the sill in the middle of the day is an indication that the occupants are away. One way to suggest that someone is at home is to leave your radio or air conditioner on and to leave several lights burning. Use porch lights, patio lights, garage lights, and garden lights, and leave some or all of them on all night.

Do improve the lighting around the house. Several lights properly positioned will minimize shadows and discourage prowlers. Form the habit of turning on your outdoor lights at night, both when you are at home and when you are out. Light, as well as noise, is a deterrent to the thief. A barking dog can be a strong deterrent; be sure your dog learns to bark at strangers. Another signal that people are away from home is an open garage door. Moreover, if there is a connecting door between the garage and house, the burglar can close the outside garage door and take his time breaking the lock without fear of being seen.

When on vacation, arrange for discontinuation of mail service and newspaper and milk delivery. Inform a neighbor of your plans and arrange for normal home maintenance. Install staggered timed light controls on several lights in your home to give the illusion that someone is home. Notify the police and a neighbor that you will be away.

Do contact your local police department and request a home security check. Inquire whether they provide etching equipment for marking of valuables. Demand credentials before admitting salesmen or repairmen. Don't leave ladders outside—lock them up securely. Don't leave the door unlocked if you are "just out for a minute," or are expecting someone. Don't try to hide an extra key anywhere on the outside of the house, and don't leave a note on the door telling a friend or relative where you have gone and when you'll return. Last, but not least, never hide valuables or large amounts of money in the house.

No protection is perfect, and it may happen that a burglar will gain entry. Should that happen, your best protection against violence is simply to say, "Just tell me and I'll give you anything you want." Your personal safety is far more important than some lost valuable.

SAFETY

The home and property are the scenes of almost two-thirds of all accidental deaths of children under five and almost half of the accidental deaths of persons 65 and over. By proper planning, your house can provide a safe environment for your family. Think safety when you are remodeling or building a new house.

Good arrangement of rooms and clear passageways between them allow safe traveling from one activity area of the house to another and can be a factor in preventing accidents. Adequate, convenient, built-in storage places encourage family members to put things away where they do not clutter passageways. If you choose a two-story house, a good design of stairways will reduce the number and seriousness of falls. Stairways need adequate lighting well-placed and convenient to control at the top and the bottom of the staircase. Be sure to provide an easily gripped handrail on at least one side of the stairs. Space the balusters close enough together so a youngster cannot squeeze his head or body through. Plan a headroom of more than 6 feet 8 inches over any point of the stairs.

Room doors should swing into rooms, not into hallways, where they may interfere with walking. Hinged doors on hall closets must open outward. A door that provides access to a descending stairway should be hinged to open away from the stairs, even if it opens into a hallway. For each room without an exterior door, plan at least one window large enough, low enough, and easy enough to open to provide an exit in case of fire if other escape routes are blocked.

No matter how well you inspect, you should always be alert to ways to improve the safety of your surroundings. Here are some hints to consider: install grab bars or handrails in the bathroom; use skidproof mats in tubs; do not leave cakes of soap in the tub or shower; anchor down all throw rugs; keep flammable articles away from fires; clear the stairways of toys and other objects; a light at the top of stairways or at the bottom step will reduce the number of falls; check gas burners often for leaks; label medicines and store them out of the reach of children; accidental poisoning has become common—young children are apt to chew woodwork, stair railings, and window sills, especially when they are cutting teeth, and if the wood is painted, the child may become ill from lead poisoning; watch where you are going—walk, do not run, on steps; light the way into a room and put lights on steps and stairs.

Kid-Proofing the Kitchen.   The kitchen can be the most dangerous area of the house. It has more equipment than other rooms, and family activities tend to be concentrated there, especially if people eat in the kitchen and it serves as a family room. The kitchen is a fascinating room to the curious toddler—but it also can be one of the most dangerous to him, for most kitchens are designed for adults, not children. "Kid-proofing" your kitchen so that you don't have to keep a watchful eye out every second is a necessity for the mother who expects to have any peace of mind or to get any family meals prepared.

These tips are from the General Electric Consumers Institute, which has been helping homemakers in the kitchen for more than half a century.

Starting at the bottom, *put plastic insert plugs in all floor level electrical outlets* when they are not in use. This will prevent anything metallic being inserted into the outlet and reduce the possibility of the child receiving an electrical shock.

Do not allow electric cords to hang below the counter or tabletop, where a child might grab them, try to eat them, or fall on the prongs. Keep such cords in good condition for your own protection; no cracked or cut cords should be allowed in a well-run kitchen.

When cooking on range surface units, *always keep pot handles turned toward the rear* so that little ones cannot reach up and tip or spill a pot of boiling water or a pan of scalding grease. Keep knives and other sharp utensils out of sight and out of reach.

Don't store soap, bleach, or other laundry chemicals where they are easily accessible to play in or drink. Insulate any undersink hot water pipes so that touching them will not result in burns. Set up a "play area" for the child well away from the range and ovens. A child playing where food is being prepared runs a greater risk of injury.

If you have a trash compactor, keep it locked when not in use so Junior can't fill it with your china, silver, or the family cat. Try to locate your refrigerator or freezer so that the back coils are not accessible to touch, as they do become hot. The dishwasher door should always be keep securely latched so that a toddler trying to stand up with the help of the handle won't pull the door down on himself. If you adopt the point of view of the child, many kitchen accidents are preventable. Removing temptation is half the battle in making your kitchen kid-proof.

Safety Precautions for the Handyman. The do-it-yourself boom is on. Many homeowners are beating the high cost of labor by doing remodeling chores themselves. As you work, follow safe practices; read the instruction manual for tools and dress for the part, protecting yourself against injury by wearing gloves, tight fitting clothes, and eye protection.

These safety rules for power tools have been endorsed by the Power Tool Institute.

Know your power tool. Learn its applications and limitations as well as the specific potential hazards peculiar to this tool. Ground all tools, unless they are double-insulated. If a tool is equipped with a three-prong plug, it should be plugged into a three-hole electrical receptacle. Keep guards in place and in working order. Keep the work area clean. Cluttered areas and benches invite accidents. Avoid dangerous environments. Don't use power tools in damp or wet locations. Keep the work area well lit. Don't force a tool—it will do the job better and safer at the rate for which it was designed.

Use the right tool. Don't force a small tool or attachment to do the job of a heavy-duty tool. Use safety glasses with most tools, and a face or dust mask if the cutting operation is dusty. Don't abuse the electric cord—never carry the tool by the cord or yank it to disconnect it from the recptacle. Keep the cord from heat, oil, and sharp edges.

Secure the work. Use clamps or a vise to hold work. It's safer than using your hand and it frees both hands to operate the tool. Don't overreach. Keep proper footing and balance at all times. Maintain tools with care. Keep tools sharp and clean for the best and safest performance. Follow instructions for lubricating and changing accessories. Disconnect tools when not in use, before servicing, and when changing accessories such as blades, bits, or cutters. Remove adjusting keys and wrenches. Form the habit of checking to see that keys and adjusting wrenches are removed from the tool before turning it on. Avoid accidental starting. Don't carry a plugged-in tool with your finger on the switch.

Finally, when you are finished, *store equipment properly.* Clean up immediately. Remove all clutter and other objects that could become a fire or tripping hazard.

SUMMARY

The American home can be a dangerous place. By planning preventive measures, you can reduce or eliminate hazards from fire, noise, burglary, and inadequate safety. Call on your local safety council and the fire and police departments for help in checking out your home for hazards.

33.
Preventive Maintenance Checklist

INTRODUCTION

Nobody wants to be a slave to a house. However, the money you have invested in your home is considerable and care and effort are necessary to secure and increase the value of your "nest egg." Unfortunately, most of us use the "squeaky wheel" technique in our approach to maintenance—doing little or nothing until failure or malfunction occurs. As a result, we are often rewarded with high repair bills and great inconvenience.

You can simplify the job of maintenance if you do it systematically instead of haphazardly. Preventive maintenance involves regular checking on those parts of the house that are liable to get out of good working order. The regular attention to the condition of our property and the early correction of possible defects will extend the life of equipment and materials as well as save you time and money in the long run.

The following preventive maintenance checklist is based on my years of experience in the home inspection field. It provides the homeowner with a general guide to inspecting problem areas in the home. For convenience, the list has been divided into interior and exterior inspection units. It may be advisable to pin the checklist on a bulletin board as a reminder.

Spring is an ideal time to make a thorough inspection of your home, since winter weather may have caused deterioration or failure in the building materials and joint sealants. Also, since spring is traditional clean-up time, the homeowner is usually in the mood to do something around the house. Fall is also a good time for home inspection, particularly if the summer weather has been severe. Remember that special checks should be made after severe wind, rain, ice, and snow storms and any resulting damage should be repaired at once.

Keep a permanent record of maintenance to the house and equipment, recording the date, the cost, and the name of the craftsman.

EXTERIOR INSPECTION—SPRING AND FALL

GROUNDS.

( ) Check driveways and walks for cracks and deterioration.

( ) Check window wells, dry wells, and storm drains.

( ) Check wooden fences.

( ) Check retaining walls for cracks, bulges, and leaning.

( ) Check all landscaping. Consult County Agricultural Agent for advice.

( ) Trim all bushes and trees.

( ) Check all out-buildings, porches, and patios for rot and infestation.

( ) Check for proper drainage.

( ) Drain exterior water lines and open taps in winter.

FOUNDATION.

( ) Check (during rainstorm) for proper drainage away from house and garage.

( ) Check for evidence of insect infestation.

( ) Check for settlement, cracks, spalling, bulges, and deterioration.

ROOF.

( ) Check for loose, damaged or missing shingles.

( ) Check soffits for signs of moisture build-up.

( ) Check flashing for lifting and poor seal.

( ) Check television antenna for sturdiness.

( ) Treat wood roofs, gutters, and siding with preservative.

( ) Remove mold from asbestos shingles.

( ) Check condition of chimney.

( ) Clean all gutters and leaders and check their condition.

SIDING.

( ) Check for finish or for paint deterioration.

( ) Check caulking at joints.

( ) Check stucco for soundness.

WINDOWS AND DOORS.
( ) Check for damaged screens or broken glass.

( ) Check weatherstripping and caulking.

( ) Lubricate window channels.

( ) Check for rot.

( ) Check for finish or for paint deterioration.

( ) Check all putty for looseness.

PORCH AND PATIO.
( ) Check all wooden supports and windows.

( ) Seal patio at foundation.

( ) Check roof for leaks.

POOL.
( ) Check all equipment for quiet and leakproof operation.

( ) Consult service manual for maintenance.

( ) Clean all surfaces periodically.

ELECTRICAL.
( ) Check condition of incoming service wire and supports.

( ) Have all exterior plugs fitted with ground fault connectors.

( ) Have electrician periodically check all aluminum wire connections.

PLUMBING SYSTEM.
( ) Check well and components.

( ) Check septic systems for possible pumping.

( ) Check all exterior taps.

CHIMNEY.
( ) Check mortar joints.

( ) Check for condition of cap.

INFESTATION.
( ) Treat for ants and other insects.

( ) Check for termites.

( ) Check for damage.

ADDITIONAL ITEMS.
( ) Check grounds for water accumulations.

( )   Check siding for cracked or lifted shingles.

( )   Check all roof flashings—a major source of roof leakage.

( )   Treat to prevent ant and other infestations.

( )   Check for dead limbs on trees.

( )   Check walks and driveway for deterioration.

( )   _____

( )   _____

( )   _____

( )   _____

INTERIOR INSPECTION

DECORATION.

( )   Check all painted and finished walls for condition.

( )   Check baseboards for finish or for paint deterioration.

( )   Check rugs for wear and tear and floor for signs of settling.

( )   Check for defective floors and walls.

( )   Check all stairs and railings.

( )   Check ceilings for leaks.

( )   Check all storm and prime windows.

ATTIC.

( )   Check for signs of roof or flashing leaks on rafters and insulation.

( )   Check chimney and chimney cap for smoke or water leaks.

( )   Check roof rafters for straightness.

( )   Check position and condition of insulation.

( )   Check ventilation openings for nests and other blockage.

( )   Check operation of vent and/or attic fan.

BASEMENT.

( )   Check for cracks or breaks in wall.

( )   Check for leaks in walls and floor.

( )   Check for condensation on walls and efflorescence.

( )   Check for rotting sills and window frames.

( )   Check for sagging floor joists.

( )   Check crawl space ventilation, insulation, and vapor barriers.

( )   Test, clean, and lubricate sump pump.

ELECTRICAL SYSTEM.

( ) Check power distribution for overloads.

( ) Check and mark all circuits.

( ) Examine lamp cords.

( ) Check circuits for over-fusing or test circuit breakers.

( ) Check all plugs and connectors.

( ) If lights flicker, fuses blow, or breakers trip, call in an electrician.

( ) Check all aluminum wire connections.

HEATING/COOLING SYSTEMS.

( ) Have heating system checked by serviceperson each fall.

( ) Clean all elements of cooling system.

( ) Check condition of hot water heater, and drain it every month.

( ) Test and clean humidifier.

( ) Test and clean dehumidifier.

( ) Service all radiators and valves.

( ) Repair breaks in insulation.

( ) Check for leaks (caulk and weatherstrip).

( ) Lubricate all pumps, fans, and motors.

( ) Inspect and service all air conditioners.

( ) Clean all elements of heating system.

( ) Check flue pipe for corrosion and leaks.

( ) Clean electronic filter.

( ) Drain and test steam boiler water level control.

( ) Clean all solar collectors.

PLUMBING.

( ) Check all faucets, drains, and traps.

( ) Check galvanized and brass piping for leaks.

( ) Check all toilet flush mechanisms.

( ) Clean all strainers and shower heads.

KITCHEN.

( ) Check all appliances for noisy operation.

( ) Clean or change range fan filters.

LUBRICATION.
( ) Check instruction booklets to see what equipment needs periodic lubrication.

HOUSE SECURITY.
( ) Check condition of all locks and general security.

( ) Check charge on fire extinguishers.

( ) Review family fire prevention and escape plans.

( ) Test smoke/fire alarms.

( ) Have police and fire officials check your home and make suggestions.

ADDITIONAL ITEMS.
( ) Check ceilings for signs of leaks and bulges.

( ) Check bathroom plumbing for leaks and drips.

( ) Check caulking around tub/shower.

( ) Check electrical outlets for poor connections.

( ) Check appliances for loose or frayed wires.

( ) Check condition of all extension cords.

( ) Change or clean all heating/cooling filters.

( ) Check humidifier for proper function and possible calcium buildup.

( ) Clean all refrigerator and dryer vents.

( ) _____

( ) _____

( ) _____

SUMMARY

Don't neglect minor repairs. Anticipate major problems by checking over your home on a regular basis using your preventive maintenance checklist. The inconvenience avoided and the money saved will be well worth the time you've invested.

Keep in mind, however, to attempt only those home repairs you know you are qualified to perform. Never attempt structural changes or repair of operating equipment, electrical systems, or plumbing unless you are skilled in these crafts.

PART IV.
SELLING YOUR HOUSE

34.
How To Sell Your House

INTRODUCTION

Welcome to the last chapter! If you are both buying and selling a home, this is the chapter you should be reading first. There are as many decisions involved in selling a home as there are in buying. Since your present home represents a needed equity, every well-planned step taken in selling your home can protect and increase that equity.

The average family in the United States moves once every five to six years. The purpose of this chapter is to make selling your present house a profitable and satisfying experience. The many cost decisions made in selling are discussed here. Remember that if these decisions are made in haste, both money and time will be lost. Above all, get good professional help (see Chapter 3). A professional can save you more than his or her fee and reduce those selling headaches. The real estate transaction is a stress provoker—so plan wisely. Know all the costs you will encounter.

LEGAL ASSISTANCE

An attorney is a must in the complex legal and financial real estate transactions in which you will be involved. In some states, an escrow agent or a title company will handle the paperwork. But even in this case, get advice from a local attorney who specializes in real estate law and closings. A good attorney can protect your interest in contract signing and in negotiating the price. Your lawyer will want to approve all contracts you sign. Attorneys are indispensable in settling any contract changes prior to—or those that come up at—the closing. He or

she will request that you supply a list of documents on the ownership of
the home. Your attorney's fee should be agreed on beforehand.

FEE AND TAX CONSIDERATIONS

Closing costs can be considerable for the seller. Before setting a price
and putting your house on the market, make a list of these costs to see
where you can control the amount.

Capital gains taxes must be paid on the profit resulting from the difference between the selling price and the costs associated with buying
and owning the house. Consult with your accountant or a competent
tax advisor for the effect the sales transaction will have on your taxes.
If you are not buying another house, or if the price of your next house is
less than that of the one you are selling, a capital gains tax must be paid
in the sales tax year. If the new house costs more than the old, the tax is
postponed. Accurate capital cost records since last purchasing your
house are a must. Call the IRS for advice and a copy of their tax
booklet on selling a house. The general rule is you can postpone tax
payment on the profit in a home sale if you buy within a year, but you
can't deduct any loss from the sale.

If you are considering going into an apartment and you are near 65,
it may pay for you to continue as a homeowner until you are 65. Note
that the tax law forgives the capital gains tax on any profits from
selling a house that was your principal residence for at least five of the
eight years preceding the sale.

In some states, a property transfer tax is imposed upon the seller
when the title to the property is transferred to the buyer.

If you recently had new sewers, sidewalks, or other improvements
made, and these are being paid off in your annual taxes as a special
assessment or charge, then the new buyer may request that the balance
be paid before he accepts the title.

Real estate taxes must be paid during the tax period that you owned
the house. The appropriate amount should be given to the new
owner—who will pay the tax bill in full when it comes due—at closing.
Your mortgage lender may have been collecting taxes from you
monthly and may, in addition, have escrow money left over that will
revert to you at closing. If not, you must come up with this tax money.

In some states, if the buyer requests a survey of the property, the
owner may have to provide it. You may also have to pay for a termite
inspection and the treatment if there is infestation.

Are there any unpaid bills for work done on your property, or are there any mechanic's liens on the property? These must be removed prior to closing.

Many municipalities require a Minimum Property Maintenance Code Inspection when you put your house on the market. If you have an older house, this could mean additional costs. One seller of a $40,000 house in New Jersey had a $4,500 repair bill to pay prior to closing to correct the violations and get an occupancy clearance. Remember: the inspector's findings can be appealed, so get the inspection done early if your town requires it.

The buyer may request that you supply the owner's present policy of title insurance. The buyer usually pays for insurance, but check with the current practice in your state.

If you sell to a buyer with an FHA or VA guaranteed loan, you often will be charged one or two points on the mortgage, depending on the current interest rate. The buyer cannot pay these discount points, so the point charges will fall on you, the seller. A point is 1% of the mortgage loan. Interest rates allowed on government-backed loans are fixed and usually lower than interest rates on conventional loans, so the lender makes up the difference by assessing the seller. If the price of your home could attract an FHA or VA buyer, then you should consider these points in the price of the home. In some instances, the buyer may have to pay points. Discuss this with your banker and lawyer.

Closing costs (discussed in Chapter 4) are normally paid by the buyer and include the lender's appraisal fee, survey cost, title search and title insurance mortgage tax, credit report, state or county mortgage and deed recording fees, and the attorney fee of the lending institution. Find out what fees you must pay.

The seller usually pays the broker's selling commission and any state taxes on the equity involved. Buyer and seller will negotiate any prepaid house insurance policies, mortgage insurance premiums, and fuel on hand. Now that you've collected all these selling costs, add them up and use the information when deciding on a price.

FINANCING

The buyer usually arranges for financing through a sales broker or bank. However, many deals fall through because the buyer cannot get a satisfactory mortgage commitment. Therefore, before putting your house up for sale, discuss financing with your broker and with the lending institution that holds your mortgage. Shop around and assess the mortgage market. If you are in an active real estate market with market prices rising each year, you may wish to consider carrying a second mortgage for about five years. If you don't need the money, this may be a good investment, so don't overlook this sales tool. Many brokers have arrangements for buying your home if they can't sell it within a time period. Relocation firms have a similar program. Get good professional advice to avoid losing a sale.

SELL YOURSELF OR USE A BROKER

I have found that those who sell by themselves usually net less than if they had the professional help of a broker. In addition, they have taken on a considerable task for which they are usually not prepared. If you are still adamant about doing it yourself, then go to the library and read some books. Also consult with friends or neighbors who have sold homes themselves. But be cautious, because if you don't sell in a month, you may have lost valuable time and prospects even if you then turn to a broker. Selling your house yourself is a large responsibility with great risks.

Be as careful in selecting a broker as you would in selecting any specialist. See if the broker has additional offices, is a member of a national realty group, is part of a multiple listing service, does a fair amount of corporate relocation work, provides an appraisal as part of the service, and will actively market your home. (See Chapter 3 on real estate brokers and how to choose them.)

When you sign the listing contract, you will agree to pay a sales commission that may range from 5 to 10% of the sales price. Never give an exclusive listing. Insist on a multiple listing and a three-month cancellation clause if you become disenchanted with the broker's service.

HOUSE FACT SHEET

The broker and MLS service will prepare a standard fact sheet on your home and give this to potential buyers. Some sellers have successfully prepared an additional one or two page handout summarizing the features of the house. Remember that buyers see many homes and can easily forget what they've seen. The resume should include the address and age of the house; a copy of the plan; the total square feet of living area; room size, number, and type; special features like heating, air conditioning, air treatment devices, pool, or fireplaces; and annual utility and tax bills. List what items do and do not go with the house, and then comment on the condition of the structure, roof, and mechanical services. The resume handout can be a useful selling tool and the facts are useful when you are setting the sales price. Leave copies on a table at the entrance to your home. You will have to price your home close to the price of the sold comparable homes, allowing 5 to 10% above this for bargaining. Here again, a knowledge of how fast the market reacts is important in setting the price and adjusting it after a period of time.

You should see all the comparables prepared by the broker. You should also check with the local tax assessor to learn what percentage of the full property value is the assessed valuation. It's a good indication of value.

If your home is over $100,000 and you are not satisfied with the broker's appraisal, you might consider getting a certified appraiser's estimate of the value. This could cost from $150 to $400. Many corporations, through their relocation services, make this available to an employee as part of the company-paid moving costs. This appraisal, combined with the broker's information, can help set the realistic price.

HOME INSPECTION

Since many buyers will be considering a home inspection by an engineer, you should review the checklist in the Part I summary to be sure you can respond to these checkpoints.

TIPS FOR PREPARING THE PROPERTY FOR SALE

Your home is an expensive sales item. The buyers are under considerable stress, so make it easy for them to buy. Just as you like a used car to be neat and in good condition, so too does the prospective buyer expect a clean and well-groomed home. If followed, these tips will make your home look like it's received all the care you've probably given it.

Scrub clean or paint the walls inside and out. If you must paint, white is preferable—it helps avoid comments like, "I love the living room but my furniture doesn't match." Also, white is easy to paint over should the buyer prefer another color. Although there is little need to paint the ceilings (they are very seldom checked), it is a wise precaution to clean or paint the inside of your closets, if they need it, since they are usually examined.

Repair those little things you've always meant to but never had the chance to do. Cracked plaster, loose door knobs, broken light switches, leaking faucets, sticking drawers, and warped cabinet doors are the small things that could be deciding factors in the sale of your house.

Keep your grounds neat and trimmed. The flower beds should be orderly, ragged shrubbery should be removed, and any debris should be cleaned up. If it is winter, be sure to clear a path to all the doors and the garage for easy access.

In the evening, keep the house well-lighted and in the daytime arrange drapes for maximum intake of sunlight.

Remember that the kitchen, bedroom, family room, and bathroom are the big four home sellers. Keep them especially neat, cheerful, and clean.

Keep the house free of clutter. Remove all unnecessary items that may have accumulated in storage areas and, above all, keep the stairways free from objects, for safety as well as appearance.

A few renovations could make the sale easier and quicker. Some suggestions are given below.

Refinish the living room floor if necessary or buy new carpeting. Choosing an inexpensive carpet in a neutral shade not only hides defects but adds a plus value to the home.

Put on new kitchen cabinet door knobs.

Install a new medicine chest in the bathroom.

Install a new kitchen stove if the old one is worn or in disrepair.

Plant new outdoor shrubs or plants. They are fairly inexpensive and create a good first impression.

If the roof is in bad condition, it would be advisable to repair it or reroof in a fresh, new color before selling.

Put the utility room or basement in neat order. Have the heating plant and air conditioner serviced and have all electrical and mechanical equipment in working order. Patch any settlement cracks. Remove all traces of water, efflorescense, and mold from the cellar walls and floors, and if you have a sump pump, be sure it operates.

Some brokers have a warranty policy available for sale that will cover malfunctions in the plumbing, heating, and electrical components. Also, many astute sellers are having a home inspection done prior to sale with a warranty. They can then repair any malfunction and offer the inspection as a sales tool. These pre-purchase inspections are a growing trend and will be as common as a survey in the coming years.

HOUSE VIEWING

The broker and member brokers and salespersons of the MLS will plan to arrive as a group some morning to view the property in preparation to trying to sell it for you. This gives the brokers a chance to view the home. When brokers have a prospective buyer, they will call prior to taking the people to view your house. Many brokers will advertise the property and have a one day open house for prospective buyers.

There are many sales methods and your broker should discuss what methods he will use to market your house. The average house takes three months to sell. In some areas, buyers ae waiting in line, but your broker can discuss the local market conditions to help in your planning.

Most important, be friendly but leave the selling to the broker. If possible, plan to be out of the house or as inconspicuous as possible. Too many words or rationalizations on your part can kill a sale. Don't react or be hurt by idle criticism of the features of your house. Your listing broker should discuss the progress of the sale effort with you each week in addition to what is being done toward actively moving the house. You must keep on top of the situation and, if necessary, regularly ask what the current state of affairs is.

NEGOTIATING

Shortly after one buyer views the house, you will get a call from the broker that a bid has been made on the property. The normal practice is for the buyer to put up earnest money (at least $100 to $1,000) to acompany the bid. If the bid is lower than your price, you must either give or stand pat. If the market analysis, appraisal, and pricing was done correctly, there will be some room to negotiate. The buyer will expect this to happen. You will have to negotiate within ten days or the deposit will be returned to the prospective buyer. If the buyer agrees to the original price, you've won; if he hedges, agree to lower the price to the figure you had previously decided to fall back on. If the salesperson handles the negotiation properly, the buyer and you will spend the next few days price bargaining with you coming down and the buyer coming up. If you can't agree within ten days, it's quite unlikely you will make a deal, and the deposit will be returned.

When both the seller and buyer agree on a price, the broker will have you both sign a sales contract or deposit receipt, and a good faith deposit of $100 to $1,000 will be paid. The form is a standard one known to your attorney. In a few days, your attorney, with the buyer's attorney's approval, will prepare a sales contract. Upon signing, the buyer will present a deposit of 10% of the purchase price.

The sales contract will state the purchase price; describe the property; set out the method of final payment; set the date of closing and satisfactory title transfer; list the conditions of sale, such as a time (15 to 30 days) for the buyer to secure a mortgage and a time (10 days) to have a home inspection and termite inspection, with an agreement of who pays for repairs over an amount (say $500); and list the extras included in the sales price. The agreement specifies that the deposit be returned if the buyer cannot get a loan or comply with the terms of the agreement.

Generally speaking, contracts are standard and brokers and escrow agents can handle the contract phase. But the best way to protect yourself and save time is to get competent advice from a lawyer.

SUMMARY

Planning your sale with the help of professionals will make both the buyer and you happy that a good deal was made. Real estate transactions are usually stress-provoking situations, but they can be made pleasant by the proper groundwork and planning. Selling a home is usually a compromise, so don't miss a sale for a matter of one or two thousand dollars.

In closing this last chapter, I want to thank you for your time and urge you to write me if I can be of help or you wish to share your experience with me and with other readers. Good luck and enjoy your home.

Appendix A.
Glossary

The following terms are used in the text. The Index can be used to find the section in which the term is used.

Absorption bed. A shallow, rectangular excavation of large dimensions filled with coarse aggregates and covered with earth. It contains a piping system that distributes the septic tank effluent so it can be absorbed.

Absorption field. A system of shallow trenches containing coarse aggregates and a distribution pipe through which septic tank effluent seeps or leaches into the soil.

Abstract of title. A summary of the public records of the title to a particular piece of land. An attorney or title insurance company reviews the abstract to determine whether there are any title defects that must be cleared before a buyer can purchase a clear and insurable title.

Aggregate. A coarse material, usually sand, stone, and gravel, used as part of the ingredients of concrete or asphalt paving.

Agreement of sale. Also known as contract of purchase, purchase agreement, or sales agreement, according to the state or municipality. It is a contract in which a seller agrees to sell and a buyer agrees to buy, under certain specific terms and conditions written and signed by both parties.

Air conditioning. The process of treating air to control simultaneously its temperature, humidity, cleanliness, and distribution.

Air return. Air returned from an air conditioned space. Return can be centrally located or located in each room.

Alligatoring. A coarse, checked pattern shown by a slipping of the new paint coating over the old coating so that the old coating can be seen through the cracks in the new coat.

Alternating current (AC). A current flow that reverses direction periodically according to a specified frequency; normally 60 cycles per second, AC current is seen in most domestic and commercial applications.

Amortization. A payment plan which enables the borrower to reduce his debt gradually through monthly payments of principal and interest.

Amperage or current. The number of amperes used in a house or in an electrical circuit. It is a measure of the amount of electricity that flows through a wire. Houses commonly have 30, 60, 100, 150, 200, or more ampere services.

Anchor bolts.   Bolts used to secure a wooden sill plate to a concrete or masonry floor or wall.

Appraisal.   An expert judgment or estimate of the quality or value of real estate as of a given date.

Area drain.   A receptacle designed to collect surface or storm water from an open area.

Areaway.   An open subsurface space adjacent to a building used to admit light or air or as a means of access to a cellar or lower area.

Artesian well.   A well with a shaft that penetrates an impermeable strata deep enough to reach water that will rise by its own hydraulic pressure.

Asbestos shingle.   A fireproof roof or siding material made of cement and asbestos fiber.

Ash pit.   A pit at the base of a chimney for cleaning out fireplace ashes.

Asphalt shingles.   A heavy felt paper saturated with hot asphalt, and covered with fine rock granules.

Assumption of mortgage.   An obligation by the purchaser of property to be personally liable for payment of an existing mortgage.

Attic ventilators.   A screened opening provided to ventilate an attic space. They are located in the soffit area as inlet ventilators and in the gable end or along the ridge as outlet ventilators.

Balloon framing.   A type of framing system where the studs extend unbroken from the sill to the roof.

Balusters.   Small, vertical members in a railing used between a top rail and the stair treads or a bottom rail.

Baseboard.   It is placed around the periphery of the room at the floor level to cover the floor-wall joint. Often, it consists of three pieces of molding: the base shoe, baseboard, and base molding.

Basement.   A space of full story height below the first floor wholly or partly below exterior grade and which is not used primarily for living space.

Batter board.   One of a pair of horizontal boards nailed to posts set at the corners of an excavation used to indicate the desired level and also to indicate outlines of foundation walls.

Beam.   One of the principal horizontal wood or steel members of a building. It can be supported at its ends by a foundation wall or a girder.

Bearing beam (girder).   A large piece of wood, steel, or other material used to support a house. It usually runs from foundation wall to foundation wall and is supported with steel lally columns or wooden poles or columns.

Bearing partition or wall.   A partition that supports any vertical load in addition to its own weight.

Berm.   A mound of earth or pavement used to control the flow of surface water. It performs the same function as a street curb and gutter.

Binder or "offer to purchase."   A preliminary agreement between a buyer and seller, secured by the payment of earnest money, to purchase real estate. A binder secures the right to purchase real estate upon agreed terms for a limited period of time. It may call for the return of the money if the buyer is unable to purchase.

Blacktop.   An asphalt product containing aggregates. It is used for driveways, streets, and sidewalks.

Blower.   A fan in a furnace or air conditioning unit that blows air through the ducts of a house.

Bluestone.   A type of crushed stone consisting of basaltic rock. It is used in driveways.

Boiler.   A heating device that heats hot water or steam for circulation in heating pipes, radiators, baseboards, or convectors.

Brick veneer.   A single course of brick secured against exterior walls of a frame structure. It does not support any weight of the building.

Bridging.   Small wood or metal members that are inserted in a diagonal position between the floor joists at midspan to brace the joists and spread the action of loads.

BTU (British thermal unit).   A measurement of heating and cooling capacity. It is the amount of heat required to raise the temperature of one pound of water 1° F.

Building line or setback.   Distances from the ends and/or sides of the lot beyond which construction may not extend. The building line may be established by building codes or zoning ordinances.

Building paper.   Heavy paper used in walls or roofs to damp-proof.

Built-up roof.   A flat or low-pitched roof composed of three to five layers of asphalt felt laminated with coal tar, pitch, or asphalt. The top can be finished with crushed slag or gravel.

BX cable.   A metal-clad electrical cable suitable only for indoor use. Plastic coated cable (Romex) has replaced this in many new homes.

Cantilever.   A projecting beam or joist not supported at one end and used to support an extension of a structure.

Caulk.   A material used to seal openings or make them water-tight.

Casement window.   A vertically hung metal or wood window that swings out horizontally on its hinges, similar to door action.

Ceramic tile.   A flat fired clay tile that comes in a variety of types and forms a decorative, hard, durable surface.

Certificate of title.   A certificate issued by a title company or a written opinion rendered by an attorney that the seller has good marketable and insurable title to the property that he is offering for sale. The protection offered a homeowner under a certificate of title is not as great as that offered in a title insurance policy, which is required by many lenders.

Cesspool.   A lined and covered excavation in the ground which receives the discharge of domestic sewage and is so designed as to retain organic matter and solids while permitting liquids to seep through the bottom and sides. It is outlawed by many communities.

Chimney cap.   Concrete capping around the top of the flue and chimney to protect the masonry from the elements.

Cinder block.   A foundation block made of cement and cinders or slag.

Circuit breaker.   An electrical circuit protection device used as a substitute for a fuse.

Cistern.   A tank to catch and store rain water. Found in older homes and usually disconnected.

Clapboard.   A long board used as siding.

Clean out plug.   A large cap in the sewer line used for cleaning out the sewer line.

Closing costs.   The numerous expenses which buyers and sellers normally incur to complete a transaction in the transfer of ownership of real estate.

Coliform count.   A test to determine the safety of drinking water. Well water should be so tested periodically.

Collar beam.   A horizontal beam fastened to rafters below the ridge pole to add rigidity and tie the rafters together.

Column.   A wood or steel vertical post used to support a floor joist or girder.

Compressor.   A pump that forces refrigerant through a air conditioning or heat pump system. In residental split systems, it is outside and contains the condenser and fan.

Concrete block.   A foundation block made of cement and water together with aggregate.

Condensate.   In steam heating, it is water condensed from steam as it cools. In air conditioning or humidifiers, it is water that drips off the cooling coils.

Condominium.   An individual ownership of a dwelling unit and an individual interest in the common areas and facilities which serve the multi-unit project.

Conduit, electrical.   A pipe, usually metal, in which wire is installed.

Construction, drywall.   A type of construction in which the interior wall finish is applied in a dry condition, generally in the form of sheet materials or wood paneling.

Contractor.   A contractor is one who contracts to erect buildings or portions of them. He may do structural work, heating, electrical, plumbing, air conditioning, or driveways.

Convector radiator.   A heat distribution system consisting of pipes with many fins attached at short intervals. The hot water or steam blows through the pipes, heating the fins, which in turn heat the surrounding air.

Convenience outlet.   A plug-in receptacle housed in a protective box with plug-in positions for attachment of portable fixtures or minor appliances.

Conventional mortgage.   A mortgage loan not insured by HUD or guaranteed by the Veterans' Administration. It is subject to conditions established by the lending institution and state statutes.

Corbel.   A horizontal projection from a wall, forming a ledge or supporting a structure above it.

Counterflashing.   A flashing usually used on chimneys at the roofline to cover shingle flashing and to prevent moisture entry.

Crawl space.   A shallow, unfinished space beneath the first floor of a house which has no basement. It is also a shallow space in the attic, immediately under the roof.

Cricket.   A small drainage-diverting roof structure of single or double slope placed at the junction of larger surfaces, such as above a chimney.

Cripples.   Cut-off framing members above and below windows.

Damp course.   A course or layer of impervious material which prevents capillary entrance of moisture from the ground or a lower course. Needed in very moist climates to prevent decay.

Damp-proofing.   A treatment of a foundation surface or structure which retards the passage of moisture.

Decay.   Disintegration of wood or other substances through the action of fungi. Sometimes called dry rot.

Default.   Failure to make mortgage payments.

Dehumidification.   The removal of water vapor from air by chemical or physical methods (air conditioner or dehumidifier).

Dewpoint.   Temperature at which a vapor begins to deposit as a liquid. Applies especially to water in the atmosphere.

Domestic sewage.   The water-borne wastes resulting from ordinary living in a house.

Double glazing.   An insulating window pane formed of two thicknesses of glass with a sealed air space between them.

Drainage system.   Includes all the piping in a house that conveys sewage, rain water, or other liquid wastes to a point of disposal.

Drip cap.   A molding placed on the exterior top side of a door or window frame to cause water to drip beyond the outside of the frame.

Earnest money.   The deposit money given to the seller or his agent by the potential buyer to show that he is serious about buying the house.

Easement.   A vested or acquired right to use land other than as a tenant, for a specific purpose, such right being held by someone other than the owner who holds title to the land. For example, the right of a sewer line or utility wires.

Eaves.   The overhanging lower edge of a roof.

Efflorescence.   A deposit of soluble salts, usually white in color, appearing upon the exposed surface of masonry. It usually indicates dampness on foundation walls.

Effluent.   Treated sewage from a septic tank or sewage treatment plant.

Equity.   The value of a homeowner's unencumbered interest in real estate.

Escrow.   Funds paid by one party to another (the escrow agent) to hold until the occurrence of a specified event, after which the funds are released to a designated individual.

Facia or fascia.   A flat board used sometimes by itself but usually in combination with moldings, often located at the outer face of the cornice or behind gutters.

Fan/limit switch.   A combination heat-sensitive switch that controls the flow of electricity to a forced warm air heating system fan motor.

Filter.   A device to remove solid material from air or a liquid.

Flitch plate.   A steel plate used on wooden girders to increase its span between columns.

Floating foundation.   Special foundations with few or no footings used where the land is swampy or the soil unstable.

Floor joists.   Wooden framing members that rest on outer foundation walls and interior beams or girders.

Flue.   An enclosed metal or ceramic pipe or chimney that is used to exhaust smoke, gases, or air.

Flushometer valve.   A device which discharges a predetermined quantity of water to fixtures for flushing purposes and is closed by direct water pressure.

Footings.   A concrete support under a foundation, chimney, or column that usually rests on solid ground and is wider than the structure being supported.

Foundation.   Construction below or partly below grade, which provides support for exterior walls or other structural parts of the building. It is used synonomous with basement wall when the house has a basement. In some areas, footing and foundation are used interchangeably.

French drain. An underground drainage system, usually with open joint pipe or drain tile, used to carry off excess water.

Frostline. The depth of frost penetration in soil. This depth varies in different parts of the country. Footings should be placed below this depth to prevent movement.

Fuse. A cartridge or plug fuse used to protect an electrical circuit.

Gable. The triangular part of a wall under the inverted "v" of the roof line.

Gambrel roof. A roof with two pitches, designed to provide more space on upper floors. The roof is steeper on its lower slope and flatter toward the ridge.

Girder. See bearing beam.

Glazing. The method of installing and securing glass or plastic in prepared openings of doors or windows.

Grade. The ground level around a building.

Grounding. A process of connecting a wire from an appliance or circuit box to a water pipe or ground rod.

Grout. Mortar made of such consistency by adding water that it will just flow into the joints and cavities of the masonry work and fill them solid.

Gutter. An open channel made of metal, plastic, or wood installed along the eave of a roof at the facia board.

Header. A framing member that goes across the top of an opening and carries the load above.

Hearth. The inner or outer floor of a fireplace, usually made of brick, tile, or stone.

Heat exchanger. A device by which heat is exchanged from one heat-carrying medium to another without contact between the two media.

Hip roof. A roof with no gables. It usually has inclined planes on all four sides of the building.

Hollow-core door. A reinforced hollow door made of two pieces of thin wood sandwiching a solid outer wood frame.

House sewer. That part of the drainage system which extends from the end of the building drain and conveys its discharge to a public sewer, private sewer, or individual sewage disposal system.

Humidifier. A device designed to increase the humidity within a room or a house by means of the discharge of water vapor. Humidifiers may consist of individual room-size units or larger units attached to the heating plant to condition the entire house.

Humidistat. An electrical control that automatically senses and controls humidity in a living space and operates a humidifier.

I-beam. A steel bearing beam or girder.

Individual sewage disposal system. A system for disposal of domestic sewage by means of a septic tank, cesspool, or mechanical treatment, designed for use apart from a public sewer.

Insulation, thermal. Any material high in resistance to heat transmission that, when placed in the walls, ceiling, or floors of a structure, will reduce the rate of heat flow.

Instantaneous hot water heater. A coil in a boiler used to heat domestic hot water.

Jack rafter. A rafter that spans the distance from the wall plate to a hip, or from a valley to a ridge.

Jalousies. Windows and doors with movable, horizontal glass slats at angles to admit ventilation and keep out rain.

Jamb. The upright wood piece forming the side of a door or window opening.

Joist. One of a series of parallel beams, usually two inches in thickness, used to support floor and ceiling loads, and supported in turn by larger beams, girders, or bearing walls.

Junction box. A plastic or metal box in which electrical connections are placed.

Kilowatt-hour. A standard unit used by utility companies for billing the power supplied to a customer over a period of time.

Knob and tube wiring. An early method of electric wiring still found in some areas today. The wire is attached to the house frame with porcelain knob insulators and porcelain tubes.

Knee wall. Vertical framing in an attic used to support a low sloping roof.

Lally column. A steel tube sometimes filled with concrete and used to support girders or other floor beams.

Lathing. Strips of wood or metal, often three-eighths of an inch thick and one and one-half inches wide, used as a base for plaster. The base today is a type of plaster board.

Lead pan. A large sheet of lead placed under a tile shower floor to keep it waterproof.

Leader. An exterior drainage pipe for conveying storm water from roof or gutter drains. Also called a downspout.

Ledger strip. A strip of wood nailed along the bottom of the side of a girder on which joists rest.

Lintel. A horizontal structural member that supports the load over an opening such as a door or window.

Live load. A variable weight to which a house is subject, such as snow on the roof, people on the floors, and furniture.

Load bearing walls. A wall or partition which assists in bearing the load of floors and roof.

Mantelpiece. A protruding shelf over a fireplace.

Means of egress. A continuous and unobstructed way of exit travel from any point in a dwelling to the exterior. There should be two means of egress in a house.

Mixing valve. A bypass valve on an instantaneous hot water heater used to temper the hot (180°F) water to a safe temperature.

Moisture barrier. Treated paper or metal that retards or bars water vapor, used to keep moisture from passing into walls or floors.

Moisture protection. Safeguarding living units against the penetration or passage of water, water vapor, and dampness.

Mortgage commitment. A written notice from the bank or other lending institution saying it will advance mortgage funds in a specified amount to enable a buyer to purchase a house.

Mortgagee. The lender in a mortgage agreement.

Mortgagor. The borrower in a mortgage agreement.

Multiple dwelling. Building containing more than two dwelling units.

Newel cap. An ornamental finish on the top of a newel post.

OHM. Unit of measurement of electrical resistance.

Overhang. The part of a roof that extends beyond the exterior wall.

Packaged chimney. A complete factory-built chimney, usually made of metal and insulation. Used primarily with pre-fabricated fireplace units.

Parapet. The part of the wall of a house that rises above the roof line.

Parging.   A rough coat of mortar applied over a masonry wall as protection or finish; may also serve as a base for an asphaltic waterproofing compound below grade.

Parquet floor.   A floor made of small blocks or squares of hardwood flooring, laid together with tongue and groove edges, and secured to a base or subfloor with mastic or staples.

Particleboard.   A composition board consisting of distinct particles of wood bonded together with a synthetic resin or other binder.

Partition.   A wall that subdivides spaces within any story of a building.

Pilaster.   A pier or column forming part of a masonry or concrete wall, partially projecting therefrom and bonded thereto.

Plaster board.   A rigid insulating board used in drywall construction. Made of plastering material, usually gypsum, covered on both sides by heavy paper.

Plenum.   A large duct or air chamber in which the hot air from the furnace builds up pressure which forces it out through the ducts to the register. The air conditioning evaporator is placed here.

Platform framing.   A type of framing where each floor is built on a platform and the studs run the height of each floor.

Plumbing fixture.   A receptacle or device which is either permanently or temporarily connected to the water distribution system and discharges used water, liquid-borne waste materials, or sewage directly to the drainage system.

Plumbing system.   This includes the water supply and distribution pipes; plumbing fixtures and traps; soil, waste, and vent pipes; and building drains within a building or structure to a point not exceeding five feet beyond the foundation walls of the building.

Post-and-beam construction.   Wall construction in which beams are supported by heavy posts rather than many smaller studs.

Potable water.   Water free from impurities present in amounts sufficient to cause disease, and conforming in its bacteriological and chemical quality to the requirements of the Public Health Drinking Water Standards or the regulations of the municipal public health authority. Well water should be periodically tested.

Private sewer.   A sewer, serving two or more buildings, privately owned, and not directly controlled by public authority.

Purlin.   An intermediate supporting member at right angles to a rafter or truss framing.

Radiant heat.   Coils of electricity or hot water or steam pipes embedded in floors, ceilings, or walls to heat rooms.

Radiator.   An exposed fixture, usually made out of cast iron, that transfers heat from the heating system by means of convection and radiation.

Rafter.   One of a series of structural members of a roof designed to support roof loads. The rafters of a flat roof are sometimes called roof joists.

Real estate broker.   An agent who buys and sells real estate for a company, firm, or individual on a commission basis. The broker does not have title to the property, but generally represents the owner.

Receptor.   A fixture or device that receives the discharge from indirect waste pipes.

Recovery rate.   A term used for hot water heaters to tell how fast the temperature of a tank of water will recover after heavy usage.

Refinancing.   The process of paying off one loan with the proceeds from another loan.

Register.   A fixture installed at the end of an air duct that directs and controls the flow of air into the room.

Reinforced concrete.   Concrete which has been strengthened by reinforcing bars embedded in the mix.

Resilient floor.   Floors covered with vinyl, asphalt tile, or linoleum.

Retaining wall.   Any wall subjected to lateral pressure other than wind pressure, or a wall built to support a bank of earth.

Ridge board.   A board placed at the ridge of the roof into which the upper ends of the rafters are fastened.

Ridge vent.   An elongated metal cap extending the entire ridge length to allow for attic ventilation.

Roll roofing.   Roofing material, composed of fiber and saturated with asphalt, that is generally furnished in weights of 45 to 90 pounds per roll.

Roof boards.   Boards or sheathing that are nailed to the rafters to which are fastened the roof covering or shingles, tiles, or other material.

Roofing cement.   An asphalt material used for patching or waterproofing roofs and flashings.

Safety valve.   An hydraulic or electrical device, the purpose of which is to block all gas flow to a system in the event of pilot outage. They are found on hot water heaters and boilers.

Sash.   The movable part of a window; the frame in which panes of glass are set in a window or door.

Sash cord.   The cord or chain that attaches the counterbalance weights to each double-hung window sash. They should be chain for a long life.

Seepage pit.   A covered pit with open-jointed lining through which septic tank effluent may seep or leach into surrounding porous soil.

Septic tank.   A covered steel or concrete water-tight sewage settling tank intended to retain the solids in the sewage long enough for the decomposition of settled solids by bacterial action to take place. The remaining effluent is discharged to a seepage pit or absorption bed or field.

Service entrance cable.   Insulated wires or conduit containing wires through which electricity is provided to a house.

Service panel.   A metal box containing fuses or circuit breakers.

Sewage ejectors.   A device for lifting sewage by entraining it in a high velocity jet of steam, air, or water. Pumps are also used if the city sewer is above the house discharge line.

Shakes.   Usually a hand (or machine) split, rough-textured wood shingle.

Sheathing.   A wood or fibrous sub-siding material nailed to exterior studs or rafters that forms the base for the finish operations of shingles or siding.

Sheathing paper.   A building material, generally paper or felt, used in wall and roof construction as a protection against the passage of air and sometimes moisture.

Sheet rock.   A trade name for gypsum wallboard.

Short circuit.   A break in wiring causing a large flow of current. The short circuit, if properly protected, will blow a fuse or cause a circuit breaker to operate. When not protected, it can cause a fire.

Shower pan.   A netal, concrete, tile, or fiberglass base or pan for catching water under a shower stall.

Siding.   The finish covering of the outside wall of a frame building, whether made of horizontal weatherboards, vertical boards with battens, shingles, or other material.

Sill plate.   The lowest member of the house framing resting on top of the foundation wall.

Siphon action toilet.   A toilet in which the flushing action is assisted by a jet of water.

Slab-on-ground.   A concrete slab made by pouring concrete directly on the prepared ground surface and over the top of the foundation and footings.

Sleeper.   A strip of wood laid over concrete floor to which the finished wood floor is nailed or glued.

Sliding doors.   Single or double pane doors that slide horizontally on tracks.

Smoke chamber.   A large void over the damper that prevents the smoke from backing up into the fireplace.

Snow guard.   Small metal catches on a roof, usually placed over a door, located above the eaves to keep snow from sliding in sudden avalanches to the ground.

Soffit.   The visible underside or overhang of structural members such as staircases, beams, a roof overhang, or an eave.

Soil percolation test.   A test to determine if the soil is suitable for a private sewage system.

Square.   One hundred square feet of roof or siding area.

Starter course.   The first row of roof shingles or shakes.

Storm drainage system.   Facilities, structures, appurtenances, pipes, channels, and natural water course improvements to collect, convey, and dispose of surface run-off to an outlet.

Storm sash or storm window.   An extra window, usually placed on the outside or inside of an existing one as protection against cold weather and drafts.

Stucco.   An exterior siding finish usually consisting of cement, lime, and sand and is trowelled on over wood or masonry siding.

Stud.   One of a series of slender wood or metal vertical structural members placed as supporting elements in walls and partitions. Studs are spaced either 16 inches or 24 inches apart.

Subfloor.   Boards or plywood laid on joists over which a carpet or finish floor is to be laid.

Subgrade support strength.   The capacity of the prepared earth surface to sustain weight, loading, strain, and wear without failure when supporting footings and a foundation for buildings, structures, pavements, or walks. It can be determined by experience or core drillings and testing.

Sump pump.   An automatic electric pump installed in a sump hole that activates as the water in the hole reaches an excessive level and pumps it out to a drainage area.

Supply duct.   A metal or plastic duct that supplies conditioned air from a furnace, a central air conditioner, or a heat pump system to rooms in a house.

Surface water.   Water from rain or seeps that collects at gound level and, if not properly channeled away, will enter a basement area.

Survey.   A map made by a licensed surveyor showing the results of measuring the land with its elevations, improvements, and boundaries, as well as its relationship to surrounding tracts of land.

Swale.   A shallow open channel for collection and disposal of excess surface water formed by intersecting slope bases—a type of gutter.

Temperature/pressure relief valve.   Safety relief valve used primarily in water heaters and activated by either a specific water vapor temperature or pressure, normally rated around 120° F or 125 psi.

Temperature, dewpoint.   The temperature at which the condensation of water vapor in a space begins for a given state of humidity and pressure as the temperature of the vapor is reduced.

Termite shield.   A protective shield, usually of metal, placed so as to interrupt the path of termites from the ground into the house.

Thermostat.   An automatic heating-cooling control. Some units are controlled by clocks to set back the temperature during certain times as a fuel-saving measure.

Threshold.   A strip of wood or metal with beveled edges that is used over the finish floor and the sill of exterior doors.

Title.   This refers to the instruments or documents by which a right of ownership is established.

Title insurance.   Protects lenders or homeowners against loss of their interest in property due to legal defects in title. Many lenders require this protection.

Ton of refrigeration.   A useful refrigerating measure equal to 12,000 BTU per hour. The average three-bedroom house has a three-ton air conditioning unit.

Trap.   An "S" bend in a waste pipe below a fixture that remains filled with water, thereby sealing sewer gases from backing up into the house.

Truss.   A triangular arrangement of framing members forming a rigid framework, usually pre-assembled and lifted intact into place between load bearing walls.

Tuck pointing.   Refilling defective mortar joints that have been cut out in existing masonry.

Underpinnings.   Concrete supports added under footings or foundations to increase the load bearing capacity of a foundation.

Underwriters' Laboratory.   An independent consumer product testing laboratory.

Valleys.   A depressed angle formed when the bottom of two roof planes meet.

Vent pipe.   A vertical stack used to vent one or more plumbing fixtures or floor drains and provide free movement of air and sewer gases.

Vapor barrier.   A material or paint applied to a wall, floor, or ceiling to prevent the passage of moisture.

Volt.   An electrical potential, usually 110 or 220 volts single phase in residential use.

Warm air system.   A heating system in which air is heated inside a furnace and distributed throughout the house either by the force of gravity or by blowers to ducts.

Waste pipe.   A pipe which conveys only waste to a sewer.

Waterproofing.   A treatment of a foundation surface or structure which prevents the passage of water.

Water supply system.   The water service pipe, the water-distributing pipes, and the necessary connecting pipes, fittings, control valves, and all appurtenances in or adjacent to the building or premises.

Watt hour.   Power over a period of one hour.

Weephole.   A small opening in a retaining wall or brick veneer to allow drainage of excess water.

Well, driven.   A well constructed by driving a pipe into the ground. The drive pipe is usually fitted with a well point and screen.

Zeolite.   A chemical used in water softeners to exchange the minerals in the water for sodium chloride.

Appendix B.
References

There are many excellent reference books on the care and repair of your home. The following books have been most useful in my work, especially the U.S. Department of Agriculture bulletins and the Circular Series of the Small Homes Council. Readers who wish to research the components of homes more thoroughly will find this reference list helpful.

The BOCA Basic Building Code—1975.   Chicago: Building Officials and Code Administrators International, 1975.

Cobb, Hubbard H. *Money Saving Home Maintenance.*   New York: Collier-Macmillan, 1965.

Daniels, George. *Home Guide to Plumbing, Heating, Air Conditioning.*   New York: Harper & Row, 1975.

Davis, Joseph C. and Walker, Claxton. *Buying Your House: A Complete Guide to Inspection and Evaluation.*   Buchanan: Emerson Books, 1975.

Dietz, Albert G.H. *Dwelling House Construction.*   Cambridge: The MIT Press, 1977.

Fala, Mario J. *Residential Plumbing Inspector's Manual.*   Cleveland: American Society of Sanitary Engineering, 1973.

Flata, Charles (Editor). *Complete Home Improvement Handbook.*   New York: McGraw-Hill Book Company, 1957.

Fox, Ron. *The Care and Feeding of Your Home.*   Dallas: A-Quality Printing Service, 1977.

Harrison, Henry S. *Houses.*   Chicago: National Association of Real Estate Brokers, 1973.

Hoffman, George. *Don't Go Buy Appearances.*   Corte Madera: Wodward Books, 1975.

Jones, Rudard, A. and Kapple, William H. *Kitchen Planning Principles, Equipment, Appliances.*   Urbana: University of Illinois, Small Homes Council, 1975.

Mencher, Melvin (Editor). *The Fannie Mae Guide to Buying, Financing, and Selling Your Home.*   Garden City: Doubleday & Co., 1973.

Moselle, Gary, Ed. *National Construction Estimator, Twenty-Sixth Edition.* Solana Beach: Craftsman Book Company, 1978.

Murray, Robert W., Jr. *How to Buy the Right House at the Right Price.* New York: Collier Books, 1972.

National Electric Code 1978. Boston: National Fire Protection Association, 1977.

Nelson, W.R., Jr. *Landscaping Your Home.* Urbana: University of Illinois College of Agriculture Cooperative Extension Service Circular 858, 1963.

O'Brien, James J., P.E. *Construction Inspection Handbook.* New York: Van Nostrand Reinhold Company, 1974.

Petersen, Kristelle, L. *How To Buy a Home.* Des Moines: Meridith Corporation, 1978.

Richter, H.P. *Wiring Simplified.* Minneapolis: Park Publishing, 1971.

Schuler, Stanley. *The Homeowner's Minimum-Maintenance Manual.* New York: M. Evans & Company, 1971.

Schwartz, Robert. *The Home Owner's Legal Guide.* New York: Collier Books, 1965.

Schweitzer, Gerald and Ebeling, A. *Basic Air Conditioning, Volume 2.* New York: Hayden Book Company, 1971.

Sherwood, Gerald E. *Renovate an Old House.* Washington, D.C.: Government Printing Office, 1976.

Small Homes Council—Building Research Council. *Circular Series.* Urbana: University of Illinois, 1977.

A Training Manual in Field Inspection of Buildings and Structures. Whittier: International Conference of Building Officials, 1968.

U.S. Department of Agriculture. *Better Lawns.* Washington, D.C.: Government Printing Office, 1974.

U.S. Department of Agriculture. *Consumers All, The Yearbook of Agriculture, 1965.* Washington, D.C.: Government Printing Office, 1965.

U.S. Department of Agriculture. *Handbook for the Home.* Washington, D.C.: Government Printing Office, 1973.

U.S. Department of Agriculture. *Home Heating Systems Fuels Controls.* Washington, D.C.: Government Printing Office, 1968.

U.S. Department of Agriculture. *Know the Soil You Build On.* Washington, D.C.: Government Printing Office, 1972.

U.S. Department of Agriculture. *Making Basements Dry.* Washington, D.C.: Government Printing Office, 1975.

U.S. Department of Agriculture. *Selecting and Financing a Home.* Washington, D.C.: Government Printing Office, 1972.

U.S. Department of Agriculture. *Shopper's Guide, The 1974 Yearbook of Agriculture.* Washington, D.C.: Government Printing Office, 1974.

U.S. Department of Agriculture. *Wood-Frame House Construction.* Washington, D.C.: Government Printing Office, 1965.

U.S. Department of Housing and Urban Development. *Home Buyer's Vocabulary.* Washington, D.C.: Government Printing Office, 1975.

U.S. Department of Housing and Urban Development. *Homeowner's Glossary of Building Terms.* Washington, D.C.: Government Printing Office, 1976.

U.S. Department of Housing and Urban Development. *HUD Minimum Property Standards 1973 Edition One and Two Family Dwellings.* Washington, D.C.: Government Printing Office, 1973.

U.S. Department of Housing and Urban Development. *Protecting Your Housing Investment.* Washington, D.C.: Government Printing Office, 1974.

U.S. Department of Housing and Urban Development. *Wise Home Buying.* Washington, D.C.: Government Printing Office, 1974.

U.S. Department of Labor. *Rent or Buy.* Washington, D.C.: Government Printing Office, 1974.

Veterans Administration. *Pointers for the Veteran Homeowner.* Washington, D.C.: Government Printing Office, 1975.

Veterans Administration. *To The Home Buying Veteran.* Washington, D.C.: Government Printing Office, 1975.

Watkins, A.M. *Building or Buying the High Quality House at Lowest Cost.* Garden City: Doubleday & Co., 1962.

Watkins, A.M. *The Homeowner's Survival Kit.* New York: Hawthorn Books, 1971.

Watkins, A.M. *How to Avoid the 10 Biggest Home-Buying Traps.* New York: Hawthorn Books, 1972.

Index

Index